The
Landrum-Griffin Act
and
Union Democracy

The
Landrum-Griffin Act
and
Union Democracy

DORIS B. McLAUGHLIN

ANITA L. W. SCHOOMAKER

Ann Arbor

The University of Michigan Press

Library of Congress Cataloging in Publication Data

McLaughlin, Doris B
    The Landrum-Griffin act and union democracy.

    Includes bibliographical references and index.
    1. Trade-unions—United States. 2. Labor laws and
legislation—United States. I. Schoomaker, Anita
L. W., 1949–   joint author. II. Title.
KF3400.M3   344'.73'0187   78-12592
ISBN 0-472-08615-4

Preface

This book grew out of a research project undertaken by the authors under a contract with the Labor-Management Services Administration of the U.S. Department of Labor. The purpose of the project was to examine the effectiveness of the Labor-Management Reporting and Disclosure Act of 1959, commonly known as the Landrum-Griffin Act after its sponsors, Phillip Landrum (Georgia) and Robert Griffin (Michigan), a statute specifically aimed at safeguarding the rights of individual union members, i.e., their right to select their officers in honestly conducted elections and, once having done so, their further right to ensure that those officers act responsibly toward them individually and in the conduct of the affairs of the organization.

We had three major objectives: (1) to determine what the impact of the Act's passage per se had been in furthering internal union democracy; (2) to learn what the effect of subsequent court decisions that defined and elaborated upon the statutory language had been; (3) to determine what role the enforcement procedures and practices of the U.S. Department of Labor have played in protecting individual union members' rights.

Initially we had thought to focus primarily on the effects of the interpretation and enforcement of Title IV, the section of the Act that governs union elections, as well as to give some attention to Title I, the so-called Bill of Rights, insofar as legal decisions arising under the latter title have had an influence on internal union affairs. However, we soon found that to do a meaningful study of our topic, we also had to give some attention to the provisions of Title III, which governs trusteeships, and to some portions of Titles II and V, which, among other things, call for the reporting and disclosure of union finances and set forth the fiduciary obligations of union officials. We also looked at two sections of Title VI: Section 601, which is the ultimate source of the Department of Labor's investigatory authority, and Section 609, entitled "Prohibition on Certain Discipline by Labor Organizations."

In the course of our study, we conducted personal interviews with some 150 people: union lawyers, officers, and staff; advocates for dissidents; dissident union members; staff of the U.S. Department of Labor charged with enforcing the Landrum-Griffin Act; as well as some management spokesmen and academicians. We would like to acknowledge our immense debt to all of them. We feel very fortunate to have had access to them. Without their knowledge, interest, and cooperation our task would have been a hopeless one.

In order to test the assessment by the rank and file of the Act's impact, we formulated questions to be included in three studies conducted by the Survey Research Center of the Institute for Social Research at the University of Michigan. By inserting questions in those three surveys, we were able to obtain information from 677 union members whom we would have had difficulty reaching in any other way. The center's staff gave generously of their time and were unfailingly helpful.

Once we received the questionnaire data derived from those three surveys, we leaned heavily on Malcolm Cohen, codirector of the Research Division of the Institute of Labor and Industrial Relations and his Labor Market Information Services staff. We very much appreciate their advice on how to integrate the data from the three surveys and analyze the information derived from the resulting mountain of computer printouts.

We should also like to thank the codirector of the Institute of Labor and Industrial Relations, Charles M. Rehmus, who was unfailingly supportive and helpful. We are also grateful for the legal expertise of our senior legal consultants, Theodore St. Antoine and Florian Bartosic. The latter gave immensely of his time, and his advice is genuinely appreciated.

The U.S. Department of Labor provided us with financial support, and members of the Department's staff encouraged our efforts. We should stress that persons undertaking projects under government sponsorship are encouraged to express their own judgments; the opinions contained in this volume are those of the authors and do not represent any official position or policy of the Department of Labor.

A number of people read the manuscript for this book, and their suggestions were most helpful. We would particularly like to thank Clyde Summers, professor of law at the University of Pennsylvania, and Beate Bloch, associate solicitor, U.S. Department of Labor.

Finally, it will become apparent that this study is replete with judgmental statements. It is customary for those writing a work such as this to absolve their advisors and interviewees of any responsibility for errors in judgment, and we make that standard disclaimer here.

D.B.M.

A.L.W.S.

Contents

Introduction 1

I. Title IV: History, Scope, and the Role of the Courts 6

II. Title IV: Enforcement by the Department of Labor 43

III. Title I: Labor's Bill of Rights 74

IV. Title III: Trusteeships 127

V. Titles II and V: Financial Reporting and Fiduciary Responsibility 149

VI. Enforcement by the Department of Labor 167

VII. Over-all Impact of the Act 178

Appendices 189

Table of Cases 281

Index 285

Introduction

There are a number of readily available texts that detail the setting in which the Labor-Management Reporting and Disclosure Act (or Landrum-Griffin Act) was originally promulgated.[1] Thus, the background of the statute will be sketched in only briefly. The method used in preparing the original report and recommendations to the U.S. Department of Labor, on which this book is based, is described in appendix B.

Public concern regarding allegations of corruption in this country's trade unions dates back at least to the 1902 hearings before the United States Industrial Commission. Intermittently thereafter, investigations into racketeering and gangsterism in a few unions continued to attract attention. Never, however, was alarm as widespread as it became in the late 1950s. Triggered by the nationally televised hearings before the Senate's Select Committee on Improper Activities in the Labor or Management Field, chaired by Senator John L. McClellan (Arkansas), the clamor for government action to regulate the internal affairs of labor unions became incessant. The McClellan Committee, as it is commonly called, heard a parade of witnesses tell of fraudulent union elections, pilfered union treasuries, employer-union collusion at the expense of rank and file members, and a host of other unsavory tales. While in fact very few unions were guilty of such misconduct, the highly publicized disclosures cast suspicion upon the entire organized labor movement. The eventual congressional response was to enact the Labor-Management Reporting and Disclo-

---

1. See for example, U.S. Department of Labor, Office of the Solicitor, *Legislative History of the Labor-Management Reporting and Disclosure Act of 1959, Titles I–VI* (Washington, D.C.: U.S. Department of Labor, 1964); Ralph Slovenko, ed., *Symposium on the Labor-Management Reporting and Disclosure Act of 1959* (Baton Rouge, Louisiana: Claitors' Bookstores Publishers, 1961); Alan K. McAdams, *Power and Politics in Labor Legislation* (New York: Columbia University Press, 1964); Aaron, *The Labor-Management Reporting and Disclosure Act of 1959*, 73 HARV. L. REV. 851 (1960); Cox, *Internal Affairs of Labor Unions Under the Labor Reform Act of 1959*, 58 MICH. L. REV. 819 (1960); Smith, *The Labor-Management Reporting and Disclosure Act of 1959*, 46 VA. L. REV. 195 (1960).

sure Act (LMRDA), a statute signed by President Dwight D. Eisenhower on September 14, 1959.

With some exceptions to be noted later, the major responsibility for enforcing the new law was placed in the hands of the U.S. Department of Labor (DOL). Within that agency, the task fell to the Assistant Secretary for Labor-Management Relations in his capacity as administrator of the Labor-Management Services Administration. (Prior to the creation of the Labor-Management Services Administration in 1963, the Act was administered by the Bureau of Labor-Management Reports.) The day-to-day administration was given to the Office of Labor-Management Standards Enforcement (current name). The Assistant Secretary's Washington, D.C. staff is supplemented by personnel in six regional offices, twenty-four area offices, and twenty resident compliance offices. Reflecting the fact that the Labor-Management Services Administration enforces a number of statutes, field office personnel are charged not only with the enforcement of the LMRDA but also with the administration of the Employee Retirement Income Security Act of 1974, the veterans' reemployment rights program, and Executive Order No. 11491, concerning federal labor-management relations. The field offices also cooperate in the President's Anti-Organized Crime Program.

While a major purpose of the Act was to protect individual members from corrupt union leaders, Congress was also mindful that unions require internal stability in order to function effectively as collective bargaining institutions, and that the government should not interfere unduly in internal union affairs. The Act was intended to regulate unions, not destroy them. A fair summary of congressional concern is the statement made by Senator Hubert H. Humphrey (Minnesota) while Congress was considering the various bills designed to regulate internal union affairs in some way. To him, the eventual statute should seek "to keep American unions clean without impairing their strength, to make them responsible without diminishing their freedom."[2]

The Act's dual function—to curb abuses affecting individual members' rights, while retaining the unions' effectiveness as instruments of collective bargaining—cannot be emphasized too

---

2. U.S. Department of Labor, *Legislative History, supra* note 1, at 58. Senator
    Humphrey's reference was to an earlier bill, introduced by Senator John F.
    Kennedy (Massachusetts). However, the aim of that legislation and that of the
    LMRDA were the same.

much. Congress was attempting to strike a reasonable balance between two possibly conflicting aims, and evaluation of the Act's
effectiveness requires consideration of both goals.

The Limits to Department of Labor Enforcement of the Act

A few points should be noted at the outset with regard to the
over-all coverage of the LMRDA. There are portions of the statute
that the Department of Labor (DOL) does not administer at all, or
in which enforcement is limited:

1. Except for Section 104, which requires that a union supply
   or make available for review a copy of its latest labor agreement to any affected employee who requests it, enforcement of Title I (the so-called Bill of Rights for union members) is by means of private civil suit alone.
2. Section 201(c), which requires that unions shall make their
   books, records, and accounts available to members if they
   have "just cause" for making such request, is enforceable
   only by means of a private civil suit.
3. Title IV is enforced by the DOL only after the election has
   taken place.
4. Enforcement of Section 501(a), which deals with union officers' fiduciary responsibility, and of Section 609, which
   prohibits discipline for exercising rights under the Act, is
   also solely by means of private action.
5. Title VII contains amendments to the Taft-Hartley Act, and
   is the province of the National Labor Relations Board. We
   are hence not concerned with that title in this study.

The Department of Justice, rather than the DOL, investigates
allegations of violations of the following sections of the LMRDA:

1. Section 501(c), which concerns embezzlement. (The DOL
   becomes involved if charges are accompanied by allegations of false reporting—as most are.)
2. Section 503(b), which prohibits any union or employer
   from paying, either directly or indirectly, the fine of any
   union officer or employee who willfully violates the Act.
3. Section 504, which prohibits certain persons from holding
   union office.
4. Section 505, which amends Subsections (a), (b), and (c) of
   Section 302 of the Taft-Hartley Act.

5. Section 602, which concerns extortionate picketing.
6. Section 610, which prohibits the use of force or violence to influence a union member in the exercise of his rights under the Act.

Furthermore, the Act does not extend protection to all union members. Public sector union members were not included in the original statute's coverage. That exclusion has been modified by Section 18 of Executive Order No. 11491 (1969) and the Postal Reorganization Act (1970). The Executive Order gives federal employees protection akin to that of the LMRDA, and the 1970 statute brings postal workers under the LMRDA. The DOL has also interpreted the LMRDA to include other public sector members if the union to which they belong contains some private sector employees. (For example, the election of top union officials of the American Federation of State, County, and Municipal Employees is covered; but the election of officers of a local of that union would not be, if that local were composed solely of public sector workers.) State and local central bodies are excluded from coverage. Thus when the AFL-CIO placed the Colorado state AFL-CIO under trusteeship and members of the Colorado organization went to court to have the trusteeship lifted, the court dismissed the case for lack of jurisdiction.[3] Moreover, the AFL-CIO itself is not covered under Title IV.

Because so many public sector union members are now covered by either the LMRDA or the Executive Order, some of those interviewed suggested that the exclusion of the remainder is now an anachronism, and that the Act should be amended to include them. We believe that their criticism of the statute as now written is valid and that if the Act were to be amended, Congress should consider whether or not such broadened coverage is warranted.

The exclusion of the AFL-CIO and state and local central bodies from some or all provisions of the Act has also received critical comment. However, we spoke to a number of people who were emphatic that Congress was interested only in regulating those labor organizations that are involved in the collective bargaining process, and purposely excluded those whose sole function is to act as spokesmen for organized labor's interests. Because of that distinction, they also differentiated between the relation-

---

3. *Colorado Labor Council v. AFL-CIO*, 481 F.2d 396 (10th Cir. 1973).

ship between the AFL-CIO and its subordinate units and that between a parent union and its subordinates.[4] The AFL-CIO, they explained, has a right to expect its subordinate units to reflect its stated policy because of the function it performs. To us, the latter position makes a good deal of sense.

---

4. An international or national union has been designated throughout as the "parent" union, organization, or body.

CHAPTER I

Title IV: History, Scope, and the Role of the Courts

Because the intent of Title IV—to ensure honest union elections—is so well known, it seems unnecessary to deal with its background at great length.[1] It is enough to say that Congress came to believe that irregularities were too common in internal union elections and that legislation was needed to ensure that, to the extent possible, the outcomes of union elections actually reflected the wishes of the voters. The result of the congressional concern was the Landrum-Griffin Act, officially known as the Labor-Management Reporting and Disclosure Act of 1959 (LMRDA). In Title I, Congress gave union members equal rights to nominate and vote for the candidates of their choice; in Title IV, Congress attempted to establish a general framework within which those rights would be safeguarded.

Title IV again reflects congressional concern that the Act serve the dual purpose of ensuring individual union members' rights and also protecting the stability of unions as institutions. Thus the provisions of Title IV set out only minimum standards to ensure democratic elections:

1. Elections of officers must be held at specified intervals.
2. Unions must comply with candidates' reasonable requests to mail out campaign literature and must do so evenhandedly.
3. Every bona fide candidate can inspect the membership list.[2]
4. Adequate safeguards for fair elections must be provided.
5. All candidates must be permitted to have their own observers at the polls and vote tally.

---

1. In addition to the works cited in the introduction, note 1, see Note, *Union Elections and the LMRDA: Thirteen Years of Use and Abuse*, 81 YALE L. J. 407 (1972).
2. This right of inspection extends only to lists of members of a labor organization which is "subject to a collective bargaining agreement requiring membership therein as a condition of employment. . . ."

6. A reasonable opportunity for nominating candidates must be given.
7. Subject to reasonable qualifications uniformly imposed, every member in good standing should be eligible to run for office, every member has the right to vote for and otherwise support the candidates of his choice without being subjected to reprisal.
8. Notices of an upcoming election must be mailed to every member's last-known mailing address at least fifteen days before that election.
9. Members whose dues are checked off cannot be deemed ineligible to be candidates or vote just because the employer has not forwarded their dues to the union.
10. No union money or employer contributions may be used for union election campaign purposes.
11. Ballots and other election records must be kept for one year after the election.

By design, much of the language of Title IV is quite broad and somewhat vague. Candidacy requirements should be "reasonable", election safeguards "adequate." Congress intended that the Department of Labor (DOL) and the courts define those terms more precisely. Moreover, in order to prevent undue outside interference in union affairs, Congress included in Title IV certain restrictions both on a union member's rights under the Act and on the DOL's enforcement powers:

1. Even if a union's elections are not held within the maximum period allowed under the Act, the DOL cannot bring suit unless a member has filed a complaint.
2. A candidate can initiate private suit under the Act in federal court before an election only if he is denied the right to inspect the mailing list, or if his request to have his campaign literature mailed out is refused.
3. Once the election has been held, a complainant's sole avenue of relief is through the DOL, and he must first have attempted to have his complaint remedied through the union's own appeals procedure and either have been denied relief or have received no final decision within three calendar months before the DOL can accept his complaint.

It should also be noted that not all union elections are covered by the Act:

1. Elections of officers of a federation of labor organizations (e.g., the AFL-CIO) and of state and local central bodies are not covered.
2. Elections of officers of unions in the public sector, with the exception of postal workers, are excluded.[3]
3. Elections of union officials, such as grievance committee-men, who are not defined as "officers" under the Act, are excluded.
4. After long debate, Congress also exempted meetings during which strike votes are taken or at which contract ratification is the issue.
5. Elections to fill vacancies and the initial selection of officers in newly formed or merged labor organizations have also been excluded by virtue of a DOL decision made subsequent to passage of the Act.

If a union elects its top officers at a convention, the election of delegates must comply with the Act.

Measuring Impact of Title IV

Table 1 indicates what statistical data we had hoped to gather in order to try to measure the impact of Title IV. Unfortunately, the unions contacted keep very few, if any, election statistics, so that we had to rely primarily on the memory and experience of those interviewed.

The first question—whether the number of opposition slates has increased, decreased, or remained constant since the passage of the Act—was designed to find out whether or not those interviewed believe that the enactment of Title IV has made dissatisfied members more willing to challenge the incumbents. In the twelve unions investigated, the union officers and their counsel from all but two of them stated that, at the local level particularly, they know that there are more opposition candidates now than there were prior to 1959. In one of the two unions in which opposition candidates were reported not to be more frequent, the spokesmen said that there had been no change whatever; in the other, the number of contested elections had dropped off. Where

3. As indicated in the introduction, federal employees are now given protection similar to that provided by LMRDA, and other public sector union elections are also covered by the Act if the organization contains any private sector members.

TABLE 1. Inferential Statistics Reflecting Effect of Title IV

Data Sought	Source*	Problems with Indicator (Validity), or Source (Reliability)	Data Actually Available
Number of opposition slates; successful vs. unsuccessful	Union Sources	*Reliability:* Unavailable in the aggregate for pre- and post-LMRDA. Even if available for sample unions, is it a *valid* indicator (i.e., is it LMRDA or the times?)	Subjective only. Parties' belief is that opposition slates have increased in most sample unions, but insofar as true, success no greater.
Number of election complaints as percentage of number of elections; results	Union Sources	*Reliability:* Unavailable in the aggregate for pre- and post-LMRDA. Even if available for sample unions, is it a *valid* indicator (i.e., is it LMRDA or the times?)	Subjective only. Parties' belief is that number of complaints has risen considerably, and that they are considered more carefully.
Number of unions having referenda vs. number having convention elections of parent body officers	Union Constitutions	*Validity:* There are numerous reasons unrelated to LMRDA which factor into a decision to go from referendum to convention election (e.g, time, cost).	In sample unions 42% elected parent body officers by referendum at top level as of 1959; 33% now do. Information on all unions not readily available through DOL.
Number of unions adopting election procedures in line with LMRDA standards	Union Constitutions	*Validity:* Constitutions are not necessarily descriptive of actual practice. However, the mere existence of the constitutional language increases members' ability to challenge.	Constitutional language changed considerably to be in conformity with LMRDA in sample unions. (See table 2.) Information on all unions not readily available through DOL.

*Before and after LMRDA.

opposition candidates are more frequent, the margin of victory may be narrower but, in the main, the incumbents still continue to win the large majority of the elections, as they always have.

Rank and file members reached through the three questionnaire surveys had the same reaction; of the fifty-nine respondents who had specific knowledge of the Act, only nine thought that opposition candidates had an easier time ousting the incumbents now than they did before the statute's enactment (appendix G, table 22).

The second question—whether the number of internal election appeals had increased, decreased, or remained constant—was included to determine whether or not passage of the Act had encouraged members to protest against improperly conducted elections and, further, to determine whether union officers are now more responsive to such complaints than they formerly were. In all but three of the unions studied, there has been an upsurge of internal election appeals in recent years. These three included the two mentioned above that have witnessed no upward movement in opposition candidates. In the third, there was reported to have been a noticeable increase in appeals immediately after the passage of the Act, but that has since died down. Parent body officers and their counsel from all twelve unions reported that internal election complaints do receive more careful consideration now, as regards both the procedures followed and the merits of the case, than they did before 1959, and they attributed this trend to the Act's passage. The complaining member can now go to the DOL if he receives no satisfaction internally, and unions try to avoid that. They considered the Act's impact less direct in connection with the increase in opposition tickets at the local level and in post-election protests. In three unions there had been a change in top leadership—in one well before passage of the Act, and in two well after—and spokesmen contended that the leadership change had been the prime influence in triggering interest at other levels. As one explained, the turnover at the top "became a role-model, a source of consciousness-raising, that filtered downward." A majority of the spokesmen from the other nine unions believed that the tenor of the times is responsible: the rebelliousness of the young as compared to the relative docility of their elders. One union lawyer explained the phenomenon in terms of the changed nature of local leaders' responsibilities. The demands of office have increased, and with them the perquisites of office. He contends that holding local office has simply become more attractive.

However, one union lawyer did attribute the increase in election appeals in his client's organization to the Act, and particularly to the law's enforcement. The impact was not immediate, he explained, and until the late 1960s an average of 12 percent of the results of all the union's local elections were being protested, as they always had been. By the late 1960s, however, members had become aware that they could turn to the DOL for help and were doing so. Because of that, about 25 percent of the union's local election results are now being challenged.

Two knowledgeable DOL officials, as well as a parent union officer directly responsible for handling election appeals, told us that the most recent upsurge in election complaints, both internal and to the DOL, is not directly attributable to the Act. Instead, it reflects the current state of the economy and the consequent rise in unemployment. As one DOL official explained, in some unions the officers hold superseniority, and in others union office is a full-time position. Either way, the winner of an election is assured of a job. The loser is thus more likely to make a formal protest than he would if the economy were booming.

As we will discuss in greater detail further along in this chapter, it is unclear to us that the election of a union's top officers by referendum ballot rather than at a convention can, in fact, be considered to reflect the will of the members more accurately. Nevertheless, because that view is widely held, we also included the third question—whether or not more unions now elect their top officials by referendum ballot rather than at a convention. That information for the universe of all unions is not readily available through the DOL. Thus our findings are limited to the twelve unions studied. In that sample, 42 percent elected their top officials by referendum before passage of the Act and 33 percent do so now. The change was attributed solely to costs.

To determine the number of unions implementing election procedures in line with the Act's tenets, comparisons were made between pre- and post-LMRDA constitutions and bylaws of each union in the sample to see whether or not the language of the sections concerned with election procedures had been revised to conform to the provisions and intent of Title IV. Considerable changes had been made in each case to bring those provisions into compliance with the Act.

Table 2 shows provisions in the constitutions and bylaws of the unions studied which may have been affected by Title IV of the Act. For each union, we have indicated whether or not a provi-

TABLE 2. Effect of LMRDA on Union Constitutions and Bylaws

Provisions in Constitution or Bylaws Relating to Local Union Officer Elections	Union											
	#1	#2	#3	#4	#5	#6	#7	#8	#9	#10	#11	#12
A. Constitutional officers defined	X	X	X	X	—	X	X	X	X	X	X	X
B. Term of office (years) at local level	3	3	3	2	3	2	3	3	3*	3	3	3
C. Number of days dues arrearage before loss of right to vote	30	90	90	30	90	120	30	60	90	30	60	60
D. Arrearage protection for "checkoff" members	X	—	X	X	—	X	—	—	—	X	—	—
E. Membership classes ineligible to vote	—	X†	X†	X†	—	X†	—	X†	—	—	—	—
F. Specified length of membership required for candidacy	X	X	X	X	X	X	X	X	X	X	X	X
G. Days notice prior to nomination (min.)	7	20	5	—	7	10	—	15	—	—	7	X§
H. Days notice prior to election (min.)	15	50	35	15	15	15	—	15	15	15	15	15
I. Secret ballot election	X	—	X	X	X	X	X	X	X	X	X	X
J. Use of union or employer money during campaign prohibited	—	—	—	—	Both	Union	—	—	—	—	—	—

						Reason-able						
K. Candidates' rights to inspect membership list (days pre-election)	—	30	30	30	30		—	—	—	—	—	—
L. Distribution of campaign literature	—	—	X	—	X	X	—	—	—	X	X	—
M. Procedures for election appeals	X	—	X	X	X	X	X	X	—	—	—	X
N. Observers allowed at polls and/or at tally of ballots	X	X	X	X	X	X	X	—	—	X	X	—
O. Months preservation of election records	12	12	12	12	12	12	—	12	—	—	X§	X
P. Publication of election results	X	X	—	X	X	X	—	—	—	—	X	—
Provisions added after the Act became effective	G,P	G,H, N,O, P	D,G, H,I, K,L, M,N, O	D,F, H,M, N,O, P	I,J, K,L, M,N, O,P	A,D, E,F, G,I, K,L, M,N, O,P	M	F,M, O	H,I	D,H, I,L, N	B,G, H,I, M,O, P	G,H, I,M
Language modified or deleted to conform to act or subsequent court decisions	B,H, M	B			G,H	B,C, D	B,C, G,H	C	E	E		C,E, F

Note: X indicates document contains provision.—indicates lack of a provision.

*Maximum.
†Apprentices.
‡Inactives.
§Indefinite.

sion currently exists for each category, and where appropriate we have specified the substance of the existing provisions. We have also shown which provisions were added after the Act took effect and which were modified to conform to the Act or subsequent court decisions.

We should stress the fact that absence of a provision in a union document does not necessarily mean that the organization is not in compliance with the Act. It may simply mean that the union, while in compliance with the Act's tenets, has not included a particular practice in its constitution or bylaws.

Listed below are the sections of the Act, alphabetically keyed to table 2. Where relevant, the specific language pertaining to each of the table 2 provisions on the chart is included.

A. Section 3(n) states " '[o]fficer' means any constitutional officer, any person authorized to perform the functions of president, vice president, secretary, treasurer or other executive functions of a labor organization, and any member of its executive board or similar governing body."

B. Section 401(b) provides that "[e]very local labor organization shall elect its officers not less often than once every three years by secret ballot among the members in good standing."

C. Section 401(b). This provision is a possible definition of "good standing."

D. Section 401(e) states that "[n]o member whose dues have been withheld by his employer for payment to such organization pursuant to his voluntary authorization provided for in a collective bargaining agreement shall be declared ineligible to vote. . . ."

E. Section 401(b). This provision is another delineation of "membership in good standing."

F. Section 401(e) specifies that "every member in good standing shall be eligible to be a candidate and to hold office (subject to . . . reasonable qualifications uniformly imposed). . . ."

G. Section 401(e) provides that "[i]n any election required by this section which is to be held by secret ballot a reasonable opportunity shall be given for the nomination of candidates . . ."

H. Section 401(e) also specifies that "[n]ot less than fifteen days prior to the election notice thereof shall be mailed to each member at his last known home address."

I. Section 401(b). See item B listed above.

J. Section 401(g) states that "[n]o moneys received by any labor organization by way of dues, assessment, or similar levy, and no moneys of an employer shall be contributed or applied to promote the candidacy of any person in an election subject to the provisions of this title. . . ."

K. Section 401(c) states that "[e]very bona fide candidate shall have the right, once within 30 days prior to an election of a labor organization in which he is a candidate, to inspect a list containing the names and last known addresses of all members of the labor organization who are subject to a collective bargaining agreement requiring membership therein as a condition of employment. . . ."

L. Section 401(c) states that "every local labor organization . . . shall be under a duty . . . to comply with all reasonable requests of any candidate to distribute . . . campaign literature in aid of such person's candidacy. . . ."

M. Section 402(a) requires a member to exhaust "the remedies available under the constitution and bylaws" or at least to invoke "such remedies without obtaining a final decision within three calendar months after their invocation" before filing a complaint with the Secretary of Labor concerning an election.

N. Section 401(c) secures "the right of any candidate to have an observer at the polls and at the counting of ballots."

O. Section 401(e) specifies that "[t]he election officials . . . shall preserve for one year the ballots and all other records pertaining to the election."

P. Section 401(e) specifies that "[t]he votes cast by members of each local shall be counted, and the results published, separately."

The information for the universe of all unions with regard to constitutional changes was not available through the DOL, and generalization is therefore impossible.

The question then arises whether or not those constitutional changes are a meaningful indicator of changes in actual practices. Were they inserted merely to pay lip service to the Act, or have they had an impact upon the way in which union elections are now conducted? One third of the union lawyers interviewed admitted that the changes were "form, not substance" at the time they were made. Nevertheless, the mere inclusion of those provisions in union constitutions and bylaws serves as a vehicle for members' protests that was unavailable before 1959. Thus, over time, form can become substance; and in the majority of the unions studied, it has. The constitutional changes are—or are in the process of becoming—an avenue by which changes in actual union election practices take place.

Additional Ways of Measuring Impact of Title IV

During the course of this study, we also sought to measure the impact of Title IV by determining how many clearly actionable complaints were filed each year. The *Compliance, Enforcement and Reporting in* [fiscal year] *Under the Labor-Management Reporting and Disclosure Act* (Compliance Reports), issued annually by the DOL, provided data on the following:

1. The number of complaints received by the DOL per year
2. The percentage of those complaints found by the DOL to be actionable
3. The percentage of complaints found actionable that resulted in remedial action

The DOL election activity on a fiscal year basis from 1960 through 1974 (the latest figures available at the time of writing) is shown in table 3. The number of election cases that reached the courts based on civil action, again on a fiscal year basis, and the disposition of those cases is shown in table 4. It should be stressed that there is no correlation between the number of civil actions filed, as listed in table 3, and the number of cases decided, as listed in table 4. The year of filing and the year in which courts render their decisions rarely coincide.

Because the DOL keeps no records concerning the outcome of elections rerun as a result of complaints brought, how often the results of the new election differed from the challenged one is unknown. Personnel of some DOL area offices were asked to estimate, even though they could not give exact figures, how often a supervised rerun resulted in an overturn of the results of the original election. Estimates ranged from a low of 10 percent to a high of 50 percent, and even those figures should be qualified. In the reruns where the results did differ from the original, the new outcome might, and often did, involve only one or a few offices

TABLE 3. Department of Labor Involvement in Union Elections, by Fiscal Year

Fiscal Year	Completed Investigations	Not Actionable (Percentage)	Voluntary Compliance (Percentage)	Civil Actions Filed (Percentage)
1960	212	83.9	16.1	0.0
1961	349	81.1	14.9	4.0
1962	126	62.7	30.2	7.1
1963	130	56.9	31.5	11.6
1964	138	56.5	25.4	18.1
1965	94	70.2	17.1	12.7
1966	150	54.0	23.3	22.7
1967	90	60.0	23.3	16.7
1968	106	62.2	16.1	21.7
1969	128	60.9	16.4	22.7
1970	127	56.7	16.5	26.8
1971	126	56.3	15.9	27.8
1972	134	61.2	21.6	17.2
1973	121	64.5	22.3	13.2
1974	185	64.8	17.3	17.9
Total	2216*	65.8	19.8	14.4

*All figures are taken from the 1974 DOL Compliance Report, at 4, table 2. The figures in this column for the years 1960 through 1963 represent the number of alleged violations investigated rather than complaints investigated. According to the Department of Labor, 30.8% of the investigations completed between 1966 and 1970 involved the twelve unions studied. U.S. Department of Labor, *Union Election Cases Under the Labor Management Reporting and Disclosure Act, 1966–1970* (January 1972), Appendix B.

rather than the entire ballot. These estimates, of course, reflect only the experience of those offices contacted, and may not be representative—even as estimates—for the country as a whole. Nor was it possible to determine why the original winners often won again in the rerun. Does it mean that members really are not interested in properly conducted elections? Or that their hostility towards the person who brought the "outsider" in to settle what to them is a "family" matter outweighs their desire for a properly conducted election? Or is it, instead, that the members make a distinction between officers who have committed a technical violation and those who have committed more serious violations (i.e., they would vote again for the former, but not for the latter)? Since only very limited statistical data are available on rerun outcomes, no analysis can be done comparing kinds of violations and election results, and those questions cannot be answered.

This lack of data is purposeful: the DOL assumes a posture of neutrality and therefore is concerned only that the election procedures are in compliance with the Act's intent. That stance, how-

TABLE 4. Court Decisions on Civil Actions, by Fiscal Year*

Fiscal Year	Number of Court Decisions	Cases Resulting in Rerun or Other Remedy		Cases Dismissed	
		(Number)	(Percentage)	(Number)	(Percentage)
1960	0	0		0	
1961	2	2	[100.0]	0	
1962	8	8	[100.0]	0	
1963	13	13	[100.0]	0	
1964	9	9	[100.0]	0	
1965	10	10	[100.0]	0	
1966	22	16	[72.7]	6	[27.3]
1967	30	20	[66.7]	10	[33.3]
1968	17	14	[82.4]	3	[17.6]
1969	16	13	[81.2]	3	[18.8]
1970	26	24	[92.3]	2	[7.7]
1971	37	34	[91.9]	3	[8.1]
1972	37	26	[70.3]	11	[29.7]
1973	25	18	[72.0]	7	[28.0]
1974	21	16	[76.2]	5	[23.8]
Total	273†	223	[81.7]	50	[18.3]

*Cases were counted in the fiscal year in which they were decided. In instances in which the higher court affirmed the lower court, we counted the first (lower court's) decision; where the higher court reversed the lower court's decision, we counted the later (higher court's) decision only.
†Of the civil actions decided, 34.4% involved the 12 unions studied.

ever, precludes keeping the kind of records that would lead any-one through the complaint maze from beginning to end. If the DOL wishes to measure the impact of Title IV in terms of the disposition of the complaints it receives, a change in the agency's present method of gathering statistical data would be required. For example, if voluntary compliance is achieved, what type of violation was involved, and what was the outcome of the election rerun in each category? If civil action was filed, what was the outcome of the suit? If the court ordered a rerun in such cases, again what was the result of the election by category of violation? In short, the information set forth in tables 3 and 4 serves as a record of election activity per se, but little else.

Interviewees' Assessment of Impact of Title IV

While some of the interviewees in this study were somewhat unfamiliar with the Act as a whole, all were acquainted with the union election provisions of the statute. Indeed, in terms of the Act's impact, one would have to say that it has been most widespread in the election area. Every union studied had changed portions of its constitution's language to conform to the provisions of Title IV; all have had at least a handful of their local elections successfully challenged by the DOL; and virtually everyone interviewed expressed an opinion concerning the Act's enforcement.

In contrast to most activities affected by the LMRDA, with respect to which modifications in constitutional language were normally made once, after the statute's enactment, in the area of union elections constitutional amendments are made continually, reflecting, for the most part, changes in DOL interpretations and subsequent court decisions.

When the Act was first passed, a flood of memoranda was mailed out from the parent union organizations instructing their locals and intermediate bodies on how to conduct elections in conformity with the new statute. Since then, four of the unions we studied have prepared election manuals and two of the four, as well as seven others, continue to send out detailed information concerning the procedures to be followed whenever an election is in the offing. Only one union investigated has not prepared special election material. Spokesmen for that union said that the constitutional provisions themselves serve that purpose amply.

Officers from 42 percent of the unions sampled contended that their particular organizations had always followed the election practices now set forth in their constitutions and bylaws and that therefore, in reality, Title IV had had no effect. On reflection, one local officer decided that the language of the statute may have had an effect in that "it pointed up things we should have done— gave us a framework within which to operate." He also noted that in a particularly "bad case, like the Mineworkers and some [other] unions," the Title also gave the members "some place to go." This observation was borne out by another local officer from a different union, a member of a group that had successfully challenged the top leadership of its parent organization. He stressed that no change had taken place in his local's election practices. But in terms of that challenge, he said, "I was glad the Act was there." Another, this time a parent union official, whose union constitution did contain the necessary language before 1959, said that since the Act was passed those provisions have been observed more conscientiously than formerly.

Other favorable comments from union representatives included one intermediate body officer's observation that the statute had relieved local union officers of the responsibility for conducting honest elections. Should a member object to the procedures as too stringent, the officer now can always use the law as an excuse. Another union official noted: "Labor leaders are very political beings. They let the Act play the bad guy in a suspicious election. Then when they're subpoenaed to testify, they tell the members they don't have any alternative." Over half of the union lawyers interviewed have found the law useful particularly if their clients have had prior experience with the bad publicity and financial costs involved in protracted litigation. Now, if their clients are contemplating changes in constitutional language or election procedures that the lawyers consider questionable, counsel need only remind the union officials of the possible consequences that might flow from those changes. The reminder alone is often all that is needed to end the matter.

One union lawyer stated that the Act made a "real contribution" when it gave unions access to the DOL's investigatory skills in Title IV matters because unions do not have the agency's expertise in investigation. In addition, witnesses to electoral malpractices feel freer to tell their stories to a government agent. They might not be so candid with an in-house investigatory team, for fear of possible retaliation.

One DOL official said that the major accomplishment of Title IV was that it gave impetus to the fashioning of a federal policy on union elections. No statute in and of itself can accomplish anything, he explained, but federal intervention can be used as a tool to further union democracy. Two DOL officials and one local officer interviewed thought that, on the whole, unions are taking more care to assure that their elections are honestly conducted, and that they are more willing to rerun an election on their own if the results are appealed internally and the violations alleged seem valid.[4]

At the other extreme, a local officer told us that Title IV had made his union's top officials less willing to order the rerunning of a local union election than they were before 1959. They find the law itself so distasteful that they refuse to try to correct the matter internally. Local union officers, knowing of the parent body's displeasure, feel freer to conduct dishonest elections now because of that. The locals are small, and "the members can make life pretty rough on the guy who tries to protest outside."

The right of the opposition to have campaign literature mailed

---

4. Union elections were rerun before passage of the Act, but it was not a common occurrence, at least among the unions we studied.

out caused the most concern among local union officers when the Act was first promulgated. Some officers still refuse to accord it. There is good reason for their reluctance. Seven local or intermediate body officers, from four different unions, all of whom had been opposition candidates, stated that the campaign literature mailing right alone spelled the difference between victory and defeat for them. Two of them had to bring private suit before the officers would agree to mail out their literature.

The provision in Section 401(e) that election notices must be mailed to each member at his last known address has, we were told, proven a burden on some unions, not only in terms of the cost of those mailings but also because an up-to-date list of home addresses is so difficult to maintain.

One very knowledgeable DOL official also reported that Title IV has made labor unions less democratic in two important respects. First, because the law specifies that local union elections must be held at least every three years, many unions that used to require that local elections be held annually or biennially now specify three-year terms. Where that has happened, elections are, of course, less frequent, which he considered an unfortunate step away from democracy. Second, because parent organization elections must be held at least every five years, a number of unions which had elected their chief officers by referendum ballot at less frequent intervals now hold elections oftener, but to ameliorate costs, they do so at convention. According to this DOL official, the change was made merely to save money by combining election and convention costs, but he noted that election by referendum which follows the one-man/one-vote principle is, in his opinion, more democratic than weighted voting at a convention.

In summary, the following facts were suggested as reflecting a salutary impact of Title IV:

1. Constitutions and bylaws of individual unions were revised to comply with Title IV's requirements.
2. Constitutional and bylaw changes, in turn, tightened election procedures where they had been lax before, and unions have become more careful to follow them (with the one exception noted, where apparently local officers pay less attention to procedures than they once did).
3. Internal complaints of election irregularities are considered more carefully.
4. The statutory language serves as a shield to protect union staff and officials when they must take unpopular action.

5. The Act has given unions access to the investigatory skills of the DOL.
6. From the dissidents' point of view, the single most important right Title IV has given them is the right to have their campaign literature mailed out.

On the other hand, the following results were suggested as reflecting an adverse impact of Title IV:

1. The requirement that notice of elections be mailed to all members at their last known home address has caused needless expense and inconvenience.
2. Local union officers' terms have been lengthened to three years.
3. Parent union officer elections have shifted away from votes by referendum ballot to votes at convention.

These criticisms of Title IV deserve comment and will be discussed in the following sections.

The Mailed-Notice Requirement

Critics, primarily legal counsel, representing almost 42 percent of the unions in our sample, contended that the provision in Section 401(e) of the Act that election notices must be mailed to each member at his last known address has proven a burden to some unions, not only in terms of the costs of those mailings, but also because an up-to-date list of home addresses is so difficult to maintain. Certainly the contention that a posted notice would be sufficient would generally be valid where the local is small, the members are at a single location, and where members are not on layoff, so that everyone has an opportunity to see those notices. Originally Congress would have exempted a union from the mailed-notice requirement if the date of the election were included in the organization's constitution or bylaws.[5] However, that exemption was eliminated and the written-notice provision retained as the only acceptable method of informing members of an upcoming election. Here, the inconvenience to the union was weighed against the members' right to be informed. In addition, the DOL has held that the mailed-notice provision has been fulfilled if the election notice is published either in the newspaper issued by the union itself (whether

---

5. U.S. Department of Labor, Office of the Solicitor, *Legislative History of the Labor-Management Reporting and Disclosure Act of 1959, Titles I–VI* (Washington, D.C.: U.S. Department of Labor, 1964), at 701.

by the local, an intermediate body, or the parent organization) or in a union publication that all interested members receive (e.g., a state or local central body's publication). In at least one case, where the incumbent officer had telephoned all of the members of his local advising them when the election was to be held, the DOL also held that that action complied with the Act's intent. That interpretation appears to be a reasonable one that takes into account the problem of costs and up-to-date mailing lists. Thus, while it is clear that keeping a mailing list current is a problem for any organization, congressional intent can be served only if the mailed-notice practice is continued.

Length of Local Union Officers' Terms

The criticism was made that local union officers are now usually elected for three-year terms, as Title IV permits, whereas before 1959 those terms were often shorter. The DOL's own 1965 study of this matter does not bear out that assertion. As that study points out, pre-1959 constitutional language prescribing terms of local office was often vague or nonexistent. Where precise language was used, the figures given in the DOL study indicate that the number of terms that became longer after 1959 was offset by the number that were shortened.[6] In our sample, three unions have revised the language to call for longer terms of local union office; two have made no revisions; and one now calls for a shorter term. The other six union constitutions had very vague language, or called for terms of minimum and maximum length. In practice, in three of those six, terms were usually for longer than three years.

Even if the contention were true that officers' terms are now longer, one could argue that longer tenure promotes greater internal stability and compensates for any loss of democracy. Five local union officers interviewed, from three different unions, complained that even the three-year term is too short. They contend that because of such short periods they must put political considerations (i.e., the next election) uppermost in their minds and cannot act responsibly enough in their dealing with employers to safeguard the members' long-range interests. Those interviewed whose tenure is even shorter—and not all local union officers have

---

6. U.S. Department of Labor, Labor-Management Services Administration, Office of Labor-Management Policy Development, *Union Constitutions and the Election of Local Union Officers* (Washington, D.C.: U.S. Department of Labor, 1965), at 20–24.

three-year terms at the present time—complained of this more forcibly still.

The complaint concerning the brevity of the three-year term was voiced most often by officers of unions which, before 1959, had traditionally accorded local officers longer terms. In contrast, a local officer of a union which had, until a few years ago, held elections every two years, disliked the new three-year terms because the old system "makes officers go back to the members more" and, to him, that was all to the good.

The legislative history of the three-year language indicates that it was a compromise between those forces in Congress that put greater stress on the stability of labor-management relations at the local level and would have preferred longer terms, and those whose primary concern was leadership responsiveness to rank and file members and thus opted for shorter tenure.[7] The three-year limitation, then, was an attempt to strike a balance between leadership responsiveness and leadership responsibility.

Referendum Ballot Election vs. Convention Election

The last criticism leveled at the Act was that it caused parent organizations to opt for electing their top officials at a convention rather than by referendum ballot, and that that change has made those elections less democratic. It should be noted at the outset that the referendum method of electing top officers was never the more popular one. A study done in 1958 showed that of the 111 unions under consideration, only twenty-five elected their top officers by referendum ballot. A follow-up study of the constitutions in effect in January of 1965, which looked only at unions with a membership of 40,000 or more, found that of the seventy-four unions studied, only seventeen still held referendum elections. By 1972, only eleven of the fifty-six unions with over 50,000 members continued to do so.[8] Between 1959 and 1972, six major unions had changed to convention election. As stated earlier, in the twelve unions we studied, one third still hold referendum elections at the present time. Prior to passage of the Act, 42 percent did. Note that this is still a higher percentage than the average among unions generally.

7. U.S. Department of Labor, *Legislative History*, *supra* note 5, at 719 *et seq.*
8. Cohany & Phillips, *Election and Tenure of International Union Officers*, 81 MONTH. LAB. REV. 1221–29 (1958); Everette, *Referendum Elections of National Union Officers*, 89 MONTH. LAB. REV. 856–59 (1966); U.S. Department of Labor, Bureau of Labor Statistics, *Directory of National Unions and Employee Associations, 1973* (Washington, D.C.: U.S. Department of Labor, 1974), at 89.

Under laboratory conditions, one could not quarrel with the assertion that election of officers by referendum is more democratic than election at convention. Such conditions are unattainable in union elections, however. All candidates and their representatives cannot possibly monitor every aspect of the electoral process in hundreds of locals. Congress recognized this in Title IV by mandating that local union elections, but not parent body elections, be governed by the one-man/one-vote principle.

Among those interviewed, the arguments went both ways. For example, local union officers from three unions tended to favor referendum election. The principle of one-man/one-vote applied to them; why not to the top officials? Moreover, they believed that the machine functions too well at a convention. More often than not, they said, at least some local union officers are ex officio delegates, and if local officers outnumber the rank and file delegates, the incumbents' chances of re-election are far greater than they would be in a referendum election. One local union official's remarks are representative of this school of thought:

> If you know how conventions are run, you know that it would take a severe lack of brains to vote against the administration. [The parent organization's president] made sure that "we" were the ones who voted for the international officers. We, who have a stake in his administration, in his being the end point of the grievance procedure, etc. It's a sure thing.

(In the unions we studied, the constitutions of five provide that at least the chief officers of the locals are ex officio delegates.)

However, others interviewed—including some local officers—from seven other unions, considered convention elections, particularly in a large union, the preferred method. The local officer delegates know something about the qualifications and capabilities of the organization's top officials since they are the ones who have contact with the officers of the parent organization. To the rank and file, they contend, the chief officers are just names. Said one, "What does the guy from Bad Axe know about the international president? The members at least know who they are voting for when they elect the delegates." Moreover, where the delegates' expenses to attend the convention are paid by the union, which is usually the case, delegate elections can be quite spirited. The policing of those elections is thus better than it would be if the members were casting their votes for remote names that mean very little to them.

Those union spokesmen contended that if a referendum election could be well supervised, with all candidates' observers present during all phases of the electoral process at each local—during the campaign, at all polling places, at every tally—it would be the more democratic method. But that situation is a physical impossibility in a union of any size. As it is, the argument continued, referendum elections can easily be stolen. This is particularly true of mail ballot elections: there is no way for the opposition to keep control of those ballots. Moreover, the mailing list problem then becomes crucial. Inevitably, the union is unaware of some address changes and some members do not receive their ballots. Those who do not are automatically disenfranchised.

The legislative history of the statute indicates that the drafters of the Act also believed that the opposition would have an easier time mounting an effective campaign against the parent organization incumbents at a convention than in a referendum election.[9]

The respondents from two unions in the sample expressed no opinion on the question of referendum vs. convention elections. Interestingly enough, in both organizations, parent body officers are elected by referendum, yet the interviewees had not thought sufficiently about the question to be willing to comment.

While we recognize that a union convention, like any political convention, may have its drawbacks, the arguments presented above in favor of electing the top officials of parent organizations at conventions are logical enough so that we cannot automatically conclude that going from referendum to convention election necessarily has an adverse impact on union democracy.

Despite the criticisms leveled at the restrictions and problems created by the enactment of Title IV, we—along with the majority of those we interviewed—believe that its over-all impact has been beneficial. Unions are now more conscientious in following correct procedures, and do give more careful consideration to election appeals. We agree with those who say that the idea of honest elections has now been firmly implanted—even if not always practiced—and, as one interviewee put it, "that idea will not go away."

Court Interpretations of Title IV

Clearly, any court decision that orders a union to rerun its election will have a certain amount of impact, if only on the organization

---

9. U.S. Department of Labor, *Legislative History, supra* note 5, at 702.

involved, and celebrated cases, such as the Mineworkers' or the Steelworkers' District 31 reruns, have had widespread repercussions. However, it would be both tedious and unprofitable to deal with decisions of that nature in this section. They are too numerous, and moreover anyone with an interest in studying them in detail has ready access to them in the DOL's annual Compliance Reports.

There are, in addition, decisions concerning the reasonableness of candidacy requirements (e.g., meeting attendance) which have been of extreme importance to the unions whose requirements have been challenged, and which have also alerted other unions to give thought to revising their own requirements. Such cases will not be discussed here unless they have caused the government to alter its enforcement policies to a noticeable degree.

The primary focus will be upon seven Supreme Court decisions which have affected the enforcement of Title IV, as well as upon significant lower court decisions. In each case where those interviewed commented on the impact of a decision, their views have been included, unless the interviewees or their unions were involved in the court action. In the latter circumstance, their opinions have been omitted for the sake of confidentiality. This fact accounts for some of the scarcity of comment on some cases; on others, interviewees simply had few or no opinions.

The seven Supreme Court cases cover a wide variety of subjects involving union elections, ranging from the complainant's efforts to be eligible for candidacy to his right to judicial review of the DOL's determination not to bring suit against his union despite his challenge. In all but one of the cases, the decisions redounded to the benefit of the complaining member.

The earliest Supreme Court decision concerning Title IV was *Wirtz v. Local 153, Glass Bottle Blowers Association.*[10] The issue involved the problem of delays between the time election results are challenged and a court's ruling with regard to that challenge. The DOL argued that an intervening election should not render the suit moot. The Supreme Court agreed. The Court's determination is a significant one, given the length of time it often takes for a case to be heard. If the Supreme Court had held the other way, most cases thereafter would never have gone to trial at all. As Professor Florian Bartosic has pointed out,

10. 389 U.S. 463 (1968).

"any competent union lawyer can delay most cases until it is time for the next election."[11]

The same day that the Supreme Court handed down its decision in the case above, it decided *Wirtz v. Local Union No. 125, Laborers International Union of North America*[12] as well. This case also involved the question of mootness, but since the Court had already rendered its opinion on that question, the only remaining issue here was whether or not the DOL could challenge the validity of the general election of union officers even though the only internal union protest had been filed against a subsequent runoff election for a single office. The Court held that it could. To the argument that the complainant had not exhausted his internal remedies, the Court countered that the union had, in fact, been put on notice of the complaint with regard to the general election by virtue of the fact that the protest concerning the runoff involved a violation which would have been present in the original election as well. The decision thus broadened the DOL's permissible scope of complaint, albeit only in a circumstance where the complaining member could be construed to have exhausted his internal remedies.

While the *Laborers Local 125* case can be said to have widened the DOL's scope of complaint under certain limited circumstances, the decision in *Hodgson v. Local Union 6799, United Steelworkers of America*[13] clearly circumscribed it. The DOL can bring suit on a violation only if that violation is encompassed in the member's original internal complaint unless the member could not have known of the violation when he filed that complaint. In this case, the member had not objected to the union's meeting attendance requirement in his internal election appeal, and since he surely knew of it the Court held that he had no right to include it later. Nor did the DOL have a right to include it on his behalf: "The obvious purpose of an exhaustion requirement is not met when the union, during 'exhaustion,' is given no notice of the defects to be cured."[14] The decision pleased union officers

---

11. *The Supreme Court, 1974 Term: The Allocation of Power Deciding Labor Law Policy*, LXII Va. L. REV. 533, 560 (1976). David Klein makes the same point in his chapter, "Public Review Boards' Place in Dispute Resolution," in Barbara D. Denis and Gerald G. Somers, eds., *Arbitration—1974: Proceedings of the Twenty-Seventh Annual Meeting, National Academy of Arbitrators* (Washington, D.C.: The Bureau of National Affairs, Inc., 1974), at 233.
12. 389 U.S. 477 (1968).
13. 403 U.S. 333 (1971).
14. *Id.* at 340.

and their counsel. Typically, their reason was, as one lawyer phrased it, that "that took care of the DOL's penchant for FBI-type investigations." One union officer, with past experience as a dissident, told us quite candidly that the decision was a good one because if the DOL has the right to investigate everything, it can always find a member to file a complaint on whatever it uncovers. He added, "I don't have to guess about such things. I know."

On the other hand, one dissident was most unhappy with the decision: "Now a complainant has to get a lawyer before he can go to the DOL, just to be sure the scope of his complaint is broad enough."

Reaction to the decision among those who enforce the Act was mixed. All of the DOL compliance officers we interviewed believed that it puts too much burden on the complainant and hampers their own investigations. On the other hand, two members of the DOL national office considered the Court's interpretation a reasonable one. They believed that the union should be on notice as to the nature of the complaint and have an opportunity to deal with it internally before the complainant comes to the DOL.

In 1968, in *Wirtz v. Hotel, Motel and Club Employees Union, Local 6,*[15] the Court was asked to decide whether or not that union's candidacy requirements could be considered a "reasonable qualification" within the meaning of the Act. It found that the qualification—which concerned prior office-holding—was unreasonable in that it prevented 93 percent of that union's members from running for office. The Court also addressed the question whether that requirement "may have affected the outcome" of the election in which it was imposed. The Court held that the requirement itself established that a violation had occurred which may have affected the outcome, since the wholesale exclusion of possible candidates in and of itself may have affected the outcome. The Court said: "[I]t is impossible to know that the election would not have attracted many more candidates but for the bylaw."[16] In such event, where a prima-facie case has been made that there was a violation which may have affected the outcome, the burden shifts to the union to prove that in fact the violation did not do so.

In subsequent lower court cases, the percentage of members made ineligible by a particular candidacy requirement has carried substantial weight in some but not all cases. In *Brennan v. Local*

---

15. 391 U.S. 492 (1968).

16. *Id.* at 508. An interesting decision which follows the rationale in this case is *Usery v. Stove Workers* (547 F.2d 1043 (8th Cir. 1977)).

5724, United Steelworkers of America,[17] where 84.8 percent of the members were disqualified as candidates because of the meeting attendance requirement, the court found the provision reasonable nevertheless. However, in *Dunlop v. Local 3489, United Steelworkers of America*,[18] where 96.5 percent were thereby excluded, the Court of Appeals for the Seventh Circuit, specifically relying on the Supreme Court's holding with regard to the 93 percent figure, found the requirement unreasonable.[19] The circuit court's decision was appealed, and the Supreme Court upheld the lower court decision both because of the large percentage of members who were disqualified from candidacy and because of the requirement that a member must attend one half of the meetings for three years prior to the election. The Court stated that "the rule's effect of requiring potential insurgent candidates to plan their candidacies as early as 18 months in advance of the election when their reasons for opposition* might not have yet emerged, established that the requirement has a substantial antidemocratic effect on local union elections." The explanatory footnote in the opinion reads: "*Regular meetings were held on a monthly basis. Thus, in order to attend half of the meetings in a three-year period, a previously inactive member desiring to run for office would have to begin attending 18 months before the election."[20] The decision leaves the issue of the meeting attendance requirement per se still unsettled. Thus, those advising unions on legal matters remain without firm guidance. The most they can do is to warn their clients that if a constitution contains a stringent meeting attendance requirement, that provision may involve the organization in protracted legal battles should a member challenge its legality.

The two additional Supreme Court decisions concerning Title IV deal with complaining members' rights. The first, *Trbovich v. United Mine Workers of America*,[21] now gives such members a right to intervene in a post-election DOL enforcement suit, as long as such intervention does not go beyond the issues raised by

17. 489 F.2d 884 (6th Cir. 1973).
18. 520 F.2d 516 (7th Cir. 1975).
19. *Brennan v. Local 3911, United Steelworkers of America, AFL-CIO* (372 F. Supp. 961 (1973)) in dictum held as did the circuit court (and, later, the Supreme Court) in the *Local 3489* case just described.
20. *Steelworkers, Local 3489 v. Usery*, (429 U.S. 305, at 306). The latter reason was also the basis of the circuit court's decision in *Usery v. Transit Union, Local 1205* (545 F.2d 1300 (1st Cir. 1976)).
21. 404 U.S. 528 (1972).

the DOL. The member is, then, allowed to have his viewpoint heard, but cannot go outside the scope of the DOL's complaint in doing so. The argument that the complainant's viewpoint was already adequately represented by the DOL acting on his behalf was dismissed on the ground that the DOL was charged with two duties: to represent the complainant against the union, and to protect the public interest. Thus, if the complaining member believes that in his case the latter obligation conflicts with the former, he has a right to intervene on his own behalf.

Those charged with enforcing the Act have not been troubled by the *Trbovich* decision, as far as we could ascertain. Nor were most of the union lawyers perturbed by it. However, some DOL officials initially feared that the impact of the decision in the last of the seven Supreme Court cases, *Dunlop v. Bachowski,* [22] might well be adverse.

In the *Bachowski* case, the DOL, after investigation, decided that the election violations Bachowski complained of could not have affected the outcome of the election and determined not to bring suit. Upon learning of this decision, the complainant filed suit asking that the DOL give a detailed explanation of the reason for its decision to him and to the court and, if the court found that the DOL acted arbitrarily and capriciously in rendering its decision, that it order the DOL to file suit.

The Supreme Court held that the decision not to sue is reviewable in order that the court can determine whether or not the decision was arbitrary and capricious, and that the DOL is obligated to provide the reviewing court and the complainant with an adequate statement setting forth the reasons for its decision. If the court finds the statement adequate, the suit should be dismissed. What the court should do if it finds, based on that statement, that the decision not to sue was so irrational as to be arbitrary and capricious, was left somewhat vague. The Court merely stated: "We prefer . . . to assume that the Secretary would proceed appropriately without coercion of a court order when finally advised by the courts that his decision was in law arbitrary and capricious."[23]

A few DOL spokesmen reported that the *Bachowski* decision could leave them in the middle: either they sue or they will be sued themselves for not suing. One possible result might be that the DOL officials would decide to sue more often in marginal

---

22. 421 U.S. 560 (1975).
23. *Id.* at 576.

cases than they have hitherto. Another might be that their limited resources would be so strained by having to defend their past actions that they would of necessity neglect current complaints, no matter how legitimate.

According to one legal scholar however, the fears of the DOL that the *Bachowski* decision will strain agency resources are grossly exaggerated. He predicted that even if there are, at first, a rash of suits to challenge the DOL's decision not to pursue a particular complaint, the number will shortly decline. The "arbitrary and capricious" test is very narrowly drawn, he explained. The courts have held that an agency can make even an "unreasonable" decision and still be upheld. Thus far, his prediction has proven accurate in the sense that, while some defensive suits were filed subsequent to *Bachowski*, the number of suits has not been as great as some had feared. It is yet too early to know whether his prediction concerning the courts' disposition of such suits will prove true. The district court decision in *Valenta v. Dunlop and United Steelworkers of America*,[24] the first post-*Bachowski* defensive suit, bore out his prediction, in that the court held that the DOL had not acted arbitrarily under the *Bachowski* standard. However, on remand to the U.S. District Court for the Western District of Pennsylvania, the *Bachowski* case itself drew a different reaction. There the judge held that the DOL had acted in an arbitrary and capricious manner.[25]

Over 12 percent of the union lawyers interviewed were troubled by the *Bachowski* decision and its potential for unwarranted harassment. One attorney—the lone dissenter from the usual opinion that the *Trbovich* decision would not have an adverse impact—thought that both *Trbovich* and *Bachowski* might prove harmful. In his experience he has found that not all dissidents are genuine reformers, and he fears that those two decisions give a variety of new options to those who are simply troublemakers.

While it is too early to assess the impact of the *Bachowski* decision on the enforcement and reach of the LMRDA, it seems clear that the decisions in four of the Supreme Court cases discussed have had a beneficial effect in terms of clarifying the scope of the Act's reach. They are: *Wirtz v. Local 153, Glass Bottle Blowers Association; Wirtz v. Local Union No. 125, Laborers In-*

---

24. 90 L.R.R.M. 3316 (D. Ohio 1975). A notice of appeal was filed but subsequently withdrawn after Valenta won the next election.
25. 413 F. Supp. 147 (W.D. Penn. 1976), appeal dismissed, 545 F.2d 363 (3d Cir. 1976). The case has since been dismissed as moot (Jan. 27, 1978).

ternational *Union of North America; Hodgson v. Local Union 6799, United Steelworkers of America;* and *Trbovich v. United Mine Workers of America.* The issues raised and decided were important in terms of both future enforcement and complaining members' rights. The two other cases, *Wirtz v. Hotel, Motel and Club Employees Union, Local 6* and *Steelworkers, Local 3489 v. Usery,* appear to have left the fundamental issue of what constitutes a reasonable candidacy requirement still undecided.

Suggested Changes in Language of Title IV

Proposals to modify the present language of Title IV of the LMRDA called for amendments that would effect the following changes:

1. Include intermediate bodies in the coverage under Section 401(c).
2. Define "bona fide candidate" and "adequate safeguards" more fully.
3. Give opposition candidates the right not only to inspect the membership list, but to be given a copy of the list itself.
4. Make the recall provisions of Sections 401(h) and 401(i) more meaningful, or, alternatively, delete those sections altogether.
5. Give the courts discretion to award attorney's fees and other expenses in Title IV cases.
6. Give the complainant the option of either going to the DOL with his Title IV complaint or filing private suit.
7. Give the DOL the power to hold an administrative hearing to determine the legality or illegality of a union's constitutional language.

The last alteration—which would provide for an administrative hearing—was suggested as an attempt to deal with two problems we will consider more fully in chapter 2: the delay between the time an election complaint over constitutional language is made to the DOL and the time the case is argued in court, and the need to give the DOL additional options in enforcing the Act. The following subsections will deal in detail with the arguments made by those we interviewed, and our conclusions regarding their suggestions.

Inclusion of Intermediate Bodies in Section 401(c) Language
Section 401(c) speaks only of "national," "international," and "local" labor organizations. Thus one might presume that intermedi-

ate bodies were excluded from coverage and, in the past, the right
of a candidate for office in an intermediate body to use the membership mailing list has, in fact, been challenged. A DOL spokesman and one dissident therefore suggested that the section be
amended to specify that intermediate bodies are covered. However, because of certain key court decisions, the DOL has already
been led to interpret that that exclusion was an oversight, and the
agency's interpretation has gone unchallenged.[26] Therefore, we
conclude that the language change is unnecessary.

Precise Definitions of "Bona Fide Candidate" and "Adequate Safeguards"

Two union lawyers regarded the term "bona fide candidate" in
Section 401(c) as too vague. Specifically, they would like the section to state by what action a member becomes a "bona fide candidate" and thus, for example, has right of access to the mailing list.
The DOL enforcement officers considered the phrase "adequate
safeguards" in Section 401(c) to be too imprecise. They found it
difficult to advise union officers seeking their guidance as to what
would constitute sufficient safeguards in their unions' elections to
comply with the Act's intent. It would be helpful to them, they
said, if the section could be rewritten to give more specific meaning to that term.

As noted previously in discussing the broad language that was
used in Title IV, Congress purposely left a number of phrases
amorphous, preferring that the courts give them more precise
meaning. The courts are in the process of doing so—e.g., the decision in *Yablonski v. Mineworkers* already sets forth the definition
of "bona fide candidate" as one who "is actively seeking both
nomination and election."[27] Thus while we can sympathize with
those who must wrestle with vague statutory language while they
await the courts' actions, those bodies are in the process of defin-
ing the language and we believe that to halt that process and start
over again would do more harm than good.

Opposition Candidates' Right to the Membership List

At one stage in the drafting of the Act, the language under consideration would have given opposition candidates free access to the

---

26. U.S. Department of Labor, Labor-Management Services Administration, *Election of Officers of Labor Organizations* (Washington, D.C.: U.S. Department of
   Labor, 1974), at 24 (interpretation and court cases).
27. 71 L.R.R.M. 2606 (D.D.C. 1969).

union's membership mailing list. Subsequently, however, Congress specifically rejected that idea.[28]

Despite the fact that Section 401(c) gives challengers the right to have their literature mailed out at their own expense, advocates for dissidents and some academicians indicated their belief that such candidates should also have a right to have a copy of the list itself. A candidate's right to inspect such a list once within the thirty days prior to an election appears to them to be a meaningless one. Particularly in an organization of any size, where the members are geographically dispersed, it does little good, they said, to have the right to "inspect" a list that contains hundreds of names. The only time such inspection would be meaningful would be when the opposition candidate already has a membership list and wants to check it against the one that will be used to mail out his literature. Moreover, if the union is a large one, even mailing rights are not very helpful—it is too costly to the candidate to do a mailing to the entire membership. (The language has been interpreted by the DOL to give the candidate the right to a limited mailing—i.e., the right to pick out just those members from the full list to whom he wants his literature mailed. However, this assumes that he already knows whom he wishes to contact.)

Ideally, the argument continues, the opposition candidate should be given the list and, moreover, the list should contain not just names and home addresses but, in addition, should indicate where each member works and whether or not he holds union office (the last is relevant if the candidate is running for intermediate body or parent union office). The incumbents already have access to the membership list and know who is influential in the union. By virtue of the fact that they are incumbents, they have every advantage in an election campaign. If the opposition candidate could be given a meaningful list, it would give him a modicum of equality with regard to access to the members that he currently does not have. If it is feared that the list might fall into improper hands, then either the Act or the union constitution should set forth stiff penalties against those who let that happen.

It was argued further that the National Labor Relations Board decision in the *Excelsior Underwear* case[29] (later affirmed by the Supreme Court) requires that an employer must give a union try-

---

28. Note, *Union Elections and the LMRDA: Thirteen Years of Use and Abuse,* *supra* note 1, at 457 n. 227.
29. 156 NLRB Dec. 1236 (1966); *NLRB v. Wyman Gordon Co.,* 394 U.S. 759 (1969).

ing to organize his workers access to employee names and addresses. Shouldn't insurgent candidates have those same rights
vis-à-vis the incumbent officers?

Officers of large, geographically dispersed, local unions who
themselves had once been opposition candidates were asked how
helpful inspection rights had been to them. Would they have
wanted the membership list itself instead? They all agreed that
inspection rights alone were relatively meaningless. The important right, in their experience, was that of having campaign literature mailed out.

One officer recalled that, after inspecting the list at the union
hall, he tried to telephone some of the members on it only to find
that they were long since deceased. If he had been given a copy of
that list, and had lost the election, at least he would have had firm
evidence on which to base an election protest. But he, along with
the rest, felt quite strongly that the membership list should not be
given out, even though it would have made it easier for him to
campaign had he had one. Without a list, they all had to rely on
personal contacts, built up over time, to help them get their mes-
sages across.

The main argument against giving out the list was that that
practice would be too vulnerable to abuse. Whenever a membership list falls into the wrong hands—and all of those interviewed
said that it does happen—it is harmful. If the "wrong hands" are
advertisers or insurance agents, for example, the members are
bombarded with junk mail, telephone solicitations, and the like,
and they should be protected from such invasions of privacy. More
important, if the list reaches a rival union—and this too has happened—it makes it that much easier for the rival union to try to
raid members from the organization whose list it now has.

Thus, while these officers fully agreed that the opposition
candidate has an uphill battle without possession of the list itself,
they still thought it best not to accord him that right.

When asked if punitive language, inserted either in the Act or
in the union's constitution, designed to forestall the list's misuse
would solve the problem, local officers said that such provisions
would have little value. If the list were given to every candidate
requesting it—and in fairness it would have to be—it would be too
difficult to prove which one of those candidates had in fact misused it.

The advocates for dissidents were not impressed with the arguments made by the local union officers cited. Everyone's pri-

vacy is invaded daily. Why give special protection to union members? Moreover, if an organization is that vulnerable to raiding, perhaps it deserves to be raided.

Having considered all of the preceding arguments, we conclude that the overwhelming advantage that incumbents have against the opposition is a worse problem than possible misuse of the lists, and that that advantage must be offset in some way. The candidate should have access to the members, and be able to visit their homes or meet them at their job sites, so that he has an opportunity to become known and get his message across. There is only one way to accomplish that: give candidates the membership list.

While a legal mandate to give out the list could be regarded to constitute still further intrusion into internal union affairs, we can also understand the position of those who advocate that the insurgent candidates should be entitled to the membership list. If the Act were ever to be amended, Congress should, in our opinion, consider revision of the membership list provision.

Recall Provisions of Sections 401(h) and 401(i)

According to some interviewees, Sections 401(h) and 401(i), dealing with the need for adequate procedures for the removal of a local union officer "guilty of serious misconduct," are not enforced and, indeed, are unenforceable. The rules and regulations that have been promulgated are far too cumbersome and difficult to interpret to be useful even if someone were to try to enforce the recall provisions. The suggestion was made that the language be changed to make the procedure workable or, alternatively, that those two sections simply be deleted.

From the legislative history of the Act, it seems clear that Sections 401(h) and 401(i) were inserted to reassure those members of Congress who would have preferred that local union officers' terms be shorter than a maximum of three years. They feared that the members would be saddled with an offending officer for too long a period, and wanted language inserted that would preclude that from happening. (Note that the language applies only to local unions. Congress believed that trying to apply those provisions to intermediate or parent bodies would be unworkable.)[30]

No DOL officials interviewed could remember a local union member ever having complained of a lack of adequate recall pro-

---

30. U.S. Department of Labor, *Legislative History, supra* note 5, at 719 *et seq.* For the fact that these provisions were intended to cover only locals, see Senator Sam Ervin's (North Carolina) remarks at page 737.

visions in his union's constitution or bylaws. Four of the unions studied have recall provisions in their constitutions, but only one union has ever used them, and then only to remove subunit officials, who are not deemed "officers" under the meaning of the Act. Otherwise, those provisions, too, have been found overly cumbersome. When the majority of the members of a local union has wanted to be rid of an offending officer before his term expired, other means have been found. The disciplinary procedure was one possibility cited. More commonly, the officer was quietly persuaded to resign.

One local union officer saw real merit in the fact that the recall provision in his union's constitution had never been invoked. (In that document, a recall vote is theoretically possible at any of the local's regular meetings.) As he put it: "Thank God it isn't enforced! Then officers might really be irresponsible, in terms of statesman-like bargaining. . . . This would so politicize a union as to paralyze it. The 'ins' and 'outs' could come out in force at every meeting and officers could be turned out every month."

Because unions do have other avenues of relief for ridding themselves of an officer guilty of serious misconduct, and because the task of drafting reasonable and workable recall provisions appears to be an onerous one, we believe it would not be practicable to recommend that the language of those two sections be changed. As to the suggestion that the two be deleted entirely, that, in effect, is what has already happened.

Discretionary Awarding of Attorneys' Fees

Even though Title IV is silent on the subject of a court's right to award attorneys' fees to union members filing Title IV complaints, at the time we conducted the interviews for this study, payment of such fees had been held to be appropriate where a member brought private suit under Section 401(c).[31] However, a number of those interviewed, both inside and outside the DOL, believed that, as the statute is written, such fees could not be awarded to the complainant in cases brought on his behalf by the DOL because the Act has already provided the complainant with the legal services of the agency, and any additional services by private counsel would be viewed as merely a duplication of effort and thus not compensable. However, as the Supreme Court noted in

---

31. *Yablonski v. United Mineworkers*, 466 F.2d 424 (D.C. Cir. 1972), *cert. denied*, 412 U.S. 918 (1973).

the *Trbovich* case, the DOL has two roles to play and, in fact, the complainant does often require outside legal counsel. Given that, some academicians, advocates for dissidents, and dissidents themselves, suggested that the language of the Act be amended to provide for the discretionary awarding of attorneys' fees to the complainant in Title IV suits initiated by the DOL.

Since the time of our interviews, two circuit court decisions have held that attorneys' fees may be awarded to complainants acting as intervenors in suits brought by the DOL,[32] thus laying to rest the doubts of those who suggested the need for that amendment. What the courts will do with regard to the awarding of fees in suits filed against the DOL for determining not to litigate or with regard to DOL-initiated cases where the complainant does not act as an intervenor has not finally been determined.[33]

Complainant's Right to Two Options

Related to the question of the awarding of legal fees is the proposal that the complainant should have the option either of going to the DOL or of filing private suit in a Title IV matter. One reason given for this proposal was that if the complainant were to win the private suit he could collect substantial damages. To the argument that Congress granted exclusive jurisdiction to the DOL so that the agency could screen out frivolous complaints, the proponents of the proposal replied that the complainant's lawyer would be just as effective a screening mechanism. He would not take the case unless he thought he could win and collect his fee.

One variation on the theme was that the complainant should have the right to go to court if the DOL refused to process his complaint. Another variant would have the individual go to court with the understanding that the court, before taking any action, would give the DOL thirty days to investigate the case. If, after the thirty-day period had expired, the DOL concluded that the case had merit, it would join with the complainant in bringing suit. If, on the other hand, the DOL determined that the case was without merit, the court would not consider the agency's findings determinative but would instead take a fresh look at the facts on its own. If

---

32. *Usery v. Teamsters, Local 639,* 543 F.2d 369 (D.C. Cir. 1976), *cert. denied,* 429 U.S. 1123 (1977); *Brennan v. United Steelworkers,* 554 F.2d 586 (3d Cir. 1977), *cert. denied,* 83 L.C. 10552 (1978).
33. For example, in dictum, the two circuit court decisions cited at note 29, *supra,* appear to be in disagreement as to whether or not a complainant who did not act as an intervenor could be reimbursed.

it became clear over time that complainants were winning cases that the DOL had refused to process, the agency might move more quickly and aggressively to avoid embarrassment in the future.

Over half of those interviewed, and union lawyers especially, were emphatically against implementation of such a proposal. They argued that the DOL was given exclusive jurisdiction, and bills giving members the right to private suit were rejected, because Congress believed that to do otherwise could lead to a rash of multiple lawsuits against unions in different courts. The DOL was intended to be the screening and centralizing mechanism which would eliminate frivolous complaints and avoid multiple litigation. Any other course would cause unions unnecessary harassment and expense.

We do not believe that by giving the complainant the two options the DOL would necessarily be spurred into action. As we will note in chapter 4, which deals with Title III and trusteeships, where the complainant has been given the two options, the DOL has not acted aggressively to avoid embarrassment. Indeed, it has at times refused to pursue Title III complaints that subsequently have been found to be meritorious by the courts.

The alternative forums argument also presumes that the courts would disagree with the DOL's judgment on the merits of the majority of cases, as has been true with regard to Title III cases. However, the DOL apparently made a policy decision that, given its limited resources, it would give low priority to Title III complaints. It cannot do that regarding enforcement of Title IV. The statute mandates the DOL's immediate attention to Title IV complaints in a manner absent with regard to the other titles.

We understand the concern of those who believe the complaining member should have an alternate means of seeking redress if the DOL refuses to process his complaint—i.e., private civil suit. However, as evidenced by the decision in the *Bachowski* case, the courts have already pointed the way to the member if the DOL does not find merit in his election complaint. The decision in the *Bachowski* case at least opens the door; how widely, it is too early to tell.

Provision for Administrative Hearing Procedure to Settle Constitutional Questions

One rather extensively reasoned suggestion, made to solve the problem of lengthy delays between the time a complaint is brought and the case is heard in court, was that the Act should provide for some kind of expedited administrative hearing to rule on election provisions of questionable legality. (Complaints related to specific election violations would still be investigated as they are now.) In order to be effective, the statute would also have to make explicit that the hearing be held within a specified period and that the decision be rendered within a stipulated time following the hearing. At the same time, such a procedure would broaden the options available to the DOL in enforcing Title IV.

The proposed procedure would have the DOL and the union go before an administrative law judge and let him make a determination as to the legality or illegality of the constitutional language. The judge's decision would be binding, pending appeal to the courts. The union thus would not have to defend those provisions in an election setting, and the incumbents would be spared possible embarrassment and the expense of litigation. In one proponent's opinion, "the more that settlements can be taken out of an election setting, the better."

According to all the DOL spokesmen to whom this proposal was presented, there would be serious disadvantages in that procedure. First, who would act as the administrative law judge in such cases? Would he not be as subject to political pressure as the current top officials of the DOL are now alleged to be? Over time, would not the judge become biased either in favor of or against organized labor's officialdom? Furthermore, are there not disadvantages to considering the constitutional provisions in a theoretical setting rather than in an actual case? And would it not be difficult to prove or disprove what impact the challenged provision would in fact have on an election?

We agree that it would be advantageous to everyone concerned if debate over constitutional language could be taken out of an election setting. And, where the union is open to suggestion, this can be accomplished under the present statutory language. (Obviously, in the case of obstinate unions, nothing can be done; in the words of one DOL area office spokesman, "they won't budge.") Thus we agree that at the present time there would be no practical advantage to be gained from implementing such a proposal.

We note, however, that under Section 18 of Executive Order No. 11491, which covers federal employees and gives them rights akin to those accorded to workers covered under the LMRDA, administrative hearings are provided for under certain circumstances. If experience with those hearings proves beneficial, it may well be that the DOL should take a fresh look at the proposal made to us.

Other Suggestions

Four additional suggestions were made with regard to changes in language:

> Local union officers' terms of office should be lengthened from three to four years or more.

> The DOL should be given express authority to investigate pre-election complaints.

> The DOL should be empowered to supervise elections whenever requested to do so.

> The DOL should be given the option of seeking injunctive relief, rather than rerunning the election, if it so chooses.

We have already discussed the arguments for and against the first of the above proposals. The other three reflect their proponents' concern that the DOL's enforcement powers are too restricted, particularly in view of the 1964 Supreme Court decision in *Calhoon v. Harvey*.[34] (As we will note in greater detail when discussing that case in its Title I context, the decision restricts a member's right to pre-election relief.[35]) The federal courts, except with regard to the limited rights available under Section 401(c) (the right of the opposition to inspect the membership list, and to have its campaign literature mailed out), cannot act. Theoretically, the state courts are not precluded from granting pre-election relief, but in practice they rarely do.

While those making the three suggestions believed a change in statutory language would be necessary, others interviewed believed that the DOL has those powers as the Act is now written. All that is required, they contended, is a change in the agency's interpretation of its enforcement powers. We will thus discuss those proposals as they pertain to DOL enforcement of Title IV, in chapter 2.

---

34. 379 U.S. 134 (1964).

35. To compound the problem, the circuit courts are divided as to whether or not an internal pre-election appeal precludes a post-election complaint which, if unheeded, can be taken to the DOL. See *Hodgson v. United Steelworkers* (459 F.2d 348 (3d Cir. 1972)), which barred a member from taking a post-election complaint to the DOL because he had appealed internally prior to the election, and therefore his four-month time limit had expired. In *Usery v. Transit Union, Local 1205* (545 F.2d 1300 (1st Cir. 1976)), the court held the other way on the ground, among others, that since the *Calhoon* decision precludes DOL entry pre-election, the time runs from the date of the member's post-election complaint.

Chapter II

Title IV: Enforcement by the Department of Labor

This chapter is devoted to a description of Department of Labor (DOL) enforcement of Title IV, both pre- and post-election. It also includes the comments received in the course of the interviews concerning the agency's administration of Title IV, as well as a discussion of comments made with regard to the use of the investigatory authority given the DOL under Section 601 and its possible use in a pre-election setting. Our own evaluation of the merits of the interviewees' comments, particularly those that were critical of the DOL's enforcement practices, is also presented here.

Role of the Department of Labor in Union Elections

The national office staff of the DOL takes the position that it has no authority under the Act to make a formal investigation of pre-election complaints. However, four of the six area office directors interviewed, while they make no formal investigation pre-election, believed that given the close relationship between alleged pre-election violations and the agency's post-election role, they should look into pre-election complaints, and in fact they do make some effort in that area. That effort may be rather perfunctory, however, and may consist simply of advising the complainant of the internal appeals procedures to follow and sending a letter to the union officers involved. The letter merely informs the officers that the DOL has learned that an election is in the offing, and reminds the officers in general terms what procedures should be followed in the conduct of that election. Two of the four area offices go beyond that. Upon receipt of a complaint, those offices will contact the union officers by phone, advise them of the nature of the complaint, attempt to discern if there is any basis for it and, if it appears to be a valid complaint, will ask what steps the union intends to take to remedy the matter. If the officers seem reluctant to do anything voluntarily, the agency official warns them of the possible post-election consequences. In addition, the area offices assist the complainant in formulating his written internal complaint.[1] According to those DOL staff members who do attempt to remedy violations before the election, if the alleged violation is a specific one (e.g., failure to post notices regarding nominations, or failure to mail out election notices), most unions are willing to correct the error because "they don't like reruns either." However, if the complaint involves "the more nebulous areas," such as candidacy requirements, "they won't budge."

The personnel at the other two DOL area offices visited did not believe that they were empowered to play any role whatever with regard to pre-election complaints, and a few of their superiors in the national office stated that that position is, indeed, DOL policy. The rest of those interviewed at the national office level, however, reported that the DOL has always encouraged the area offices to take pre-election remedial action, and cited Regulation 617.016 in the *Administrative Manual:*

> *617.016 Pre-Election Complaints.* If the allegations are that a labor organization is engaging, or is about to engage, in acts which violate election provisions of the Act, the [area administrator] shall, without disclosing the source of information, either (1) informally disclose to the labor organization that he has received allegations indicating possible violations of the election provisions of the Act, or (2) direct a letter . . . to the organization calling its attention to the election provisions of the Act.

Thus the staff at the area offices who believe they cannot play any pre-election role whatever have been misinformed. On the other hand, those who do more than write a letter or "informally" contact the union, go beyond the scope of the regulation.

The area offices visited also receive requests from unions asking that the offices supervise an upcoming election or, in at least one instance, all future elections. Area office administrators and compliance officers in the field offices claimed lack of authority to provide supervision, and have consistently refused.[2] However, if

---

1. Such assistance has been condoned by the courts. See Note, *Union Elections and the LMRDA: Thirteen Years of Use and Abuse,* 81 YALE L. J. 407, 485 n.343 (1972).
2. Until sometime in 1976, it was general policy for the DOL not to become involved in observing an election even if the parties requested that it do so, although the agency did send two staff members to observe the McDonald-Abel election. On that policy, see Note, *Union Elections and the LMRDA: Thirteen Years of Use and Abuse,* 81 YALE L. J. 407, 481 n.330, 482 nn.331 & 332 (1972). Sometime after we submitted our report and recommendations to

asked, they will review the constitutional language governing elections to see whether procedures are spelled out adequately. In addition, they will issue procedural guidelines. In many cases, the persons seeking guidance are not the insurgents but the incumbents.

At the present time, then, the DOL's pre-election practices vary. A number of area offices visited are willing to play a limited role; others play none at all.

As to post-election complaints and the disposition of them, all of the area office staff contacted agreed that the election complaints are the most time-consuming part of their LMRDA duties. (As noted earlier, they have other DOL-related assignments in addition to their LMRDA work.) Estimates as to time spent on election complaints ranged from 20 percent to 50 percent of total office time, the bulk of it consumed by investigations and supervision of elections.

Once it has been determined that the complainant has exhausted his internal remedies, the complex process of investigating the allegation, weighing its merits, and determining how to proceed is begun. In brief, the procedure involves the area office, the regional office, the regional solicitor's office and, in the national office, the Branch of Elections and Trusteeships, the office of the director of Labor-Management Standards Enforcement, the Solicitor of Labor's office, the Secretary of Labor's office and, if the case is to be litigated, the Department of Justice. (Whether or not the case is initially argued by a regional solicitor or a U.S. attorney differs, depending upon the region.)

The law sets strict time limits for the completion of the investigation of an election case: sixty days from the time the complaint is filed. The area offices, which do the initial in-depth investigations and make the preliminary determinations on the merits of the case are allotted, according to internal practice, a maximum of thirty days. Following that, the regional office personnel and those who make the final determination at the national office in Wash-

---

the national office of the DOL in June of 1976, the decision was made to enlarge the agency's pre-election role somewhat under certain circumstances. This was done in the interest of decreasing the financial burden, to both the union and the DOL, of possible post-election investigations and resultant election reruns. The DOL has already played that enlarged role, in which staff members advise and observe, pre-election, in connection with the election of parent union officers, in the International Union of Electrical, Radio and Machine Workers and the United Steelworkers of America elections.

ington, D.C., also have a thirty-day limit. This is the theoretical allocation. In practice, the national office may allow the area office longer than thirty days if necessary. In addition, if the area office takes the full thirty days, and its report is delayed in the mails, the regional and national offices clearly have much less than their allotted thirty days. During the original investigation, those who are to review the area office recommendations are kept informed; during the remaining thirty days, the area office is often contacted again for further information.

Many of the complaints filed are found to be without merit at the area office level. In the six offices contacted, the estimated percentage of nonmeritorious cases varied, but ranged between about 40 percent and about 80 percent. The area office recommendation is not determinative, however. In some instances reported, where the area office recommended no litigation, the national office reversed the decision. Reversals in the other direction are, however, more common. Estimates of the number of times the national office decided against the area offices' recommendations to litigate a case again varied among the offices visited, although the most commonly cited figure was 10 percent. (One office put it at closer to 65 percent, but this was quite unusual. The figures given are merely estimates and represent only the experience in the area offices we contacted. Indeed, a key DOL staff member in the national office felt that the 10 percent figure was too low.)

Once the regional and national offices of the DOL have reviewed the area office file on the complaint, the Branch of Elections and Trusteeships sends out a "summary of violations" letter to the president of the parent union organization, as well as to the president of the local directly involved.[3] That letter lists all Title IV violations that the investigation uncovered, whether litigable or not, and whether or not those violations were a part of the original complaint. Often that letter results in a meeting between representatives of the parent organization and officials from the national office. Omitting further detail concerning these meetings or subsequent decision-making processes, the end result would be one of the four possibilities outlined below.

1. The complaint is determined not to be litigable, either be-

---

3. For purposes of this description, it is assumed that the election being investigated is that of a local union. Such investigation could, of course, involve the election of officers of an intermediate body, the parent organization, or an independent union.

cause the allegation proved to be incorrect or, if accurate, could not have affected the outcome of the election.

2. It is determined that a voluntary rerun of the election by the parent organization or the local union itself is deemed to have remedied the violations which occurred.

3. The union agrees to have the DOL supervise either a rerun of the questioned election or, on rare occasions, the next regularly scheduled election.

4. Action is initiated to have the merits of the complaint itself argued in court.

If the decision is made that the complaint is not litigable, a "closing" letter is sent to the complainant, the parent organization, and the local, setting forth the reasons why no action will be taken by the DOL. (This letter, since the *Bachowski* decision, is far more detailed than it previously was.)

As to the possibility of an internal rerun election, Section 402(b) of the Act can be read to mean that the DOL need not bring suit if a violation of the statute has been remedied within the sixty-day period during which the DOL may initiate civil action. Thus, if the facts of the particular election complaint quickly establish that a violation affecting the outcome occurred, and if the parent organization is willing to rerun the election on its own and can do so within fifty days after the complaint was filed, the DOL usually will agree to that solution.[4] (The fifty-day limit is imposed so that, should there be an allegation of an electoral violation in the rerun, the DOL would still have ten days in which to take action.) The appropriate area office then keeps in touch with the local's officers to make certain that the election is in fact held during that period, and to provide whatever technical assistance the union may request. After the election is conducted, the DOL contacts the original complainant as well as other interested parties and, if there is no evidence that violations occurred that would have affected the outcome of the new election, a "determination" is sent to the complainant, the parent organization, and the local union, closing the matter.

If the DOL and the union come to an agreement that the questioned election will be rerun under the DOL's supervision, or

---

4. It should be noted that in a few cases the remedy has been something other than a rerun. For example, if the tally had been incorrect and the wrong person had been installed in office, then installation of the actual winner has been all that has been required.

that the next regularly scheduled election will be supervised, the DOL requires that the union request a waiver of the sixty-day time limit and ask instead for a specified longer period (i.e., the time actually required to conduct the supervised election). In so doing, the union is agreeing that it will not raise timeliness as a defense with regard to the period specified in the waiver. The DOL deems such agreements to be "voluntary compliance" on the part of the union with the Act's requirements. Union officials would not readily agree that it is in fact quite that "voluntary." They think of this option more as being a club that the DOL uses "to 'encourage' union settlements where such settlements might otherwise not be forthcoming."[5]

If the DOL supervises an election held as a result of "voluntary compliance" or court order, the pertinent area office is normally charged with the responsibility of such supervision. Usually, the area office staff is involved in every step of the process: nominations, election, and tally. Once the election has been held, the DOL assigns a time period during which complaints may be filed. The standard deadline is ten days after the election, although the DOL will investigate protests received during a reasonable period thereafter. For elections where the supervision resulted from "voluntary compliance," the DOL thereafter sends out a "determination." If the election was the result of a court order, the DOL certifies the election results to the court which ordered the election.

Comments on Enforcement

We asked all those interviewed for their opinions concerning the adequacy of DOL enforcement of Title IV, and what suggestions, if any, they had for changes in DOL policy or procedure that would make the administration of the Act's election provisions more acceptable to them. Even within the different levels of the DOL itself, the responses differed. Therefore, we have divided the comments into those made by DOL personnel and those made by others. Where germane, DOL policy-makers' responses to those comments have been included as well.

Comments by Department of Labor Personnel

Comments by DOL personnel regarding agency enforcement of Title IV fell into five categories:

---

5. AFL-CIO Maritime Trades Department, *A Report after Eight Years of the Landrum-Griffin Act* (Washington, D.C.: AFL-CIO, 1967), at 23–24.

1. Communication between levels of the agency and across agencies
2. Role of the Justice Department in arguing Title IV cases
3. Conduct of all union elections
4. Agency's pre-election role
5. Adequacy of staffing levels

Communication.   Personnel in the DOL area offices, and particularly the compliance officers there, were at times quite critical of the regional office, as well as of the national office. They did not question the need for a review of their recommendations at the national level (though they frequently did not see the necessity for regional review). In fact, the area officials often saw positive value in the national office review. Their concern for their particular case could, they conceded, at times blind them to flaws in the evidence they had collected. Moreover, there might be public policy aspects to be considered of which they were unaware. Nevertheless, all of the compliance officers felt that the national office made decisions without the specific knowledge the area officials had acquired during their investigations and without additional information learned subsequent to submitting their recommendations. Once they turn in their reports, they complained, they are not consulted sufficiently. At the very least, they added, when the national office decides against taking area office recommendations, those offices have a right to know why. (Upon inquiry, we learned that originally the national office did state the reasons for reversals. For a time that policy was changed, but recently the national office has reverted to its original position.)

Of all the field staff interviewed—administrators, enforcement officers, personnel at the regional solicitor's office—almost 75 percent wondered if national office decisions not to pursue a case might not be politically motivated. The top DOL officials are political appointees, they pointed out, and remain in office only as long as they make "politically right" decisions; i.e., consider the interests of the union leaders, who control contributions to governmental election campaign funds, and may have an influence upon how the union members vote in state and national elections for governmental office.

Over 80 percent commented that, political motives aside, the top DOL officials must be concerned with their effectiveness as guardians of industrial peace, and that that duty could conflict with their role as administrators of the LMRDA. For example, if these officials are trying to persuade a union to settle a strike, what sort of position are they placed in if, at the same time, other DOL officials are investigating an election complaint against the same union?

All of the compliance officers interviewed also wondered aloud whether or not the final decision of the national office not to pursue certain election complaints, particularly those against a parent union election, might not involve financial considerations. One officer, for example, told of a parent organization election that he believed should clearly have been rerun, but was not because of the costs involved. He went on to say that while the outcome in that election "probably" would have been the same had it been rerun, the "notoriety of the rerun would have been an education for the rank and file for the future."

These compliance officers, as well as two former national office staff, also stated that they often feel that the national office is more concerned with its relationship with union leaders than with honest elections and the rights of the rank and file. The comment was that "national headquarters and the internationals play footsies at the complainant's expense." Three compliance officers who felt very keenly that their duty is to represent rank and file members' rights contended that, because of the close relationship between the DOL national office and the top union leaders, the area offices and the national office work "at cross purposes."

The national office DOL personnel, past and present, who were involved in enforcing the LMRDA from the beginning, or at least for a considerable period of time, admitted that top officials are often confronted with a dilemma. Because of the dual roles they play, they have often wondered if it would not have been better to have created a new regulatory agency at the outset, separate from the DOL, to enforce the Act. Officials of such a newly created agency could at least have administered the Act without the external pressures that both political and public policy considerations create.

One national office representative agreed that the DOL takes a particularly hard look at whether or not the outcome would have been affected when a complaint comes in with regard to a parent organization election, and he did justify that in terms of the "staggering" costs of rerunning such an election.

The concern for rank and file rights is generally of high priority for those in the field. For example, national office personnel told us to be prepared for a negative reaction from the compliance officers to queries on the thirty-day limit imposed upon them in election investigations. Instead, we found that, while compliance officers had little enthusiasm for the pressures those bounds imposed, they nevertheless considered them imperative. ("Some poor guy is sticking out his neck.") While the time limit could well mean that their case write-ups suffer—an additional reason for their desire to be consulted once the reports are turned in—in no case did they express the desire to have the stricture lifted. Instead, it was strongly urged that additional personnel be provided so that a more thorough investigation could be done within the time prescribed.

The compliance officers also expressed the wish that the national office would keep them informed of changes in interpretation of the Act made either by the DOL itself or as a result of court decisions. As it is, compliance officers sometimes base the answer to an inquiry upon outmoded rules, only to have the inquirer learn subsequently that those rules are no longer operative. Some thought that if each area office could have a staff lawyer with whom the compliance officers could be in daily contact during the course of their investigations, it would avoid the present problem of having the compliance officers' recommendations sometimes fly in the face of court interpretations of which they are totally unaware. Three compliance officers came up with a suggestion to deal with the problem: the national office ought to prepare, and continually update, a digest of precedents—court rulings, national office policy interpretations, and other area office policy interpretations—for the guidance of those in the field. They noted that such a system has been developed to guide them in enforcing the veterans' reemployment rights program and is very helpful.

We can corroborate the fact that the area office personnel are often unaware (as they themselves admit) of even key Supreme Court decisions concerning interpretations of the Act. The national office does send out periodic newsletters that inform area offices of some court decisions dealing with LMRDA issues, but not all. While the national office also provides funds to permit each area office to subscribe to a reporting service, such as those published by the Bureau of National Affairs and the Commerce Clearing House, given the workload and the small number of people in some area offices, many staff members never have the time or opportunity to study those publications.

The suggestion that the national office of the DOL issue and continually update a digest of precedents is a very useful idea and should be implemented. A copy should be issued to every person who is assigned any responsibility for enforcing the LMRDA. Such a digest should include all material directly related to the LMRDA and its enforcement and, in addition, should include information regarding other labor legislation which would be useful to the area office staffs. Not only would such information broaden the perspective of area office staff members, but it would enable them to advise those seeking help in some area of the law other than LMRDA as to what alternatives might be open to them.

Role of the Department of Justice. Criticism of the role of the Department of Justice in arguing Title IV cases before the courts came not only from concerned DOL personnel at all levels of the agency, but from six union lawyers as well. The thrust of the lawyers' comments was that the Justice Department staff must be generalists in the law and cannot take the time to develop the expertise that DOL lawyers have concerning the Act. Capable though the Justice Department's lawyer may be, once a judge starts to probe the intricacies of the Act's language and its legislative history, that lawyer is at a loss. Such inadequacies have resulted in the dismissal of perfectly meritorious cases. The union attorneys, along with the DOL representatives, urged that the DOL argue its own cases instead.

Investigation of the criticism of the Justice Department went beyond the scope of this study, but because knowledgeable people both inside and outside the DOL voiced it, it is clear that the issue should be seriously considered by those responsible for establishing DOL policy.

Supervision of all elections. As noted earlier, area office staff are often asked by union officers and/or their opponents to formally supervise elections, but believe that they are not now empowered to do so. A third of the personnel in the field considered this policy wrong, and thought they should be able to provide supervision if so requested. Indeed, a few believed that, as a matter of policy, they should supervise all union elections. If DOL supervision became a regular practice, they contended, union members would not view the government's presence at an election with suspicion and it would not be harmful to the incumbents. Rather, it would just be considered as a routine way of ensuring the peaceful transition from one term to the next. One proponent of this plan also added that unions could not argue against the practice of third party involvement since a number already use the services of an outsider, such as the American Arbitration Association or the Honest Ballot Association, to supervise their elections.

The other two thirds of the area office personnel thought that the DOL should not supervise elections upon request. The DOL presence would have "a chilling effect" even under those circumstances. As to supervising all elections, one national office member summed up the top level reaction to that idea by throwing up his hands and asking: "Where are the bodies supposed to come from?"

We do not agree with those who would like to change the present DOL policy. If it became normal practice to supervise any union election upon request—and "upon whose request?" already poses a problem—then, over time, such requests would become commonplace. From a practical standpoint alone, such a policy would be unrealistic, for it would require an enormous increase in staff. Moreover, any incumbent who did not ask for DOL supervision would automatically be under suspicion. Beyond that, should there be violations despite the government's supervision, a post-election investigation would be necessary. Not only would that situation cast suspicion upon the DOL's ability to supervise elections adequately, but it would obviously involve the government still further in unions' internal affairs. If it became policy for the DOL to supervise all elections automatically, the problems just recounted would be compounded.

Although some unions now use outsiders to supervise elections, the voluntary decision to do so makes for an entirely distinct type of third party involvement.

Greater pre-election involvement. In the two DOL area offices which follow a policy of complete noninvolvement in the pre-election setting, personnel often expressed the wish that they could do something about pre-election complaints. If they could, they contended the violation could be corrected when it occurred and an election rerun would be unnecessary. A few persons in those two offices also expressed the belief that they should conduct investigations of those complaints before the election, just as they now do following an election. On the other hand, in the area offices that do play a minimal pre-election role, the staff believed that the action they now take is all that should be done. If each allegation were to be investigated every time a union member complained, they explained, "it's quite possible that we'd get twenty-two different complaints at twenty-two different times, and then we'd be in there all the time." Such extensive DOL involvement would really throw suspicion on the incumbents, whether warranted or not, and could in itself have an effect on the outcome of the election. Moreover, Congress intended that unions be given the opportunity to remedy violations internally. When these area offices make an informal inquiry, as they now do, the union is aided in taking remedial action if it chooses to. Any more formal involvement could entail greater government interference in internal union affairs and thus violate congressional intent.

The same arguments can be made against formal pre-election involvement as those made against supervising all elections: such action might throw unwarranted suspicion upon the incumbents and could entail greater government involvement in internal union affairs.

However, the playing of a limited and informal role pre-election is in accordance with DOL regulations, and permits the union to take remedial action without undue outside interference. Insofar as the agency's role is informal, does not involve the physical presence of DOL officials in any phase of pre-election activity, and is designed to give impartial assistance when sought, it benefits everyone.

Increased staff. As indicated earlier, efficient administration of the Act is hampered by the problem of inadequate staffing. The area offices would like more staff in order to conduct the election investigations more thoroughly within the time limits imposed. No one within the DOL quarrels with that desire. The problem is simply one of very limited resources.

It was suggested that retired enforcement officers be utilized on a temporary basis during periods of peak workload. They are experienced investigators and observers, and would require minimal retraining. DOL spokesmen noted that on some occasions retired enforcement officers have been employed as election rerun observers, and that that arrangement proved to be quite satisfactory. However, since time limits are imposed on investigating elections, it was often not feasible to utilize retirees for investigations because of the time-consuming paperwork required to rehire a retiree on a temporary basis. Moreover, the number of retirees available at any given time is small, and even when retirees are available, their personal commitments might interfere with the ability to complete their DOL assignments. Physical stamina might be another inhibiting factor.

More commonly, if an election rerun requires more personnel than the field office can supply, personnel from the national office are called upon to help. Those currently working in the national office are readily available, and using them lessens the costs of supervising such elections. Perhaps more important, there is a positive value in acquainting the national office staff with the kinds of work done in the field. Not only is the field work a learning experience for them, but their presence serves as a morale booster to those who usually have the full responsibility for supervising election reruns. At the same time, of course, while the national office personnel are in the field, their own work suffers.

We recognize that, given budgetary constraints, it may be impossible for the DOL policy-makers to look favorably upon the idea of increasing the area office staffs. At the same time, we strongly urge that larger field staffs be looked upon as a desirable goal. If, as is often contended, election investigations are not being conducted thoroughly enough because of inadequate staff, then the results of those investigations, and the recommendations made based on them, could well be doing a disservice to everyone concerned.

Comments by Others

As previously noted, union attorneys suggested that the DOL, rather than the Department of Justice, argue Title IV cases. The other comments by persons not connected with the DOL (i.e., by lawyers, academicians, union officials, and dissidents) on the subject of DOL enforcement fell within two broad categories: the "how" and "why" of election investigations, and the DOL interpretations of Title IV. Those topics are subject to further subdivision, as follows.

Investigations
1. Pre-election investigations under Section 601
2. Conduct of investigations
3. Policy of not pursuing cases where the violations found could not have affected the outcome of the election
4. Policy of seeking remedies other than a supervised election rerun when violations are found that would have affected the outcome
5. Alleged practice of "picking and choosing"
6. Time lag and the role of waiver granting
7. Conduct of rerun elections
8. Purpose of rerun elections

Interpretations
1. Uneven DOL responses to inquiries when the agency's guidance is sought
2. Published DOL interpretations and the need for general guidelines

Investigations of elections by the Department of Labor. *Pre-election investigations under Section 601(a).* Section 601(a) contains the following language:

> The Secretary shall have power when he believes it necessary in order to determine whether any person has violated or is about to violate any provision of this Act (except Title I or amendments made by this Act to other statutes) to make an investigation and in connection therewith he may enter such places and inspect such records and accounts and question such persons as he may deem necessary to enable him to determine the facts relative thereto.

The DOL is thus empowered to investigate a pre-election situation even if no formal complaint has been made. As already noted, however, as a matter of general policy, the agency does not use that investigative authority on the ground that the mere presence of a DOL investigator casts suspicion upon the incumbents and therefore that presence alone may affect the outcome of the election. That policy, while ordinarily looked upon favorably by a substantial majority of those interviewed, came under sharp attack in the wake of the Yablonski murders.[6] The vast majority of the union officers and lawyers interviewed, the group which usually was the most adamant that the DOL not use its Section 601 powers pre-election, was quite critical of the DOL for not having taken pre-election action in that case. As one parent union officer phrased it, "the whole labor movement shouldn't have to pay for the sins of the Mineworkers." But he, like the rest, then quickly added that only under the most exceptional circumstances—a situation where there has been a pattern of violence, a blatant misuse of union funds, or where it is obvious that the election violations are of such magnitude that there can be no doubt that the election will have to be rerun if nothing is done—would DOL pre-election action be warranted. In such a case, said one local union officer, "the Secretary shouldn't need to be hit with a baseball bat to recognize the exception. There, the argument that inter-

---

6. For a detailed report concerning that tragedy, see Trevor Armbrister, *Act of Vengeance* (New York: E.P. Dutton & Co., Inc., 1975).

vention could upset the balance in the election can easily be answered with the argument that if the incumbents had been behaving there would be no need for intervention in the first place."

However, DOL officials pointed out still another problem in using Section 601 powers in a pre-election context. That section states only that the DOL "may report to interested persons or officers . . ." whatever it has found during the course of the investigation. When the DOL uses Section 601 to investigate nonelection matters (e.g., to enter the union offices to look at financial records), the phrase "interested persons" has variously been defined as the Congress, the public (reached through news releases), the union members, or the union officers. In the case of an investigation of a local union's records, it is often the officers of the parent organization who are most concerned. But in a pre-election investigation, the question as to who the "interested persons or officers" would be becomes a difficult one to answer. Certainly the opposition candidates would be "interested" in every sense of the word if the DOL did find pre-election violations. But if the incumbents had agreed to correct the violations found, how could the DOL maintain its stance of neutrality if it gave the opposition that information and the opposition misused it (e.g., broadcast the violations but failed to state that they had been corrected)? If the incumbents refused to correct minimal violations, should the opposition be told? Or, in the case of a local election, where the incumbents had corrected their mistakes or where the errors were of little consequence, need the parent body be told? Unless the situation uncovered was horrendous, should the public be informed? DOL officials raised those questions to demonstrate why they are so reluctant to use Section 601 investigatory powers before the election is held.

The DOL's policy of using Section 601 powers sparingly in a pre-election setting is the correct one to follow, in our opinion. Unless a strong case can be made that intraunion activities occurring before the election will result in violence or in an election so blatantly fraudulent that a rerun election will be required if no DOL action is taken, the agency should not use Section 601 to conduct its own investigation. In those exceptional cases, however, the DOL has the power to act, and should use it.

The fact that the information uncovered during the course of a pre-election investigation would have to be handled in an extremely gingerly fashion lends support to the conclusion that such Section 601 investigations should be conducted only under very unusual circumstances. However, if an election campaign is so exceptional as to warrant pre-election intervention, then all members of the union that is under investigation have a right to know the results of that inquiry.

Conduct of investigations.   Criticisms of the DOL's election investigations were quite diverse. A substantial majority of the union officials and their counsel thought that, despite the strictures of the *Steelworkers' Local 6799* decision, the agency's investigators still played "cops and robbers" and looked into everything. One area office director who had been enforcing the LMRDA since its enactment conceded that in the beginning agency personnel did indeed act like "cops and robbers." "We overdid it." However, he felt that over time the DOL interpretations and policy had become "more realistic." Two national office spokesmen also spoke of the "damning" quality of the old version of the "summary of violations" letters—the letters which are sent to the parent organization and the local union involved after completion of the field investigation, but before the review and final determination by the national office.[7] But these spokesmen hastened to add that the language of those letters has now been softened considerably and stresses the preliminary nature of the findings. The change in the language of the letters has tempered, but not eliminated, the earlier hostility to them. Typical was one parent union lawyer's comment that "they still drive my clients nuts."

Two union lawyers differed from their colleagues, as did the dissidents and their advocates. They approved of the fact that the letters are sent. To them, the more precise the list of uncovered violations, the better. That way, the incumbent cannot pretend that the election was entirely free of taint. Moreover, even if the DOL decides not to bring suit, if the members gain access to those letters, they are alerted to the kinds of violations that took place and can watch for them in future elections.

The fact that a complaining member can go to the DOL and get what was termed "a free ride"—i.e., free legal services— caused a certain amount of concern to a few union officials. As one grumbled: "For a five-cent postcard, the guy can get a million-dollar lawyer."

---

7.   For criticism of the earlier letters, therein called "last clear chance" letters, see AFL-CIO Maritime Trades Department, *A Report after Eight Years, supra* note 5, at 23–24.

One lawyer for a parent union which has been involved in numerous investigations said that he resented the fact that the DOL assumed a posture of secretiveness and refused to tell him what was being investigated, while at the same time, details of the investigation mysteriously found their way to the news media. Since the complaining union member must first exhaust his internal remedies, the union normally has already been put on notice of the violations alleged. Thus the lawyer's statement that he should receive that information from the DOL officials is perplexing. But one can hardly quarrel with his assertion that he should not have to find out what the investigation is about by reading about it in the newspapers. Agency spokesmen pointed out, however, that while someone in the DOL may have been responsible for the particular news leaks the lawyer referred to, frequently other persons, such as the complainant in the case or his advocate, are responsible for giving out confidential information to the news media. Under such circumstances, there is little the DOL can do.

Agency personnel were also scored by over half of the union officers and lawyers for conducting incomplete and "sloppy" investigations. Furthermore, they said, the DOL personnel "concentrate on the little things," are "oblivious to the fact that elections are run by workers in the plant, not technicians," and "gag at gnats, but miss the real point."

The top officials in two area offices, both with long experience in administering the Act, were inclined to agree with some of the criticism. Their private views were that they should "not go in like gangbusters." Indeed, they personally felt that elections should not be rerun at all if the violations were only technical ones.

One national office DOL official admitted that the agency "concentrates on the little things," but attributed that to the fact that it lacks flexible remedies and procedures. He contended that DOL officials do all they can, given the statutory constraints under which they must work.

The compliance officers' universal desire for more personnel in order that investigations could be more thorough contains the implicit admission that those investigations currently are at times imperfect. Five area office administrators agreed. A few union lawyers and other labor officials sympathized with the compliance officers' plight: their own organizations have trouble with time limits, too. One lawyer suggested that perhaps the time limits should be lifted because "fraud should be actionable at any time."

But he quickly added that if the limits were lifted, he would want to be certain that the DOL investigators kept the *Steelworkers' Local 6799* decision's strictures firmly in mind: "They shouldn't come in there and investigate *everything!*"[8]

All of the dissidents and their advocates felt that the DOL does a "sloppy" job of investigating complaints. Indeed, from their point of view, the DOL does nothing at all. According to them, the DOL considers all dissidents to be "crackpots." Said one dissident: "They'll rap with you all day, as long as you don't interfere with their coffee break. They think you're quaint. But they don't *do* anything." Interestingly enough, all of the dissidents interviewed have at one time been or now are union officers. They give the Act full credit for their victories, but give none at all to the Act's enforcers. On its face, there is a certain lack of consistency in their position.

There seems to be no doubt that the investigations are of uneven quality. The majority of the compliance officers believed that at times a thorough job of investigating within the thirty-day time limit is not possible with the resources now available. On the other hand, they did admit that they do—albeit infrequently—go beyond the scope of the complaint in search of violations that the member could not have been expected to know of when he filed his complaint.

We have already recommended an increase in staff to aid the cause of thorough investigations. At the same time, the practice of broadening the inquiry beyond the scope of the member's complaint is subject to abuse, and we received enough confidential information on that topic to feel certain that, in a few cases at least, it has been followed injudiciously. We urge that the DOL investigators be cautioned to exercise their right to look beyond the violations complained of only with great care.

The DOL has made an effort to stress the preliminary nature of the findings listed in the "summary of violations" letters. Perhaps more could be done in that regard but, on balance, we agree with those who argue that such letters should continue to be written, that the union members have a right to know what the investigation uncovered, and that those letters serve an educational purpose.

---

8. The DOL still claims the right to investigate everything, on the ground that the Court ruling excepts those violations that the member could not have been expected to know about when he filed his complaint. U.S. Department of Labor, Labor-Management Services Administration, Office of Labor-Management and Welfare-Pension Reports, *LMRDA Interpretive Manual.*

We strongly urge that, insofar as the DOL can control the situation, direct news leaks, or improper communications to favored persons which indirectly lead to news leaks, should simply not be permitted.

We have noted more than once that the DOL investigators themselves were not wholly satisfied with the conduct of their own inquiries, and that some of them believed that undue stress is laid on technicalities. Furthermore, we were given enough examples of elections in which actual fraudulent practices had gone undiscovered by the DOL to be convinced that such situations do occur.

We found no basis, however, for believing that there is any deliberate effort made by the DOL investigators to overlook fraudulent practices while they uncover the minor or technical ones. We concluded that in some instances technical violations may receive undue emphasis, and that more serious violations are at times overlooked, but that those problems should be laid at the feet of human fallibility rather than attributed to conscious policy.

Policy of not pursuing cases where the violations found could not have affected the outcome of the election. Three advocates for dissidents, and a few academicians, were critical of the DOL's policy of not pursing election cases if the violations found could not have affected the outcome of the election. In their opinion, even if the eventual outcome would have been the same in terms of who won or lost, the election should still have been rerun. That way, the losers would know what their real strength had been in that election and, if the winners' margins of victory had in reality been slim, the losers would take heart and be encouraged to make the effort once more. The advocates of that position would prefer to read "may have affected the outcome" to mean that the election violations may have had an impact upon the margin of victory rather than solely upon who won or lost. They conceded, however, that the latter interpretation has been in force for so long that to reinterpret the language now in the way they would prefer would raise more problems than it would solve.

Approximately one quarter of the local union officers, as well as the dissidents and their advocates, a few academicians, and even some DOL staff, found disturbing the fact that the agency does not pursue election complaints in cases where the violations found could not have affected the outcome. "If it's wrong, it's *wrong*," was a recurring theme. While most of them could see the

logic of not rerunning the election in such a case, they nevertheless felt that something should have been done to ensure that such
violations do not take place in the future. The most common suggestion, made by those knowledgeable in the law, was that injunctive relief should have been sought.

The DOL response to the injunctive relief argument was that,
while such relief has on rare occasion been sought, it has been
requested only "under very special circumstances." That is so
because, while the enforcement provisions of Titles I, II, III, and
V include injunctive relief, the applicable provision of Title IV
does not.[9] DOL officials read that fact to mean that the omission
from Title IV was purposeful. In addition, they argued, had Congress specifically granted injunctive relief in Title IV, it might
have given the DOL a "hunting license" concerning union elections that could be used at any time, rather than solely in an actual
election context. That possibility would have constituted undue
interference in the internal operation of labor unions.

However, since the DOL has requested—and received—injunctive relief in Title IV cases, the argument that the statute
precludes that remedy in such cases seems thin.[10] One must conclude, as did Senator Barry Goldwater (Arizona), that "the jurisdiction of the court to grant relief in cases of violations which do not
affect the outcome of an election is not clear . . . nor is the authority of the court to grant injunctions."[11] The DOL, then, does not
have a clear mandate one way or the other.

*Policy of seeking remedies other than a supervised election rerun
when violations are found that would have affected the outcome.* Even if the DOL determines that election violations have
occurred that could have affected the outcome of the election, the
agency is sometimes satisfied with supervising the next regular

9. For relevant enforcement provisions, see LMRDA §§ 102, 210, 304, 402,
   501(b), 29 U.S.C. §§ 412, 440, 464, 482, 501(b) (1959) (73 Stat. 519 (1959)).
10. See *Wirtz v. Local 1752, International Longshoremen's Association,* 56
    L.R.R.M. 2393 (S. Miss. 1963); *Wirtz v. Teamsters Industrial and Allied Em-
    ployees Union Local 73, International Brotherhood of Teamsters, Chauffeurs,
    Warehousemen and Helpers of America,* 257 F. Supp. 784 (N.D. Ohio 1966);
    Wirtz v. Hotel, Motel and Club Employees Union, Local 6, 265 F. Supp. 510
    (S.D.N.Y. 1967); *McDonald v. Oliver,* 400 F. Supp. 660 (S.D. Miss. 1974), aff'd
    525 F.2d 1217 (5th Cir. 1976), *cert. denied,* 429 U.S. 817 (1976).
11. U.S. Department of Labor, Office of the Solicitor, *Legislative History of the
    Labor-Management Reporting and Disclosure Act of 1959, Titles I–VI* (Wash-
    ington, D.C.: U.S. Department of Labor, 1964), at 830.

election, rather than rerunning the one investigated. Alternatively, if the violation involved illegal constitutional language, and the union agrees to change that language, the DOL has at times accepted that remedy rather than insisting that the election be rerun. Both alternatives have their critics.

Supervising the next regularly scheduled election instead of rerunning the suspect one troubled a small minority of people interviewed. One local union officer, for example, was completely bewildered by an agreement reached between the DOL and his parent organization that the DOL would supervise his local's next election rather than order a rerun. As a part of that agreement, those officers whose election maneuvers had been called into question were precluded from running again. The local officer (who was not among those barred from candidacy in the future election) could not fathom the rationale behind that agreement at all. If the suspect election did involve sufficient violations of the Act, *that* election should have been rerun. Supervising the next one, in which the alleged culprits were specifically excluded from candidacy, struck him as "simply ridiculous—there's no logic to it at all."

All of the advocates for dissidents were critical of this practice, not so much because they considered it illogical as that it afforded no immediate protection to the member whose rights had been violated—the one who had had the election stolen from him. Protecting his rights in the upcoming election, they said, did little good. By that time, the incumbents would be firmly entrenched, would have co-opted the opposition's following and, in any event, would have discouraged the defrauded candidate to such a point that he would be unwilling to spend the energy, time, and money it would take to try again.

The DOL officials countered the above arguments by pointing out that if they do decide to litigate to set aside an election, particularly that of a local union where the term of office is at most three years, they must calculate very carefully the time required to bring the case to trial. They are aware of, and have to consider, the possible legal maneuvers the union's lawyers can employ to stall the case, and have to evaluate the possibility that the next election could already have taken place by the time the case is heard. If there is a good possibility that that may occur, then they believe that, from everyone's point of view, it makes more sense to supervise the next election. Moreover, if the local is a large one, the financial burden on the union of conducting the additional election is so great that it offsets whatever advantage the rerun might give the complainant. These officials also noted that rerunning the questioned election may, in fact, work to the disadvantage of the complainant. If the union members resent, as they well may, the fact that the loser of the original election went to the DOL—an outsider—to complain, his margin of defeat in the rerun could be even more substantial than that in the original election.

The other alternate remedy which the DOL will accept, as already noted, arises when the original election complaint focuses upon illegal constitutional language concerning candidacy requirements or election procedures. In such a case, the DOL is satisfied that the violation has been remedied if the union agrees to alter that language to conform to the Act's intent. Here again, the critics of agency acceptance of that remedy argued that the complaining member's rights were sacrificed. The reply of the DOL officials was that even if the complainant's rights have been sacrificed, the long-range benefit to all members of that union in future elections offsets the short-range disadvantage to one or, at most, a handful of members.

On balance, we agree with the DOL's position.

Alleged practice of "picking and choosing." Lawyers representing dissidents, as well as a few national office staff members and nearly half of the field personnel, criticized the DOL's alleged practice of what they termed "picking and choosing." For example, when a number of locals of a particular parent organization hold their elections at the same time, and numerous complaints from members of various locals come in to the DOL, the agency will, according to those critics, not file suit regarding some of those complaints, even though the agency investigations showed that the complaints were valid. The DOL has adopted this practice on the ground that to pursue all complaints would have a steamroller effect, disrupting the entire labor organization. Here again, the criticism of that alleged practice centered on the fact that it sacrifices the rights of those members who have filed legitimate complaints but have been turned away by the DOL. One national office staff member specifically rejected the steamroller argument in one case he described, on the ground that the valid complaints involved locals that were so geographically diffuse that processing all of them would not have had an adverse effect on the parent organization. Moreover, he believed that the DOL inaction made the agency "look bad" to those whose complaints had not been pursued, and made them and their followers distrustful of turning to the DOL for help in the future.

The other DOL officials questioned categorically denied that they ever "pick and choose," even though it might appear to outsiders that they do.

Our own conclusion is that, given the agency's limited resources, it is difficult to believe that there are not times when DOL policy-makers, inundated with valid complaints, must decide how best to deploy those resources and in so doing, consciously or unconsciously, they do make choices. This problem, however, is a matter of adequacy of funding, which must be left to Congress.

Time lag and the role of granting waivers. The fact that election cases take so long to come to trial troubled almost everyone interviewed. Advocates for dissidents and the dissidents themselves tended to blame that situation on the DOL. The agency, in their view, is too willing to consent to a union's request for a time waiver, i.e., a waiver by the DOL of the sixty-day time limit in return for which the union signs a letter of waiver of defense on claims of time requirements. Again, the critics pointed out that time is all on the side of the incumbents. While in theory the union must request such waivers, in fact, the dissidents and their advocates said, the DOL encourages this practice. Upon asking union lawyers if this assertion were true, we were told that more often than not the DOL officials prepare the waiver requests themselves. One union lawyer stated that of the total number of waivers he supposedly has requested, he in fact sought only one on his own. The club the DOL used to get him to agree to the rest was "sign or we'll go to court."

Most DOL officials were reluctant to admit that their own requests for such waivers were common occurrences. In any event, they went on, the giving of waivers is not a key factor in the lag between the time the agency brings suit and the date the case is heard. The greatest delays occur when the case is before a district court in a large city, where the proceedings become mired in "the docket crunch." Even if the union's lawyers do not engage in stalling tactics, they explained, the inherent barriers to a quick decision in such a situation are virtually insurmountable.

We asked DOL spokesmen if they ever requested summary judgment to speed up the proceedings, and were told that they do do so in certain instances. One problem is that often the union's lawyers will not agree to stipulate to the facts. Moreover, there is some question—although there is by no means general agreement among the courts—as to whether the language of Section 402(2), calling for a "trial upon the merits," precludes the use of summary judgment.[12]

Without undertaking a more thorough investigation of the use and alleged abuse of the granting of time waivers, we cannot determine the merits of that criticism. It may be true that, particularly when the DOL is flooded with election complaints, the agency is too ready to grant such waivers. Under those circumstances, the DOL's lack of investigative personnel and the union's desire to avoid litigation costs and attendant bad publicity may well combine against the interests of the individual complainant. We are, however, not prepared to do more than raise that point as a likely possibility.

Conduct of rerun elections.   We received varying comments concerning the conduct by the DOL of election reruns from union officials who had been involved in them. A few—about 20 percent—of the union officials thought that the DOL observers were of high caliber and very fair. The other 80 percent were quite critical. The majority of the latter contended that the observers were hypertechnical in carrying out the rules established for the election. A few reported that the DOL observers did not follow the rules at all.

The rules themselves received adverse comment. A preliminary determination of these rules is made at a meeting between the area office staff that will supervise the election and all other interested parties, e.g., those who won the original election, those who lost, any of their followers who care to be present, counsel for either side. The preliminary rules are then reviewed by the national office, and that office can and does make changes in them. We were told that even then the rules may not be firm. They can and have been changed further, "right down to the wire."

Officials of the DOL could not explain the failure of the observers to follow the rules except in terms of human fallibility. As one told us quite candidly: 'Who says the DOL can run a better

---

12. *Hodgson v. District 5, UMW,* cited in *Brennan v. Teamsters Local 639* (494 F.2d 1092, 1094 (D.C. Cir. 1974)), is the only case found that held that "trial on the merits" means just that. The *Brennan v. Teamsters Local 639* decision, as well as other cases cited in that decision, held the other way.

election than the union?" They could explain why the original set of rules was sometimes—though, they contended, rarely—changed upon review by the national office. Such changes occur when the preliminary rules contradict national office policy or recent court interpretations of which the area office staff are unaware. (Note that this seems to substantiate or at least bolster the repeated complaint of area office personnel that they are not kept sufficiently apprised of interpretive changes.)

We also heard adverse comment regarding the DOL's practice when its representatives appear in court to have the results of a supervised election certified. One advocate for dissidents asserted that he has repeatedly been told that he would be notified by the DOL of the date for that court appearance only to find that the day has come and gone without the promised notification. In each case, he had compiled evidence of election violations which he wanted to present to the court to try to convince it not to certify the results. Upon reading the court record, he found that the DOL representatives had recounted those complaints to the court in every case, but always did so in such a manner as to make them appear to be of no consequence. When we asked DOL officials about this practice, we were informed that since the late 1960s the agency has adopted the policy of always informing the complainant beforehand of the date on which certification is to be sought. Thus, if the dissidents' lawyer was describing recent experiences, then the DOL representative who failed to keep his promise was in blatant violation of agency policy.

On the basis of the incidents cited to us, we have concluded that the DOL's supervision of union elections, like its investigatory ability, does vary in quality and that, despite the government's presence, election violations can and occasionally do occur. We also conclude from the instances reported to us, which were partially confirmed by DOL spokesmen, that the changing nature of the rules established for a particular supervised election does, at times, constitute a problem or at least an unnecessary annoyance. An attempt should be made to keep such changes to a minimum.

Purpose of rerun elections.   Since the DOL itself admits to imperfections in its supervision of union elections, and since the winners of the original election often win the rerun as well, one is led to ask what purpose is served in having the DOL rerun elections at all. The DOL officials insisted that, despite the imperfections of the reruns or the actual outcome of the new elections, the reruns are nevertheless useful. They argued that the violations in elections supervised by the DOL are rarely of any consequence. Moreover, the rules established and the procedures followed in those reruns may be more stringent than the minimal requirements, e.g., additional precautions are taken, such as requiring voters to sign in so that the number of signatures can be checked against the number of ballots cast. The DOL officials indicated that such additional rules serve an educational purpose, and said that the guidelines, as well as the very presence of the government's observers, "add formality" to the proceeding that the members will long remember. Their point is well taken.

Interpretations of Title IV by the Department of Labor. *Uneven Department of Labor responses to inquiries.* A lawyer who acted as counsel for one of the unions in our sample said that during the course of the internal election appeals procedure, where the complaint involved the legality of a constitutional provision, he had asked the DOL to state the agency position with regard to the challenged language, and had been refused an answer. The refusal was made on the ground that the DOL itself might later receive an election complaint on that language, and it did not want to prejudge the merits of that complaint. Another lawyer, representing a different union, reported that he sought advice on constitutional language first from the area office, then from the regional office, and finally from the solicitor's office. He never received anything but a vague answer at any level. Nine other lawyers, advisors to still other unions, complained that, even where they do get answers, the responses can vary from level to level of the DOL. We should point out that varying answers at different levels can at times work to the advantage of the lawyer. One attorney told us: "You can go to the lower guy and not get the answer you want, but do what you want to anyhow. Then you can go over the guy's head to his superior, and get an okay on having done it ex post facto."

A substantial majority—well over half—of all union lawyers interviewed also said that a firm answer in one year does not mean that the same answer will be forthcoming two years later. These lawyers found to their dismay that all too often when union members filed a complaint to the DOL concerning the precise issue on which the lawyers had earlier sought agency guidance, DOL response to the complaint showed that the agency had completely reversed its earlier position.

The DOL's alleged penchant for giving out no answer, or an ever-changing one, was particularly grating to those who sought guidance concerning acceptable meeting attendance requirements. While one local union officer said that he thought the government had no business ruling on the issue at all, the rest of the union officials interviewed simply wished that the DOL would take a firm position on the matter. They pointed out that until July of 1973, the requirement that a candidate must have attended half of the regular union meetings over a two-year period preceding the election was acceptable to the DOL if liberal excuse provisions were included. In July of 1973, however, the DOL announced that the reasonableness of that attendance requirement would thenceforth be determined on a case-by-case basis. As several critics pointed out, the purpose of the DOL's regulations is to serve as a guide, and the agency's current interpretation with regard to the meeting attendance requirement simply does not fulfill that function.[13]

A DOL spokesman agreed that the agency does appear to have a wavering policy with regard to the meeting attendance requirement. However, he pointed out, the courts themselves have been inconsistent. Until the courts take a firm position, the DOL has no choice but to remain flexible.

We must agree with those who contended that the DOL's response to questions posed can vary from level to level, and time to time. We ourselves encountered that problem in the course of this study, and found the practice both annoying and confusing. At the same time, we should stress that, where the courts have not clearly delineated the policy to be followed, it is unfair to place blame on the DOL for taking a cautious approach.

Published Department of Labor interpretations and the need for general guidelines.   The DOL's published interpretations generally were also the topic of critical comment, not only by union members seeking guidance in the conduct of their own elections, but also by DOL staff members who must use those interpretations in enforcing the Act. Title 29, Part 452 of the *Code of Federal Regulations* (1973) was issued in booklet form by the DOL in 1974 under the title *Election of Officers of Labor Organizations.* These regulations supersede some, but not all, sections dealing with Title IV found in the older *LMRDA Interpretative Manual.*

---

13. The offending regulation is 29 C.F.R. 452.38 (1973).

On the whole, the 1973 regulations are considered better than those of the manual (which has been described by union lawyers and advocates for dissidents as "an unholy mess") but the manual must still be consulted for interpretations not covered in the 1973 regulations.

Our reading of the *LMRDA Interpretative Manual* confirmed that it is not a particularly useful tool for ascertaining current DOL interpretations. Subsequent policy decisions and court interpretations have substantially altered, if not reversed, some statements made in the manual, and yet that volume has not been updated to reflect those changes.[14] Nor, as already reported, are those who use the manual informed of the changes on a regular basis.

Lawyers both for unions and for dissidents often suggested that it would be helpful to everyone if the DOL were to issue general guidelines detailing procedures to be followed in all union elections. Those who made that suggestion pointed out that the language of Section 402(b) already gives the DOL the authority to issue rules and regulations with regard to election reruns. If the agency were to do even that much, it would be useful.

The DOL policy-makers conceded that some of the criticism leveled against the current printed interpretations have merit. However, they argued that the issuance of general election guidelines might do unions more harm than good. They noted that electoral practices vary greatly from union to union, depending upon the nature, history, and structure of the organization. Thus, trying to develop a framework into which all such practices could be fitted would be very difficult indeed. It would be far more useful, they said, if a strong technical assistance program could be developed at the area office level, so that the staff in those offices could help organizations seeking advice on election matters, on an individual basis.

The DOL officials reported that, when the Act was first passed, labor organizations were willing to use technical assistance from the area offices, but only to learn how to fill out the necessary financial reports. This allegation was confirmed by union officials. The unions shied away from any outside advice on the conduct of their elections. Some unions still do so, but others are now willing to look to the DOL for aid. Thus the implementa-

---

14. For examples of outdated statements, see Entry 476.100 and 476.500. In addition, language of some interpretations is at times quite cryptic, e.g., Entry 452.96.

tion of a strong technical assistance program on Title IV matters would fill a real need.

We agree that the DOL should do more than it now does to keep its field staff and others seeking guidance apprised of changes in policy. Moreover, despite DOL protests that the variability of union elections is such as to prevent construction of a meaningful framework into which all current election procedures could be fitted, it is our belief that such a framework can be established. Local union election procedures within a single parent organization vary greatly in many instances, yet a number of unions have been able to fit those local practices into the election manuals they have issued. The policy which the DOL adopted subsequent to the filing of our report and recommendations—to "advise and observe" parent union election procedures under certain circumstances when so requested—gives some indication that the agency itself does recognize that the task is not an impossible one.

While the problem of attempting to develop a framework into which all union election procedures could be fitted would undoubtedly be difficult, it does not appear to be beyond the realm of possibility. Such a framework would, of course, have to be bent if subsequent court decisions so dictated; but designing such a framework, even one subject to modification, has much to be said for it.

Summary

Of all the titles of the LMRDA administered in whole or in part by the DOL, that agency's enforcement of Title IV has had the greatest impact. There is good reason for this. Congress assigned primary responsibility for ensuring democratic union elections to the DOL. Thus the Act requires that each election complaint the DOL receives—no matter how flimsy—be investigated. Moreover, the inquiry must be completed within specified time limits. As already indicated, there are instances in which the agency evades those time limits by means of waivers, but the goal, even when not met, remains.

One beneficial impact of the DOL enforcement of Title IV is that internal election appeals have been considered with greater care since 1959 because union officers know that if they dismiss a meritorious complaint out of hand, the member has an alternate forum to approach in an attempt to get a fair hearing. Moreover, union spokesmen said that members are aware of the additional option they now have open to them and are therefore more ready to file those appeals. Another favorable impact, then, is that members know that a complaint regarding a fraudulent union election is no longer necessarily an exercise in futility, as it often was before the DOL became the guardian of union democracy.

On the other hand, the DOL sometimes administers its guardianship in an uneven manner. Indeed, it can at times play an adverse role rather than a beneficial one. While we limited our interviews to six area offices, we chose them carefully, basing our selections on the reports we had received concerning the high quality of their enforcement of the Act. Nevertheless, we would have to characterize the personnel in one of those offices as callous toward dissident members, who, for no reason, they automatically classify as "perennial whiners." To the extent that the agency lightly dismisses dissidents' legitimate complaints—and we received enough examples of that attitude from the dissidents and their advocates to believe that such treatment is not altogether uncommon—it discourages not only those complainants but other would-be dissenters who hear about what the DOL did, or rather did not do. Thus, valid complaints that should be filed are not. There is much merit to the statement made by one dissident who had consistently been refused help: "There are so few of us that the DOL should not constantly discourage us."

We should emphasize that we do not believe that the automatic dismissal of dissidents' complaints is DOL policy, but rather that it is a practice in one area office we visited. In four of the other five, dissidents' complaints are dealt with in a fair and evenhanded manner. On the other hand, the staff in the remaining area office went so far out of their way to protect and aid the complaining member that the prevailing attitude there would have to be classified as antiunion. One staff member in that office even told us flatly that he hates labor unions. Union officials who complained of the "cops and robbers" attitude or "FBI mentality" on the part of some enforcement officers are, to that extent, voicing an accurate assessment. Some effort should be made to install in all area offices the balanced approach now taken only in some.

We must also add that the imbalance we noted in some of the field offices—the tendency either to dismiss the dissident or automatically to assume that the complaining member's union is guilty as charged—is not limited to that level of the agency. For example, one highly placed national office staff member grumbled that the complainants come to the agency solely for the free legal services available through it. Another, in an even more important position, consistently referred to union representatives as "the opposition." We found both statements astounding. Neither assumption is correct, and neither should be automatically applied to an entire group.

In summary, then, the DOL's enforcement of Title IV has had a favorable impact to the extent that, to avoid contact with that enforcement, many unions are now more conscientious in dealing with internal election appeals. On the other hand, insofar as the DOL's threat to take an election complaint to court has at times led unions to agree to rerun elections merely to avoid litigation rather than because the unions' own investigation showed that the election had been improperly conducted, thus causing unnecessary internal disruption and needless expense, the impact of Title IV enforcement has been adverse.

Much also depends upon the attitude of the investigator in any given case. If he takes a balanced approach towards the election complaint he is considering, he will be effective in furthering the cause of union democracy; conversely, if he favors either the complainant or the union, he will impede that cause.

Chapter III

Title I: Labor's Bill of Rights

In terms of safeguarding the rights of individual union members, Title I is the most basic section of the LMRDA. It mandates equal rights to nominate candidates for office, to vote in union elections, and to participate in union meetings. It also safeguards the members' right of free speech, disallows unilateral increases in dues and assessments, protects members' rights to sue their unions, and prohibits improper disciplinary action.

With one exception, all complaints concerning violation of union members' rights under Title I must be redressed by means of private civil suit. The exception is Section 104, which is enforced by the DOL and states that the union must provide a copy of the current collective bargaining agreement to any employee who requests it. In only one instance has the agency had to sue a union in order to make it comply with that section.[1] In all other instances, a telephone call to the complainant's union is all that has been required for a copy of the contract to be supplied. The reason access to the document was denied is rarely anything more serious than that the union was temporarily short of copies.

Because all other complaints concerning the violation of rights safeguarded under Title I must be redressed by means of a private civil suit, the courts' role in protecting Title I rights has loomed large. The following discussion is not intended to be a complete and exhaustive survey of the legislative history of Title I, but seeks merely to point out the highlights of the title's history and those court decisions which have had the greatest impact on internal union affairs.

The earliest lobbying activities for legislation to regulate internal union affairs were directed at promoting internal union democracy. Undertaken by the American Civil Liberties Union at the time of congressional deliberations surrounding the enactment of the Taft-Hartley Act, the effort was aimed at the passage of a bill of rights for union members. However, Congress ignored until 1959 demands for federal legislation to ensure internal union de-

---

1. *Wirtz v. Independent Service Employees Union.* [E.D.N.Y., Civil Action 65 C 471, December 15, 1965].

mocracy. Moreover, the courts generally adhered to the idea that the citizens' rights enumerated in the U.S. Constitution—freedom of speech and press, freedom from discrimination, etc.—were not guaranteed to union members as such. As long as unions did not violate their "contracts" with their members—i.e., their constitutions and bylaws—they were allowed to govern according to rules that they themselves established, which included the regulations governing the disciplining of members. It was not until about 1950 that the state courts began to show any concern for the protection of the free play of ideas or for the need for democratic practices within labor unions. Only then did those courts begin to consider member criticism of union officers and the organization of opposition groups within unions to be worthy of protection.[2]

Neither the final House bill which was ultimately enacted, nor any of the many other congressional proposals which were deliberated in the years prior to passage of the LMRDA, contained a section outlining the internal union rights of members. In fact, according to one scholar of the legislative history of the Act, of the three major purposes of the LMRDA—to provide internal union democracy, to eliminate union racketeering, and to permit unions to function effectively in the collective bargaining sphere—Congress gave the first the least thoughtful attention.[3] Interest throughout the early stages was focused primarily upon specific areas of perceived abuse in union administration: mishandling of union funds, fraudulent election of officers, unnecessary imposition of trusteeships, and racketeering. When Senator McClellan's bill of rights amendment passed in the Senate,[4] supporters and opponents of the pending legislation were taken by surprise.[5]

The original McClellan amendment guaranteed to union members the right of free speech and assembly, equal rights and privileges in voting and meeting participation, and impartial review as a final step in the administration of the internal grievance

2. Summers, *The Usefulness of Law in Achieving Union Democracy*, 48 ANN. ECON. REV. 44, 52 (1958); Summers, *The Law of Union Discipline: What the Courts Do in Fact*, 70 YALE L.J. 175 (1960); Beaird & Player, *Free Speech and the Landrum-Griffin Act*, 25 ALA. L. REV. 579, 582 (1973).
3. Aaron, *The Labor-Management Reporting and Disclosure Act of 1959*, 73 HARV. L. REV. 851 (1960) (hereafter cited as *The LMRDA of 1959*). For discussion of the legislative history of LMRDA, see Cox, *Internal Affairs of Labor Unions Under the Labor Reform Act of 1959*, 58 MICH. L. REV. 820 (1960).
4. The amendment passed by a vote of 47 to 46, with then Vice-President Richard M. Nixon breaking the tie.
5. Aaron, *The LMRDA 1959, supra* note 3, at 858.

process. It also invested the DOL with the authority to investigate any complaint concerning the violation of these rights. The sweeping provisions of the original amendment provoked opposition from northern labor sympathizers, who saw it as unreasonable interference in union affairs and preferred enforcement by means of private suit. As one parent union lawyer explained quite candidly: "Most unions felt that if it were left to individuals, they'd never have enough money anyway, so it would pose no problem." Opposition to the amendment was shared by southern solons, who were concerned that it would open the door to federal intervention in civil rights matters.

The two forces quickly joined to back California Senator Tom Kuchel's amendment which, among other things, replaced DOL enforcement with redress by individual private suit, and deleted the requirement of third party review as the final step in the appellate procedure.

Preceded by hasty, informal consultations, the Kuchel amendment passed in the Senate overwhelmingly. In the House, that amendment's language was grafted onto the bill sponsored by Congressmen Phillip Landrum and Robert Griffin, and was approved in the House without consideration in committee. Thus, as one of the Act's draftsmen reported, "these sections never received the careful technical review and clarification which comes from scrutiny by a congressional committee and its legislative staff ... [and] the draftsmanship left much to be desired."[6]

Because of the diversity of subject matter covered in Title I, the individual sections will be treated separately. The rights of union staff members under Title I are given separate attention because the subject involves not only several sections of Title I, but also Section 609 of Title VI.

Section 101(a)(1)—Equal Rights

Section 101(a)(1) of the LMRDA provides that union members shall be accorded equal rights to nominate candidates for union offices, to vote in union elections, to attend membership meetings, and to participate fully in the business of those meetings, subject only to reasonable rules and regulations provided in the union's constitution and bylaws. The intent was that any rights in these areas accorded by a union to any of its members would be granted

6. Cox, *Internal Affairs of Labor Unions Under the Labor Reform Act of 1959*, *supra* note 3, at 833.

to all of its members. Congress did not intend to alter internal union policies by granting members any new substantive rights they did not already have.[7]

Few changes in constitutional language were necessary to comply with the section's intent, because in many instances the courts interpreted the language of the section in light of and consistent with unions' prior practices and written rules. Instances of blatantly discriminatory language in union constitutions were few and any constitutional amendments that were enacted after the Act's passage were largely included to codify existing practice.

In the cases which have been brought under Section 101(a)(1), representing approximately one third of all Title I litigation, the courts have sought to maintain a proper balance between the individual member's "equal rights" and the union's right to "reasonable rules and regulations." Two thirds of the decisions handed down have involved nominating and voting rights; the remainder have concerned restrictions on union membership (15 percent), the right to participate in union meetings (14 percent), and allegations of job discrimination leveled against the employer and/or the union (4 percent).

Nominating and Voting

A few suits challenging a union's nominating procedures have been brought by members who questioned the legality of their unions' regulations per se—for example, a protest against a union rule permitting a candidate to run for only one office.[8] None of those cases has been decided in the complainant's favor. As would be expected, the great majority (80 percent) of nominating and voting procedure challenges has been filed by would-be candidates who have been denied the right to run. Virtually all of those also have failed. Consistent with congressional intent,[9] the courts

---

7. U.S. Department of Labor, Office of the Solicitor, *Legislative History of the Labor-Management Reporting and Disclosure Act of 1959, Titles I-VI* (Washington, D.C.: U.S. Department of Labor, 1965), at 41, 48–49. See also Atelson, *A Union Member's Right of Free Speech and Assembly: Institutional Interests and Individual Rights*, 51 MINN. L. REV. 403, 410 (1967).

8. *Lenhart v. International Union of Operating Engineers*, 68 L.R.R.M. 3084 (D. Colo. 1968).

9. In response to a question as to the scope of Section 101(a)(1), and how it would affect the right to run for office, the author of the original bill of rights amendment responded: "I do not believe that in any fashion the equal rights section touches what the provisions of the constitution or by-laws might be with respect to the right to run for office." See U.S. Department of Labor, *Legislative History, supra* note 7, at 288.

have dismissed such suits for want of jurisdiction, on the ground that Section 101(a)(1) protects the member's right to nominate, but not his right to be a candidate. This reading of Section 101(a)(1) was upheld in 1964 in the Supreme Court decision in *Calhoon v. Harvey.*[10]

Two issues were before the Court in *Calhoon:* whether or not the union's "self-nominating" procedure, allowing a member to nominate only himself for office, was reasonable, and whether or not the union's candidacy requirements were just. Rather than deciding on the reasonableness of the self-nominating procedure issue per se, the Court ruled on the equity of its application. It found that the complainants had not been discriminated against vis-à-vis other union members because all other members had been similarly disqualified by the required procedure. The plaintiffs therefore had not been denied an equal right to nominate under Section 101(a)(1). As to the reasonableness of the candidacy requirement, the Court ruled that that issue fell outside the scope of Section 101(a)(1), and was instead a Title IV matter.

The limitations of Title IV enforcement (i.e., post-election complaint to the DOL), coupled with the *Calhoon* decision as to the coverage of Section 101(a)(1), have left a curious vacuum: the only question that a member can raise in federal court with regard to a union's nomination procedure prior to an election is whether or not such procedure, per se or in practice, is discriminatory.[11] If discrimination is not the issue, he has little choice but to wait until the election is held.[12] The member does retain the legal right

---

10. 379 U.S. 134 (1964).
11. See, for example, *McNail v. Meatcutters*, 549 F.2d 538 (8th Cir. 1977). Since procedures are rarely discriminatory per se, only in cases of blatantly biased application are they found to be illegal by the courts. In *Garret v. Dorosh* (77 L.R.R.M. 2651 (D. Mich. 1971)), an injunction was issued against an election because the nominations had been held while the opposing caucus was locked out.
12. Two federal court cases are exceptions. In *Libutto v. Dibrizzi* (337 F.2d 316 (2d Cir. 1964)), the appellate court, in a ruling handed down just weeks before *Calhoon* was decided, had granted pre-election relief in a candidacy denial complaint. After the *Calhoon* case, the court reviewed and revised its original decision, again granting relief, but on other grounds. It found the union in violation of its own constitution and thus in violation of state law rather than of Section 101(a)(1) (*Libutto v. Dibrizzi*, 343 F.2d 465 (2d Cir. 1965)). In *Depew v. Edmiston* (386 F.2d 710 (3d Cir. 1967)), the court reversed a lower court's dismissal of a candidacy denial complaint, finding that, in the unique circumstances of the case, it was really the candidate's membership status that was at issue, rather than the union's eligibility requirement.

to challenge the reasonableness of a candidacy requirement per se in a state court. However, since the *Calhoon* decision, those courts, too, have dismissed pre-election protests on the basis that they fall exclusively within the jurisdiction of Title IV.[13] Only if a would-be candidate is willing to protest his exclusion from candidacy after the election is held does he have any chance of having the procedure declared invalid.[14]

The provisions of Section 101(a)(1) require that members be accorded equal rights with regard to voting "in elections or referendums of the labor organization." This covers all voting rights accorded members in their union constitutions. Most common among these, in addition to the election of union officers, are votes to approve or disapprove the promulgation of, or amendments to, union constitutions, and those to ratify or reject newly negotiated contract terms. In voting situations other than those involving election of officials, the courts have assessed the reasonableness of the procedure or its application on grounds that go beyond the outright discrimination test applied to officer elections. With regard to contract ratification votes, unions have sometimes been able to justify voting arrangements that on their face have the appearance of unequal treatment. Also, groups of members have successfully challenged as unequal the practice of permitting all members to vote on contract terms that affect only the particular group.[15] With regard to votes on union constitutional language, the

---

13. See Note, *Union Elections and the LMRDA: Thirteen Years of Use and Abuse,* 81 YALE L.J. 407, 554 n. 669 (1972). Therein are listed twenty-two pre-election cases brought in state courts; in only six was any relief provided. Six other state court cases were called to the attention of the DOL Compliance Report compilers. Five of these were dismissed on jurisdictional grounds. In the other case, *Holdeman v. O'Callaghan* (83 L.R.R.M. 2172 (N.Y. Sup. Ct., 1973)), the court ordered the union to hold an election to fill a vacancy created by the death of an incumbent whose election was under investigation by the DOL. In so ordering, the court denied the defendant's motion to dismiss the case pending the outcome of the DOL's investigation.

14. E.g., *Hodgson v. Operating Engineers Local 18,* 440 F.2d 485 (6th Cir. 1971), *cert. denied,* 404 U.S. 852 (1971). See also the election suits discussed in chapters 1 and 2, dealing with Title IV.

15. In *Williams v. I.T.U.* (423 F.2d 1295 (10th Cir. 1970)), for example, the court held that the union's creation of two classes of members (those "working at the trade" and those "not working at the trade") was valid under Section 101(a)(1). In *Taxi Rank and File v. Van Ardsdale* (86 L.R.R.M. 2362 (S.D.N.Y. 1974)), the court found that the union had violated a preliminary injunction by scheduling a contract ratification meeting for all members, including those not covered by the new agreement's terms.

courts have gone even further to determine whether or not the voting procedures ensure meaningful participation.[16]

The issue of whether or not deceitfully represented or fraudulently conducted referenda other than officer elections are covered under Section 101(a)(1) has not been fully litigated.[17] The issue of fraudulently conducted contract ratification has not been litigated at all under Section 101(a)(1), although legal scholars believe that such activity probably would be covered. In any event, where participation in contract ratification is a right accorded by a union constitution, violation of that right can be the subject of suit in state courts.

Restrictions on Admission

Whereas the legislative history is often vague and ambiguous—if not completely silent—with regard to many portions of the LMRDA, on the topic of union admission policies it is quite clear: it was not the intent of Congress to dictate terms of union membership eligibility. This posture has been the subject of strong criticism, on the ground that it did not attempt to end race or sex discrimination practiced in some unions.[18]

The courts have not found the common union practice of refusing admission to affiliates of the Communist Party violative of Section 101(a)(1). However, they have usually read that section more broadly once a member has been initially admitted to membership.

---

16. For example, in *Sheldon v. O'Callaghan* (497 F.2d 1276 (2nd Cir. 1974)), the court held that it was a denial of equal voting rights for the union to publish misleading information and to deny the opponents "equal time" by refusing them permission either to state their objections to the new constitution in the union's newspaper, or to have access to the mailing list to transmit their objections in that manner to other members.

17. In *Arnold v. Meatcutters* (60 L.R.R.M. 2018 (D. Minn. 1965)), the court held that where a contract ratification is business properly before a membership meeting, it is within the jurisdiction of Section 101(a)(1). Similarly, in *Stettner v. Printing Pressmen* (278 F. Supp. 675 (E.D. Tenn. 1967)), the court held that the counting of constitutionally improper ballots in a referendum is a dilution of members' equal rights to vote, and is therefore a violation of Section 101(a)(1). See also *Lucy v. Richardson* (67 L.R.R.M. 2638 (N.D. Cal. 1967)), in which the court found the results of a mail referendum questionable because the members had received varying information with regard to the proposal at various stages of the balloting.

18. Griffin, *The Landrum-Griffin Act: Twelve Years of Experience in Protecting Employee Rights,* 5 Ga. L. REV. 622, 624–25 (1971); Previant, *Have Titles I–VI of Landrum-Griffin Served the Stated Legislative Purpose?* LAB. L.J. 28–40, 32 (January 1963).

Suits brought against a local union for refusing to accept a transferred member, or against a parent body for denying reinstatement following suspension, have generally been successful, where the member had otherwise fulfilled membership requirements.[19]

Participation in Union Meetings and Allegations of Job Discrimination

An anomaly exists in Section 101(a)(1): the law states that members have an equal right to attend and participate in union meetings, but nothing in the statute requires that such meetings even be held.[20] If the union's constitution specifies that regular meetings must be held, the members can bring suit at the state court level for violation of the contract between the union and its members.[21] However, they have no such rights under the LMRDA.

Generally, the courts have been reluctant to interfere with unions' procedures in the conduct of meetings, despite members' allegations that such procedures constitute denial of rights of participation.[22] However, some courts have held that unruly meetings constitute a denial of the right to participate.[23]

The courts have also been reluctant to deal with members' complaints of unequal treatment by union representatives within

---

19. E.g., *Ferger v. Local 483 Iron Workers*, 342 F.2d 430 (3d Cir. 1965); *Lusk v. Plumbers*, 84 L.R.R.M. 2266 (4th Cir. 1973), *cert. denied*, 415 U.S. 913 (1974); *Axelrod v. Stultz*, 391 F. 2d 549 (3d Cir. 1968). In *Lux v. Blackman* (546 F.2d 713 (7th Cir. 1976)), the court held that it was not unequal treatment for a union to remove an officer from his post when it was found that he had been a member of the Communist Party where the union constitution barred those who have been members of the Communist Party within the last five years from holding office. In *Gavin v. Ironworkers* (553 F.2d 28 (7th Cir. 1977)), the court held that would-be transfer members were not denied equal rights where the union constitution specifically gave discretion to locals to accept or deny transfers.

20. One circuit court has held that the inclusion of the right "to meet and assemble freely" "was not intended to create a right to call meetings of the union membership," but rather, "was intended to enable union members to meet outside their regular union meetings for the purpose of discussing internal union affairs without fear of reprisal by union officials. *Yanity v. Benware*, 376 F.2d 197 (2d Cir. 1967), *cert. denied*, 389 U.S. 874 (1967).

21. E.g., *Bausman v. National Cash Register Employees' Independent Union*, 74 L.R.R.M. 2950 (Ohio Ct. App. 1970).

22. E.g., *Allen v. Local 92 Iron Workers*, 47 L.R.R.M. 2214 (W.D. Ala. 1960).

23. E.g., *Vestal v. International Brotherhood of Teamsters*, 81 L.R.R.M. 2732 (C.A.D.C. 1972).

the work place. The few cases brought under Section 101(a)(1) alleging job discrimination have all been dismissed.[24]

Because instances of blatantly discriminatory nominating and voting procedures were not widespread, the courts have had little occasion to interfere in labor organizations' internal affairs under Section 101(a)(1). However, union spokesmen might quarrel with the assertion that the section's impact has not been disruptive, contending instead that far too many unmeritorious cases have been brought under Section 101(a)(1). They would note that in only a fourth of all such suits have the courts ultimately upheld the complaining member.

The aggrieved members and their advocates, however, would argue that the courts' denial of relief in the other three fourths of the suits brought under Section 101(a)(1) reflects the courts' narrow reading of its language, rather than the lack of real merit in the cases heard. Unless the procedures complained of have been blatantly discriminatory, the courts have refused to take jurisdiction.

To us, the latter group's contention is the more valid, given that in over 75 percent of the cases brought under Section 101(a)(1) that have been dismissed, the courts have ruled that they lack jurisdiction rather than that the complaint is without merit. While it is impossible to know in what proportion of those cases the plaintiff's appeal would have been upheld had the court ruled on the merits, it is clear from a reading of the opinions that, in a large number of them, the judge's sympathy clearly lays with the complainant.

Section 101(a)(2)—Freedom of Speech and Assembly

Unlike Section 101(a)(1), which was included to protect equality of treatment with regard to procedures, Section 101(a)(2) was intended to give union members substantive rights of free speech and assembly. The proviso to the section, however, subjects those rights to reasonable union regulations, i.e., regulations which restrict certain union member activities in order to protect the union

---

24. *Stout et al. v. Construction Laborers Council*, 226 F. Supp. 673 (N.D. Ill. 1963). In *Hill v. Aro Corporation* (275 F. Supp. 482 (N.D. Ohio 1967)), the court said there were no grounds for action on an unfair labor practice charge under LMRDA, but retained jurisdiction based on *Vaca v. Sipes* (386 U.S. 171 (1967)). In *Thomas v. Penn Supply and Metal Corporation* (55 L.R.R.M. 2861 (E.D. Pa. 1964)), the court retained jurisdiction where there was an allegation of a Section 101(a)(2) violation.

as an institution. In evaluating the reasonableness of the regulations, the courts determine whether or not the restricted activity would actually interfere with the union's contractual and legal obligations.

A very heavy burden has been on the union to show that the member's action impaired the union's ability to function as an institution, or to meet its contractual obligations. Even where the member has been responsible for promoting a wildcat strike, the courts sometimes have found for the member. Furthermore, when a member has made an allegedly slanderous or libelous statement about an officer, or made false allegations with regard to a union's policies, the discipline is virtually always overturned. The case most often cited in the latter context is the 1963 decision of the Court of Appeals for the Second Circuit in *Salzhandler v. Caputo*.[25]

The Salzhandler *Decision*

This most controversial of all the cases coming under Section 101(a)(2) involved Sol Salzhandler, a union officer who had been disciplined by his local's trial board for having made allegedly libelous statements against another officer. The discipline imposed was a five-year suspension of Salzhandler's right to attend union meetings and vote in union elections. The court, in finding such discipline improper, stated:

> Salzhandler had a right to speak his mind and spread his opinion regarding the union's officers, regardless of whether his statements were true or false.... The Congress has decided that it is in the public interest that unions be democratically governed and toward that end that discussion should be free and untrammeled and that reprisals within the union for the expression of views should be prohibited.[26]

As interpreted by the decision, the proviso in Section 101(a)(2) imposed two conditions on members' rights of free speech: a member is obliged to accept the "organization as an institution" and to refrain from acts that would impair the union's performance of "its legal or contractual obligations." Salzhandler's alleged libeling of an officer, in the court's opinion, fell into neither category. Furthermore, the court regarded local trial board procedures as "peculiarly unsuited" to the rendering of an impartial judgment

---

25. 316 F.2d 445 (2d Cir. 1963), *cert. denied,* 375 U.S. 946 (1963).
26. 316 F.2d 445, 451 (2d Cir. 1963).

as to whether or not a member's statements constituted valid criticism or defamation. The *Salzhandler* decision was appealed, but the Supreme Court denied certiorari.

The case has had a pronounced effect on subsequent decisions, both at the district and circuit court levels, in cases where the courts have been called upon to determine what constitutes free speech.[27]

Impact of the Salzhandler *Decision*

Critics of the *Salzhandler* decision contend that it has had a decidedly adverse impact on the nature of union meetings. They describe the meetings as more disorderly and say that as a result members' attendance has dropped. They attribute the disorderliness to officers' alleged reluctance to defend themselves against disruptive elements within the union, or to discipline members who make false accusations against them. These views were convincingly countered by the majority of the local union officers interviewed, as well as by the respondents in the three surveys.

Nature of union meetings. The vast majority of local union officers, those most directly involved in interacting with the rank and file members, felt that there had been no significant change in the nature of local union meetings since the *Salzhandler* decision was handed down. Fully 70 percent said that members have always felt free to voice their opinions at meetings and that rarely if ever had discipline been imposed for any type of free speech activity before or since enactment of the LMRDA. Parent union officers and their counsel, on the other hand, were largely critical of the Act's protection of free speech rights and especially of the interpretation accorded it by the *Salzhandler* decision. Although these parent officials recognized that most local officers are not troubled by rank and file disruption, their concerns focused on those few who are. Said one parent union officer: "It isn't the guy who is in great shape that I'm worried about. I'm concerned about

---

27. In *Reyes v. Laborers Local 16* (464 F.2d 595 (10th Cir. 1972), *aff'g*, 327 F. Supp. 978 (D.N.M. 1971)), the district court had said that free speech receives greater protection under the LMRDA than under the U.S. Constitution. Nevertheless, the court found against the plaintiff. See also *Farowitz v. Associated Musicians of New York, Local 802*, 241 F. Supp. 895 (S.D.N.Y. 1965); *Hall v. Cole*, 412 U.S. 1 (1973); *King v. IAM*, 335 F.2d 340 (9th Cir. 1964), *cert. denied*, 379 U.S. 920 (1964); *Boilermakers v. Rafferty*, 348 F.2d 307 (9th Cir. 1965). All the foregoing are in accordance with *Salzhandler*.

the good, conscientious leader who hasn't had a whole lot of experience in quelling unbridled attacks. Not all leaders can have everything going for them." The views of the 30 percent of the local union officers who felt that meetings were less orderly now divided evenly in their assessment and explanation of that situation. A third of them attributed the change to the Act and felt that the change was for the better: "Members know that officers can't just tear up their work cards anymore, [whereas before] members who raised the kind of challenge they now do would have been kicked out of the meeting."

Another third of those who believed meetings are now more unruly also attributed it to the Act and/or the *Salzhandler* decision but, in contrast to the first group, they considered the change to have had an adverse effect. They felt that officers were too often left defenseless against disrupters and dissenters. Interestingly, they themselves did not feel inhibited in dealing with dissent, but rather talked in terms of other officers' problems. Moreover, some of them attributed their colleagues' troubles to a misinterpretation of the scope of Section 101(a)(2): the officers who feel constrained in dealing with disruption believe that they are precluded from taking any disciplinary action. In fact, however, if the union's constitutional provisions are reasonable and are followed, officers may still discipline disruptive members with impunity.

The remaining local officers who perceived the meetings as more unruly now did not attribute the change in the tenor of the meetings to either the *Salzhandler* decision or the statute. The explanations they gave pointed to the generally younger, better educated membership and, in some cases, to the "leftist elements" with which some unions have always had to deal. These local officers also expressed confidence in the ability of competent leaders to overcome dissension, and even admitted to "waltzing out the loudmouth" on occasion and imposing discipline when they felt it necessary, despite the *Salzhandler* ruling.

One issue this group of officers raised was the length of time it takes for a slandered or libeled officer to seek redress by filing suit, especially during an election campaign, when such attacks are usually made. They contend that, no matter how well officers can fend off mudslinging, they simply should not be subjected to it. Said one: "The average competent guy who is trying to do a good job can't cope with outright attacks—and he shouldn't have to." Again, however, the officers who were most critical of the Act's free speech provisions denied ever having been hindered by them, and most were unable to identify specific local union officers who had.

The officers who had had personal experience with false accusers shrugged the incidents off as "a daily fact of life" and a "spontaneous piping off" that they find annoying but not dangerous. Some responded with variations of "I call him an S.O.B. right back," although most contended that they simply "roll with it." One, for example, responded to insinuations that he was using union funds to "live high and dress fancy" by proclaiming: "Yes, indeed. Your latest dues increase paid for these shoes. This suit was paid for out of the health and welfare fund. Thank you, one and all."

At election time, however, even these officers take false accusations more seriously, unless they know they "have it made" despite the charges. One local officer countered his accusers by publishing and distributing a denial at his own expense. Others said the alternative is to appeal to a local election committee or to call a special meeting to clear one's name.

Despite the concerns raised by the parent union officers and their counsel, as well as by a handful of the local officers, the protection of free speech rights within the organization appears not to have worked to the detriment of the internal functioning of the unions studied. Criticism against Section 101(a)(2) made in terms of its effect on weak or marginal officers only serves to highlight the need for such a provision. As one parent officer pointed out: "It's the weak local officer who is most apt to be undemocratic. He's too insecure to withstand open opposition." Union democracy is most vulnerable in a situation in which the organization is administered by an incompetent leader. He is less apt to be attuned to the members' desires and even less able to fulfill them. Because he is insecure, he is intolerant of the free expression of opinion. If he comes under attack he cannot fend off his accusers and, as a consequence, he reacts by trying to silence them. Either he succeeds in repressing his opponents, or he is overrun by them. Either way, the cause of union democracy is not served. In such instances of poor leadership at the local level, the situation can become so chaotic that the parent organization has to impose a trusteeship in order to restore stability. In such cases, all union members' rights suffer as a result of officer weakness.

Moreover, even if disciplinary measures for libel and slander are available to the weak union officer, he still is not protected from the silver-tongued member who, according to several officers, is more of a threat than the vitriolic slanderer. The gifted orator can veil half-truths and derision with his glowing eloquence. Thus confronted, the local officer has no justification for discipline of any kind and must rely on his own ability to talk down or otherwise withstand the attack.

The survey responses of rank and file union members were consistent with the view expressed by the majority of the union officers: members do feel free to speak up at union meetings. More union members (93 percent) responded affirmatively to "Could you speak up at union meetings?" than to any other inquiry about LMRDA rights (appendix G, table 14). Three percent of the union member respondents said they did not know if they could speak up. Among those who either did not feel they could speak out at union meetings (22 or 4 percent of the total) or who at the same time in the past felt they could not (85 or 13 percent of the total), the reasons given were largely unrelated to the union. Fully 75 percent of these 107 respondents gave personal reasons for their failure to voice their opinions. (appendix G, table 18). Among the personal reasons given were general inactivity, language problems, or timidity, rather than "trouble with leaders" or "trouble with co-workers." Of the 107 respondents who indicated ever having been reluctant to speak out at meetings, only two explained their hesitancy in terms of a belief that they did not have a right to speak up (appendix G, table 18).

However, only fifteen (or 28 percent) of the fifty-nine survey respondents who were familiar with the LMRDA felt that the Act had contributed to the members' feeling of freedom to speak up. Just slightly more than that—about 33 percent—said it made officers more inclined to listen to members (appendix G, table 22). Among the twenty-eight respondents who were over forty-four years of age and who knew of the LMRDA and thus were more likely to have been union members at the time of the Act's passage, only 29 percent said it was easier to speak up now, but 40 percent said officers were more inclined to listen when they did (appendix G, table 23B). Thus, while speaking up at union meetings remains formidable to a small proportion of union members, the situation has been improved in terms of officers' willingness to listen.

It may well be that there are cases of which we are not aware in which an officer, because he was newly elected and untried, or because his particular local had an unusual amount of factionalism, has in fact been hampered because of the courts' zealous protection of free speech rights. However, no such instances were called to our attention.

We were also given hard evidence that in some cases members' free speech rights are not sufficiently protected, and that members exercising such rights have been subject to unjust discipline. Based on that evidence, we must conclude that the courts' solicitude in protecting the free speech rights of union members has had a beneficial effect in promoting union democracy, without interfering unduly with the unions' ability to function.

Impact of Section 101(a)(2) on Meeting Attendance

Attendance at local union meetings is poor, and has gotten steadily worse over the past fifteen years. Whereas formerly, member turnout ranged from 50 percent in the larger locals to 95 percent in the smaller units, it now ranges from a low of less than 1 percent to a high of 20 percent.

Why is attendance generally down? Only three of the officers interviewed attributed the decline even partially to the LMRDA. They believed that the statute encouraged the young, who are already aggressive, to be even more so, and that this drove other members away. That theory was countered by an equal number of officers who said that it is the livelier meeting that attracts members.

The vast majority of officers at all levels cited reasons other than the Act for the lack of interest in local meetings. Locals are being consolidated for efficiency reasons, and large locals have always had the worst meeting attendance records. Members' homes are farther away from the meeting hall and, moreover, there is less community of interest among members. In two of the largest locals we visited, the officers had been unable to get a quorum at any regular meeting since the last election. Because their union constitutions require a quorum for the conduct of business at such meetings, the officers had had no alternative but to administer the unions without any member participation in the decision-making process.

Some of the officers contended that external factors are basically responsible for low attendance: the union is no longer as central, socially or politically, to its members' lives as it once was. Moreover, higher incomes have given members more options for their leisure hours, with television cited the most often as an ever-present diversion.

Dissidents argued that the problem is largely internal. Unions have become so bureaucratic, with most business conducted in executive session, that members have little incentive to attend meetings where so little of import is actually decided. There is some support for that argument since the special meetings called to discuss contract terms and to ratify newly negotiated agreements, where members do have an opportunity to make meaningful decisions, are better attended. At those meetings, attendance in the locals we contacted ranged anywhere from 25 percent to 95 percent, and averaged about 50 percent.

However, the information obtained from the three surveys of rank and file members tends to support those who contend that external factors, rather than internal reasons or the LMRDA, are to blame for low attendance at local union meetings.

None of the survey questions focused on meeting attendance per se. Several questions, however, were designed to assess general activity levels and reasons for specific instances of failure to exercise rights specifically protected under LMRDA, e.g., failure to vote in union elections or to protest expenditures for political purposes, etc.

Union member respondents were asked to characterize themselves as either inactive, fairly inactive, somewhat active, fairly active, or very active.[28] Over-all, the largest proportion of respondents characterized themselves as not active (31 percent), and the smallest number considered themselves very active (13 percent). (See appendix G, table 8 for further analysis of activity level.) In addition, when members indicated inability to act on a right protected by the LMRDA—either at present or at some time in the past—their reasons for feeling unable to act were largely personal, usually the result of their own inactivity (appendix G, table 19).

Union members who had specific knowledge of the LMRDA tended to consider themselves more active within their unions than those unfamiliar with the statute: 56 percent of the former

---

28. The categories themselves were not defined more precisely because the type of union to which the respondent belongs has considerable bearing on how activity level is perceived. For example, a person who might be considered relatively active within a large industrial union local might seem relatively inactive within a small craft union using a hiring hall. Therefore, the respondent's own perception of his activity level was considered more revealing than any objective criteria such as the percentage of meetings he attended per year, or the number of times he spoke out at a union meeting when he disapproved of an action taken by his elected representatives.

described themselves as "very" or "fairly" active in contrast to 31 percent of the latter. But which came first? Are members more active because they are familiar with the Act and therefore know that certain activities are protected? Or, in contrast, because they are more active, for whatever reason, are they made more aware of labor legislation such as the LMRDA? Conversely, are the less involved members inactive because they are unaware that certain actions are protected and thus hesitant to exercise rights they in fact have? Or are they simply disinterested, and less likely to be familiar with their rights under the law for that reason alone?

As one would expect, there was no single explanation for the diffidence of those respondents who considered themselves inactive. However, the reasons they gave for choosing not to exercise certain rights protected by the LMRDA did shed some light on the subject. Thirty-six percent of the inactive respondents attributed the lack of participation to a previous history of noninvolvment: "I didn't speak up at the meeting because I'm not active enough." When those giving "other" reasons for nonparticipation are added to that 36 percent, which can be justified on the basis that most "other" answers involved personal reasons, fully 50 percent of the explanations given for inactivity suggested disinterest. Such a large percentage of apathetic responses weakens the contention that members are not involved in union affairs because other members discouraged them from participating, or because they believe involvement would be futile. The respondents were given the specific option of blaming their nonparticipation on the "system," their leaders or their co-workers, and yet the majority chose instead to put the blame on themselves.

However, the argument that members are inactive because they feel participation is futile was given some support by the survey responses. "Can't beat the system" accounted for over 30 percent of the explanations given for not acting on one of the six LMRDA-protected rights listed. While this might suggest leader unresponsiveness or intimidation or co-worker opprobrium, since the respondents were given the explicit opportunity to cite the officers or their co-workers as the inhibiting factor, the fact that they pointed instead to the system seems to indicate that they believed the system to be so entrenched that an attempt at positive action or change would be in vain. Only 12 percent named union officers as the deterrent; another 5 percent singled out their co-workers; and 3 percent simply said, "I don't have the right" (appendix G, table 18).

Thus it seems fair to conclude that the LMRDA has had little impact on meeting attendance and, further, that the causes for decreases in attendance are largely external. Even officers elected on reform platforms that promised participatory decision making reported little success in generating a higher turnout. The only instances in which the statute was cited as having a direct and adverse impact on meeting attendance were in fact instances in which the statute had been misinterpreted. Several officers reported that they no longer fine members who do not attend meetings because they believed that such fines could be considered discipline prohibited by Section 101(a)(5). Similarly, in one union, the policy of giving bonuses to members who do attend has been discontinued because of concern that the practice might constitute unequal treatment in violation of Section 101(a)(1). The fact is, however, that courts have upheld the imposition of reasonable rules with regard to meeting attendance.[29]

Other Section 101(a)(2) Court Cases

Approximately 18 percent of all Title I cases have been brought under Section 101(a)(2). If the litigation involving the free speech issue which has been brought under Section 101(a)(5)—"Safeguards Against Improper Disciplinary Action"—is included, the figure comes closer to 20 percent.

The decisions under Section 101(a)(2) have been much more favorable to the complaining member than have those in cases brought under Section 101(a)(1). Whereas under the latter section, the decisions favored the union approximately 75 percent of the time, under Section 101(a)(2), the individual member succeeded at that rate.[30] The only Section 101(a)(2) suits won by the unions have been those in which, like the bulk of the Section 101(a)(1) cases, the challenge was brought on the ground that the procedures in the conduct of meetings had been improper. In such litigation, the

---

29. For example, in *Kalish v. Hosier* (256 F. Supp. 853 (D. Colo. 1965), *aff'd per curiam,* 364 F.2d 829 (10th Cir. 1966), *cert. denied,* 386 U.S. 994 (1966)), the plaintiff challenged the union's practice of assessing each member an extra dollar a month in dues, and rebating that amount if he attended the monthly meeting. The plaintiff had refused to pay the extra assessment, and the union therefore prohibited him from voting in an officer election. The circuit court upheld the union's right to institute such a system. See also *Gartner v. Soloner,* 384 F.2d 348 (3d Cir. 1967), *cert. denied,* 390 U.S. 1040 (1968); *Graham v. Soloner,* 220 F. Supp. 711 (E.D. Pa. 1963).

30. This figure includes 5 percent which were dismissed as moot because the union had already remedied before the case came to trial.

courts have been reluctant, again as is the case with Section 101(a)(1) suits, to interfere where there is no suggestion that the union has applied its procedures in a discriminatory manner.[31]

The courts have been least likely to uphold the union in cases involving the discipline of a member or members because of their opposition to actions taken by the officers or to union policy generally.[32] For example, relief has been granted where a member was disciplined for the following activities:

1. Questioning the amount of the officers' salaries
2. Provoking opposition to a union's allegedly illegal method of collecting dues
3. Picketing a union to protest the imposition of discipline
4. Soliciting support from other locals to oppose the imposition of a trusteeship[33]

Numerous courts have acknowledged the existence of the proviso to Section 101(a)(2) saying in dicta, that free speech is a "variable" right, and that not all speech activity would be protected, given the proviso's language.[34] Defendant unions, however, have been hard pressed to convince the courts that any actions taken by members actually have been injurious to the union as an institu-

---

31. In *McFarland v. Building Material Teamster Local 282* (180 F. Supp. 806 (S.D.N.Y. 1960)), the court ruled that it was not a violation of the plaintiff's free speech rights for the local officer to refuse to put the plaintiff's motion to a vote when the motion was in violation of the union's constitution. Similarly, in *Broomer v. Schultz* (356 F.2d 984 (3d Cir. 1966)), the court held it was not a violation to disallow a motion on an issue which had been voted on and settled at the last meeting.

32. Where the challenging members were also union employees, and their activity centered on internal union politics, the courts have sometimes upheld the union, a topic which will be dealt with more fully in a subsequent section of this chapter.

33. *Sordillo v. Local Union No. 63 Sheet Metal Workers*, 53 L.R.R.M. 2791 (D. Mass. 1963); *Farowitz v. Associated Musicians of New York, Local 802, supra* note 27; *Gartner v. Soloner, supra* note 29; *Barbour v. Sheet Metal Workers*, 401 F.2d 152 (6th Cir. 1968). In *Allen v. Iron Workers, supra* note 22, a local had ordered a member to appear before a union meeting to defend himself against possible discipline because he had requested that the handling of union funds be investigated by the local's executive committee. The member filed suit to protest that order, and the court found for him. The need to defend himself before the entire membership was deemed so unusual as to be intimidating, and thus a violation of the member's free speech rights.

34. *Deacon v. Operating Engineers Local 12*, 59 L.R.R.M. 2706 (S.D. Cal. 1965).

tion.[35] Only if the action taken by the member does quite obvious harm to a union's interests, such as in the case of a local officer provoking an unauthorized strike, have the courts held for the union.[36] Otherwise, if the organization's interests appear to conflict with a member's free speech rights, the latter has carried the greater weight.[37]

Section 101(a)(3)—Dues, Initiation Fees, and Assessments

To protect members against unilateral or coercive increases in dues, initiation fees, and assessments, Congress included the provisions of Section 101(a)(3).[38] By the terms of the section, such increases must be approved by the members either by secret ballot (in the case of a local union) or by vote at convention or by referendum.

The section deals solely with procedures. It puts no limits of any kind on the amount of such increases. Rather, that issue is left to the discretion of those voting. The section does require that if an increase is to be voted upon at the local level, the members must be given reasonable notice that such voting is to take place. The section says nothing about prior notification of either locals or

---

35. E.g., *Giordani v. Upholsterers' Union*, 403 F.2d 85 (2d Cir. 1968); *Farnum v. Kurtz*, 50 Lab. Cas. 13,216 (Los Angeles Mun. Ct., Los Angeles Jud. Dist., County of Los Angeles, Calif. 1968). See also *Morrissey v. National Maritime Union*, 92 L.R.R.M. 3211 (2d Cir. 1976). Even in the *Deacon* case cited at note 34 *supra*, upon the plaintiff's return to court after having been found guilty by the local trial board, the court found for the plaintiff. In the interim, Mr. Deacon made clear at a press conference that he had sued the local business manager, not the local, and his earlier statement had been retracted by the newspaper. *Deacon v. Operating Engineers Local 12*, 273 F. Supp. 169 (C.D. Cal. 1967). See also *Stachan v. Weber*, 535 F.2d 1202 (9th Cir. 1976).
36. E.g., *Degan v. Tugmen's and Pilots' Association*, 84 L.R.R.M. 2569 (N.D. Ohio 1973).
37. The most controversial issue has been to what extent, if at all, Section 101(a)(2) protects members' activities in support of another union. In *Johnson v. IBEW* (181 F. Supp. 734 (E.D. Mich. 1960)), the court disallowed discipline of members who had participated in a meeting held for the purpose of petitioning for the chartering of a new local. Opposition activity during organization campaigns has been protected by some courts, based on Section 101(a)(2). See *Nix v. Fulton Lodge*, 452 F.2d 794 (5th Cir. 1971); *Lodge 702, IAM v. Loudermilk*, 444 F.2d 719 (5th Cir. 1971). However, in *Sawyers v. Grand Lodge IAM* (279 F. Supp. 747 (E.D. Mo. 1967)), the expulsion of union members for opposition activity was upheld.
38. See U.S. Department of Labor, *Legislative History, supra* note 7, at 251, 269, 341.

their members where the issue of a dues increase is to be approved by delegates at a regular convention. Notification is required prior to a special convention.

Impact of the Enactment of Section 101(a)(3)

In our sample unions, very little change in union practice was initially necessitated when Section 101(a)(3) came into force, since the procedures it set forth were already common practice in all of them. The two most important constitutional inclusions were the need for secret ballot vote and the requirement that members be notified in advance. In only one of the unions we investigated was there any change in actual practice: in that organization, the parent body had traditionally set the dues unilaterally for members of locals not affiliated with an intermediate body. Following passage of the Act, the members of such locals were permitted to determine dues rates themselves.

Prior to 1959, the constitutions of only a few of our sample unions provided that dues increases were automatically tied to wage increases. In those instances, no prior approval by the members was required, presumably on the ground that they had already given tacit approval to the arrangement when their representatives to the parent body convention agreed to the constitutional amendment that made dues rates dependent upon wage rates. At present, all but two of the twelve sample unions have specific constitutional provisions authorizing the sliding scale method of increasing dues, or at least contain language making such a practice possible. None of the spokesmen for the unions that added that language after 1959 attributed the addition to the LMRDA. Rather, they contended, the method was just considered to be more equitable. Whether or not the practice is technically in compliance with the intent of Section 101(a)(3) has never been litigated.[39]

There were virtually no complaints raised by the union spokesmen we interviewed concerning the requirements of this section. The only objection was voiced by a dissident who felt that there should be additional language requiring unions to notify their members when a proposal to increase dues was to be considered at an upcoming convention. He contended that parent

---

39. In *Painters Union Local No. 127 v. District Council of Painters, No. 16* (415 F.2d 1121 (9th Cir. 1969), *cert. denied,* 397 U.S. 972 (1970)), the circuit court ruled against what was essentially a percentage dues structure, because of a procedural defect in arriving at the structure, not against the structure per se.

unions could persuade delegates to approve any proposal, including a dues increase, no matter how the members they represent might object. However, our review of union convention proceedings indicates that the one issue that is likely to arouse heated debate, even in an otherwise lifeless convention, is that of an increase in dues.

Court Interpretations of Section 101(a)(3)

Approximately 10 percent of all Title I court cases involve alleged violations of Section 101(a)(3). Of those, 90 percent are concerned with dues increases, rather than with initiation fees or assessments. The cases have revolved around one of two questions: (1) Was the procedure used in raising dues proper? and (2) Was the action taken by the union an "increase" under the meaning of Title I?

Cases determining proper procedure.   Decided by the Supreme Court in December of 1964, *American Federation of Musicians v. Wittstein*[40] is the most important of the cases involving the issue of proper procedure under Section 101(a)(3). In question was whether or not an increase in per capita dues assessed against each member, approved at a convention at which each local's delegates cast the number of votes equal to the approximate number of members in the local they represented, was a violation of Section 101(a)(3). Those bringing suit argued that the Act's language calling for "a majority vote of the delegates voting at a regular convention" should be read to mean that each delegate casts "but one vote, no more or less, and the affirmative votes cast add up to a majority of the delegates voting."[41]

The Court disagreed: "Where the 'vote' cast at a convention is weighted according to the number of people the delegate represents, that vote, we think, is a vote of a delegate."[42]

Over-all, the courts' reading of the procedural requirements of Section 101(a)(3) has been narrow. As with Sections 101(a)(1) and 101(a)(2), they have shown reluctance to interfere with existing union procedures.[43] Despite their hesitancy to intervene, the

---

40. 379 U.S. 171 (1964).
41. *Id.* at 176.
42. *Id.*
43. For example, the courts have held that local reratification of a dues increase voted on at convention is not required; that a combined vote on wage increase/dues increase is not improper if an opportunity is provided to decide on each

courts have been mindful that member participation should be meaningful. One court, for example, has held that the term "vote" connotes a determined expression of will and should be unambiguous. Thus, a show of hands or a standing vote was held to be too imprecise a method of determining the results in a close vote.[44]

Cases determining statutory construction. The courts have frequently had to deal with the question of whether or not the action taken by the union should be regarded as effectuating an "increase" in the context of Section 101(a)(3). They have consistently held that if the action resulted in a direct increase in assessments of any kind for members, it is an increase.[45] On the other hand, if the over-all assessment structure remained the same, but the amount of an individual member's dues rose due to his own change in job classification, the result of that action has not been considered an increase.[46]

---

issue separately, but that it is improper when stated as a single yes/no proposition; and that where a constitution that includes a dues increase provision is passed by delegates at convention and is to be subsequently approved by a membership referendum, the union is not required to hold a separate vote on each constitutional provision in the referendum "where separate vote on some of these provisions and the rejection of others might result in an unworkable document and [throw] the operation of the union into confusion." See *Ranes v. Office Employees Local 28,* 317 F.2d 915 (7th Cir. 1963); *Ford v. Carpenters, Metropolitan District Council of Philadelphia,* 323 F. Supp. 1136 (E.D. Pa. 1970); *Sertic v. Carpenters District Council,* 423 F.2d 515 (6th Cir. 1970); *Sheldon v. O'Callaghan,* 497 F.2d 1276 (2d Cir. 1974).

44. *Rota v. Railway Clerks,* 489 F.2d 998 (7th Cir. 1973), *cert. denied,* 414 U.S. 1144 (1974).

45. Thus, a checkoff procedure negotiated between the company and the union was held to be an unauthorized "assessment" because it imposed a direct financial burden on the members using procedures other than those set forth in Section 101(a)(3); a local's action to end a longstanding tradition of covering dues of certain members from its own funds was held illegal in that it resulted in an increase in payments by the formerly exempt members; and a parent union's directive that certain of its locals affiliate with a newly established council was null and void insofar as it required the members of those locals to pay dues or per capita tax to the council where that assessment had not been enacted according to the procedures of Section 101(a)(3). See *Steib v. Local 1497, ILA,* 436 F.2d 1101 (5th Cir. 1971); *Wesling v. Waitresses Union, Local 305,* 74 L.R.R.M. 3068 (D. Ore. 1970); *King v. Randazzo,* 346 F.2d 307 (2d Cir. 1964).

46. E.g., *Williams v. Typographical Union,* 423 F.2d 1295 (10th Cir. 1970); *Schwartz v. Associated Musicians of Greater New York, Local 802,* 340 F.2d 228 (2d Cir. 1964).

The courts are divided on the issue of whether or not per capita taxes assessed of locals rather than of individual members should be considered dues, and thus fall within the scope of Section 101(a)(3) coverage.[47] This has not been a widespread problem, however, because most parent bodies raise per capita tax payments at convention, a procedure regarded as in compliance with Section 101(a)(3).[48]

In instances where correct procedures have not been observed, the courts have construed their remedial authority quite broadly. In addition to issuing temporary restraining orders or injunctions to halt the collection of illegally increased dues, as the statute specifically authorizes, and to restrain a union from disciplining a member for nonpayment of such dues,[49] the courts have ordered unions to return the improperly collected increases to the members.[50] We were told by one union officer that the last-named remedy has a distinct disadvantage. In his experience, those to whom the rebate would be due are hesitant to request repayment, for fear of reprisal. Perhaps because of that possibility, another court in a similar situation did not order refunds to individual members but, instead, left it to the entire membership to determine the disposition of the total amount overpaid.[51]

The instances of unilateral imposition of an increase in dues or other levies, as reported to Congress during its deliberations concerning the Act, were not widespread. Thus, the major impact of Section 101(a)(3) has been one, not of bringing about membership participation, but rather of ensuring that voting at the local level is by secret ballot and thus takes place without fear of coercion.

---

47. Per capita taxes assessed of locals were held not to be covered by Section 101(a)(3) in *King v. Randazzo, supra* note 45, and *Ranes v. Office Employees Local 28, supra* note 43. *Contra, Telephone Workers Local 2 v. International Brotherhood of Telephone Workers*, 362 F.2d 891 (1st Cir. 1966), *cert. denied,* 385 U.S. 947 (1966). See also *Jenette v. Ammons*, 60 L.R.R.M. 2154 (M.D. Tenn. 1965).

48. Some legal scholars have raised the question whether or not, under Section 101(a)(3), a parent body convention may increase local dues rates or minimums without submitting the issue to a vote of the members of the affected locals. The courts thus far have held that they can. See *Ranes v. Office Employees Local 28, supra* note 43. See also *King v. Randazzo, supra* note 45.

49. E.g., *Steib v. Local 1497, ILA, supra* note 45; *Painters Union Local 127 v. District Council of Painters No. 16, supra* note 39.

50. E.g., *Telephone Workers, Local 2 v. International Brotherhood of Telephone Workers, supra* note 47; *Peck v. Food Distributors, Local 138*, 237 F. Supp. 113 (D. Mass. 1965); *White v. King*, 319 F. Supp. 122 (E.D. La. 1970).

51. *Sertic v. Carpenters District Council*, 423 F.2d 515 (6th Cir. 1970).

Section 101(a)(4)—Protection of the Right to Sue

Section 101(a)(4) embodies both of Congress' overriding concerns
in enacting the LMRDA: the protection of union members' rights
and the concurrent preservation of union self-government without
outside interference. Although the main body of the section protects the individual member by prohibiting restriction of his right
to seek judicial or agency assistance, the concern for the preservation of union self-government is manifest in both of the section's
two provisos. The first states that a member who intends to sue his
union "may be required" to exhaust his internal remedies for up
to four months before doing so. The second prohibits employers or
employer associations from encouraging a member in any way to
bring such action.

The first proviso has received the courts' primary attention.
Thus, a broad guarantee of a union member's right to institute suit
against his union was coupled with a strong suggestion that the
union first be given an opportunity to resolve the grievance within
its internal trial and appellate procedures. The time limit was
imposed to preclude interminable delay on the part of the union
in its attempt at internal resolution.[52]

Internal Exhaustion Requirement

The foremost question to be brought before the courts under Section 101(a)(4) has centered upon the "may be required" language
of the first proviso. To whom is the apparent discretion to require
or excuse the four-month exhaustion accorded: to the courts or to
the unions? If it is to the courts, then the proviso is in essence a
statement of policy that *under normal circumstances* the courts
should refrain from taking jurisdiction until the plaintiff has
sought internal relief for four months. If, on the other hand, the
discretion was intended to be accorded to the unions, then the
proviso is tacit acknowledgment that the union may discipline a
member who fails to attempt to seek internal redress for at least
four months before filing suit.

The legislative history of the "may be required" language
being unclear, judicial decisions have been interpretive (table 5).

---

52. The time period was finally set at four months, rather than six, as initially
    suggested, in order not to interfere with a member's right to file unfair labor
    practice charges with the NLRB. The latter has a six-month statutory limitation.
    See U.S. Department of Labor, *Legislative History, supra* note 7, at 307–308.

TABLE 5. Issue of Exhaustion of Internal Remedies in Private Suits Brought under Title I, LMRDA

Section Under Which Suit Primarily Brought	(a) Suits in Which Exhaustion Was an Issue (percentage)	(b) Suits in Which Exhaustion Was Excused (percentage of col. a)
Section 101(a)(1): Equal right to nominate	21	68
Section 101(a)(2): Right of free speech	27	92
Section 101(a)(3): Right to vote on dues	20	85
Section 101(a)(5): Right to due process	21	55

The Supreme Court has not directly addressed itself to that question in an LMRDA case, but that body's view with regard to the subject of exhaustion of internal remedies is clear. In ruling on that topic in a different context in *NLRB v. Marine Shipbuilders*,[53] the Court did make reference to Section 101(a)(4) to support its position: "We conclude that 'may be required' is not a grant of authority to unions more firmly to police their members but a statement of policy that the public tribunals whose aid is invoked may in their discretion stay their hands for four months while the aggrieved person seeks relief within the union."[54] In addition, the Court said "that unions were authorized to have hearing procedures for processing grievances . . . provided these procedures did not consume more than four months of time, but that a court or agency might consider whether a particular procedure was 'reasonable' and entertain the complaint even though those procedures had not been exhausted."[55]

Circuit court decisions interpreting Section 101(a)(4) issued after the *Marine Shipbuilders* case came down have not countered the Supreme Court interpretation. If a member has a right to bring suit prior to the expiration of the four-month period, it follows that he should not be vulnerable to discipline for exercising that right. This is implicit in the *Marine Shipbuilders* decision and is true whether or not the case is ultimately decided in his favor. Section

---

53. 391 U.S. 418 (1968).

54. *Id.* at 426.

55. *Id.* at 428. For earlier court decisions in agreement with *Marine Shipbuilders*, see *Detroy v. American Guild of Variety Artists* (286 F.2d 75 (2d Cir. 1961), cert. denied, 366 U.S. 929 (1961)), and *Parks v. IBEW* (314 F.2d 886 (4th Cir. 1963)).

609 of the Act, which prohibits retaliation for exercising the rights protected under the statute, buttresses that view.[56]

In the cases in which the courts have not required the member first to exhaust his internal remedies, only approximately 15 percent of the complainants returned to the courts after having appealed to their unions. It is difficult to assess the meaning of the low percentage of returns. It could mean that the internal appeal procedures of the union involved were meaningful and that the member was satisfied with the final decision. Or, it could signify that the knowledge that the member would return to the court if he received no satisfaction within the union influenced the decision reached internally in his favor. On the other hand, the court's initial rebuke and the opprobrium of the complainant's fellow members because of his action may have discouraged him from trying the court again, no matter what the outcome of his internal appeal. There is insufficient evidence, however, to come to any conclusion.

Impact of Section 101(a)(4)

Despite the courts' predominant interpretation, unions consider exhaustion of internal appeals procedures to be obligatory upon the member. Accordingly, the vast majority of the unions covered under the Act, and all of the unions in this study, have constitutional language detailing the steps a member must take to fulfill that obligation. A 1963 government survey found that of the 158 union constitutions analyzed, 153 contained internal appellate procedures of some kind.[57] All but one of the unions studied had constitutional language covering internal appeals procedures prior to passage of the Act. Eight of the twelve had explicit exhaustion requirements and, of those eight, four authorized discipline for failure to follow that requirement. The other four had a general discipline authorization for violation of any constitutional provision.

---

56. The prevailing view is perhaps best expressed in the decision in *Ryan v. IBEW* (361 F.2d 942, 946 (7th Cir. 1966)), a case in which the member was disciplined for bringing a suit that was ultimately unsuccessful: "The right of free access to our courts is too precious a right to be curbed by the risky prediction that the judge's discretion may, like a lucky roll of the dice, turn up in favor of the suitor." See also *Parks v. IBEW, supra* note 55; *Ross v. IBEW,* 544 F.2d 1022 (9th Cir. 1976); *Wiglesworth v. Teamsters Local 592,* 552 F.2d 1027 (4th Cir. 1976), *cert. denied,* 95 L.R.R.M. 2575 (1977).

57. U.S. Bureau of Labor Statistics, Department of Labor, Bull. No. 1350, *Disciplinary Powers and Procedures in Union Constitutions* (1963), at 4, as cited in AFL-CIO Maritime Trades Department, *A Report After Eight Years of the Landrum-Griffin Act* (Washington, D.C.: AFL-CIO, 1967), at 6 n. 3.

•

In the constitutions of the twelve unions, the most important change relating to Section 101(a)(4) was the tightening of the procedural language to take account of the four-month exhaustion limitation, adding to or shortening the amount of time allowed at each appellate level.[58] Basically, the aggrieved member is now required to appeal from local action to the parent body within a specified period of time, usually thirty days. This language was added to prevent the member from delaying his appeal to the parent until the four months have almost run out, and then lodging his complaint with the parent body and the court almost simultaneously.

Most union representatives we interviewed did not find these time limits onerous. Indeed, none of them found fault with the four-month limitation under ordinary circumstances. One parent union officer did consider the period too short in extraordinary circumstances, where a careful investigation would be required; and one local union officer found the time limits difficult to meet when he had a flood of simultaneous cases. Neither considered the limits unreasonable merely from the point of view of the union; under those unusual circumstances, they felt they could not consider the merits of the complaints fully enough.

Despite the fact that such time limits are imposed, a number of local union officers with long experience in their unions stated that those strictures have made no difference at the local level. Complaints at that level have always been handled expeditiously and informally. The only difference they saw since the limits were imposed is that appeals from decisions of local unions are now handled more quickly. In other words, the impact of the four-month limitation has been felt most keenly by the parent unions.

The majority (75 percent) of the union lawyers considered it reasonable that a member be required to exhaust his internal remedies before turning to the courts, regardless of the type of complaint or the futility of attempting to seek redress internally. Fur-

---

58. Following enactment of the LMRDA, three unions added specific exhaustion language; two expanded the requirement to include exhaustion prior to resorting to "any agency" for relief. Only one union deleted its authorization for disciplining for nonexhaustion. Four modified their discipline language, two made nonexhaustion subject to trial rather than to automatic discipline, and two others authorized discipline "subject to applicable law."

Prior to passage of the Act, seven of the twelve sample unions had constitutions which imposed specific time limits on at least some step of the trial and/or appellate procedure. Only one had time limits at each level. After the enactment, three in the sample shortened those periods and five, which had previously had none, imposed a time limit at some point in the procedure.

thermore, they maintained that discipline for failure to exhaust was standard practice prior to passage of the Act and, absent clear congressional intent to the contrary, unions should still retain the right to discipline a member who has strayed in that manner. In their view, the interpretation that the courts have discretion in the matter has virtually gutted the unions' constitutional provisions requiring the member first to turn to his union for a remedy. One union lawyer observed that the courts look solely at the merits of the complaint and if, in their view, it is meritorious, they completely ignore the union's exhaustion requirement, thus denying the union any opportunity to remedy the matter internally. Another attorney found the courts' attitudes to be based solely on personal biases: "The court's stance depends entirely on the judge you get. Those of the old school are not inclined to interfere in internal union affairs. Others are gung-ho on getting union officers. Often it is a political decision. If the judge is with you, he'll require exhaustion; if not, he won't."

A surprising 25 percent of the union lawyers interviewed found the courts' ad hoc approach reasonable and correct. To them, excusing exhaustion in cases where the member's attempt to use the internal procedures would be futile made good sense. They nevertheless stressed that in instances where a union's appeals procedures are meaningful, and invoking them would not be futile, the member should be required to exhaust the internal remedies.

Despite the fact that 75 percent of the union lawyers objected in principle to the courts' interpretation of the first provision of Section 101(a)(4), none reported that this interpretation had caused nonexhaustion to become the rule, or even a frequent occurrence, in suits against his union. One parent union officer, who said aggrieved members in his union had always taken cases to court without first having exhausted, went on to say that the courts had invariably dismissed those cases and required the plaintiff first to appeal his case through the internal appellate mechanism. No union officer attributed an increase in court litigation to the judicial interpretation of Section 101(a)(4).

Employer Noninterference

The Congressional intent behind the second proviso of Section 101(a)(4) was to prevent employers from using the subterfuge of member suits to attack the unions. Litigation under this section has been sparse, only six reported cases. However, interest in the provision has been growing: five of the six cases have been brought since 1973. Thus far, the courts have held that, if an employer finances a suit brought by a member against his union charging that the organization has violated his LMRDA rights, such suit is itself a violation of Section 101(a)(4), and is therefore dismissed.[59] However, the proviso has been held not to preclude an employer from financing a member's defense against a suit brought against him by his union.[60]

Two critical questions are currently before the courts. First, does the proviso prohibit the employer from financing only those suits brought under Title I, only those brought under LMRDA, or, instead, all suits brought by members against their unions? As to that issue, the courts are at odds.[61] The second question is: does the term "interested employer" preclude employers other than the member's own from financing his suit? In the first case brought under the proviso, the court construed the term "interested" rather narrowly, holding that employers were not sufficiently interested in suits brought by a member expelled for his opposition to a union tax to be precluded from financing these suits, even though the employers had previously litigated against that tax themselves.[62] However, the scope of the term "interested employer" is currently being litigated again in a suit brought by ten unions against the National Right to Work Legal Defense Foundation, which has sponsored suits by dissident members against their unions. A portion of the foundation's income comes from employer contributions, and the complainants contended that therefore the foundation should be considered an "interested employer association" as defined by the Act. The court repeatedly ordered the foundation to allow the unions to examine selected sections of its contributors list and, after the foundation consistently refused to do so, held that the foundation could indeed be considered an "interested" association. In a later ruling, however,

---

59. E.g., *Adamczewski v. Local Lodge 1487 IAM*, 86 L.R.R.M. 2594 (7th Cir. 1974).
60. *IBEW v. Illinois Bell Telephone*, 496 F.2d 1 (7th Cir. 1974).
61. See *Adamczewski v. Local Lodge 1487 IAM*, *supra* note 59; *Verville v. IAM*, 89 L.R.R.M. 2122 (D. Mich. 1975); *Ransdell v. Local Lodge 1904 IAM*, 390 F. Supp. 203 (E.D. Wis. 1975); *UAW v. National Right to Work Legal Defense and Education Foundation*, 376 F. Supp. 1060 (D.D.C. 1974).
62. *Farowitz v. Associated Musicians of New York, Local 802*, *supra* note 27. The employers in this case were orchestra-leader members of the union who had previously won suits against the union which resulted in their exemption from paying the tax. Because they were already exempted from paying the tax, the court in *Farowitz* held that they were not "interested" in whether or not Mr. Farowitz and the other musicians were exempted from the tax.

while appearing to agree with the complainant unions that the foundation had violated the second proviso of Section 101(a)(4), the judge went on to say that that proviso was itself unconstitutional because it "interferes directly with the first amendment rights of petition, association, and speech of the Foundation and its contributors." At the time of writing, the unions planned to appeal that ruling.[63]

Thus far, the number of court decisions dealing with the second proviso is so small that it is impossible to assess the proviso's effect. However, it is clear that if, upon appeal, either the language of the proviso is found to be unconstitutional or the unions' contention that the proviso prohibits any employer subsidy of any member's action taken against his union is found to be correct, then the impact—especially in the area of right-to-work litigation—may be far reaching indeed.

Sections 101(a)(5) and 609—Internal Union Discipline

The primary focus of this discussion is on Section 101(a)(5) of the LMRDA, but because Section 609 also deals with internal union discipline, we have included treatment of that section here. Section 101(a)(5) states, in part, that "[n]o member of any labor organization may be fined, suspended, expelled, or otherwise disciplined except for nonpayment of dues . . . unless such member has been (a) served with written specific charges; (b) given a reasonable time to prepare his defense; (c) afforded a full and fair hearing."

Unions use their disciplinary power—often called the criminal law of internal union government—for both internal and external purposes. Within the organization, those powers are used to maintain order and ensure that members will fulfill their obligations to the union. Discipline is also applied to prevent violations of contract obligations or an undermining of the union's collective bargaining strength. In addition to those legitimate purposes, some unions have also disciplined members in order to suppress criticism and quell political opposition. When discipline is used

---

63. Among the many decisions rendered in connection with this case are *UAW v. National Right to Work Legal Defense and Education Foundation, supra* note 61, and *UAW v. National Right to Work Legal Defense and Education Foundation,* 91 L.R.R.M. 2270 (D.D.C. 1976). The quotation in the text is from *UAW v. National Right to Work Legal Defense and Education Foundation* (95 L.R.R.M. 2584, 2588 (D.D.C. 1977)). That case also cites all of the decisions that bear on the case thus far.

for such reasons, union democracy—the ultimate objective of LMRDA—is stifled.

In 1947, Congress attempted, in the Taft-Hartley Act, to protect union members from loss of employment resulting from internal union discipline by including the provisions contained in Sections 8(a)(3) and 8(b)(2) of that law. Twelve years later, with the passage of the LMRDA, the members' right to participate in internal union affairs without fear of reprisal under the guise of union discipline also was safeguarded. Section 101(a)(5) deals solely with the procedural aspects of union discipline. Section 609 is substantive, prohibiting retaliatory measures of any kind for the exercise of LMRDA rights, and specifying how an aggrieved member should proceed to seek redress.

The language of both sections was modified substantially during the course of congressional debate. As originally drafted, the disciplinary provision of the bill of rights stated that a union could impose discipline only for "breach of a published written rule of such organization." Moreover, the accused member would be given the opportunity to have "final review on a written transcript of the hearing by an impartial person or persons" selected jointly by the union and the member, or by "an independent arbitration association or board."[64] The first requirement, that only violations of a published written rule could be the basis for discipline, was rejected as too restrictive. It was deemed impossible for a union to list all conceivable bases for discipline. The independent review provision was also found objectionable; unions would feel constrained from disciplining for any but the most serious of disruptive actions.

An earlier Senate proposal would have made retaliatory discipline a criminal offense. This was rejected on the ground that it, too, would have had too much of a deterrent effect on legitimate union discipline. Moreover, it would have provided no relief for the unjustly disciplined member. As finally enacted, Section 609 permits the member to file civil suit in the appropriate federal district court. Section 610 makes the use of violence or force to prevent a member from exercising his LMRDA rights a criminal offense, subject to fine and/or imprisonment.

Impact of the Enactment of Section 101(a)(5)

Relatively few of the unions in our sample altered the internal disciplinary procedures substantially to comply with the Section

---

64. See U.S. Department of Labor, *Legislative History, supra* note 7, at 276.

101(a)(5) procedural requirements. Spokesmen described those changes in constitutional language that were made as "clarification" or "specification" of long established practices. At the same time, the fact that they inserted the clarifying language was attributed to the passage of the Act, or to the subsequent court decisions interpreting Section 101(a)(5). Two parent unions already have issued, and others at the time of interview were contemplating the issuance of, trial procedure manuals as additional and more detailed guides to their locals in the conduct of hearings on internal disciplinary matters.

The most important aspect of the disciplinary proceedings, and the one most vulnerable to criticism, is the composition of the trial board itself, particularly at the local level. Frequently, those boards are composed of the elected officers or their appointees. Often the officers themselves, either directly or indirectly, brought the charges. The common practice of excusing "interested" parties from serving on the trial board does little to lessen criticism because those who remain on the board are usually aligned with him. Even if the local takes the precaution of having the trial board chosen from among the membership by lot, or of having the board's recommendation voted on by secret ballot at a membership meeting, critics contend that the whole procedure can still be "a popularity contest." The decision, they say, is based on personalities rather than upon a determination of the merits of the case.[65]

In part because of the possibility of local board or membership bias, ten of the twelve unions we studied authorize the parent organization to take original jurisdiction in a disciplinary proceeding if an unfair decision at the local level seems likely. (This practice, if not the constitutional language, ordinarily preceded passage of the Act.) In some of those ten unions, the parent body officers learn of trouble spots through their representatives in the field, and can move quickly to correct potential injustices. Indeed,

---

65. In the sample unions, eight of the twelve either specify that the local executive board shall be the trial board or leave the composition of the board to the discretion of the members. A ninth union has the local executive board appoint the trial board. Since the Act's passage, two unions have liberalized their provisions, going either from elected trial boards or general membership trial decisions, to random selection, with provisions for challenging those selected. Two unions have changed to more conservative procedures, one going from random selection to the specification that the local executive board act as the trial board, while the other has changed its provisions so that the local president, rather than the parent body president, now appoints the trial board.

they often know of the problem before disciplinary action has been initiated at the local level and, through informal communications, can settle the case without need for a trial. The other two unions studied shy away from taking any part in local disciplinary proceedings, and become involved in the proceeding only if the original decision is appealed.

Section 101(a)(5) deals only with procedures for imposing discipline and not with bases for which discipline may be imposed. Nonetheless, there have been more constitutional changes of provisions specifying the grounds for discipline than there have been changes of any other constitutional provisions. In every case, the constitutional changes entailed either an elaboration of the activities which would be subject to discipline or an expansion of the language concerning members' obligations to their unions, the violations of which are subject to discipline[66]

At the local level, the number of disciplinary trials has generally not increased since passage of the Act.[67] Where there had been few or none before, that is still true. Where such trials were frequent before, they continue to be. The most striking thing to us was that in the majority of the locals visited such trials were, and always have been, a decided rarity. Estimates quoted as to the number held were often given in terms of "one in fifteen years"; "six or eight charges brought per year, but never any trials"; or "on the average, one trial a year." The officers explained that if one member accuses another of violating the constitution or work rules, they prefer to just sit down with the parties and work out a settlement informally. The matter goes beyond the discussion stage only if it cannot be reconciled in that manner.

In the locals where trials are more frequent—primarily in the building and construction trades—the charges brought usually have involved the violation of work rules or fighting on the job. Even in those, violations of work rules often have not resulted in

---

66. Disciplining for nonpayment of dues was a practice in all twelve unions prior to 1959. One union added language to cover that practice after enactment of the LMRDA, and a few organizations modified their provisions to make nonpayment "subject to" discipline, rather than a cause for automatic suspension or expulsion. Other unions modified the type of discipline imposed for dues arrearage.

67. Union officials at all levels were asked for statistics, pre- and post-LMRDA, on the number and outcome of local trials, as well as on the number and results of appeals at all levels. Only one parent union in our study had even partial figures to offer. The rest had few if any statistical data. Thus, the text discussion is based on estimates and observations by those interviewed, as well as on a reading of the action taken on appeals at union conventions.

formal action. Officers told us that peer recrimination is a more effective deterrent. One said, "They punish themselves. It's difficult to go back to work with people after you've shown yourself willing to eat them up."

Very few locals in the sample reported having had an increase in disciplinary cases in recent years. Again, those that did record more cases were all building and construction trades unions. According to the officers of those unions, the increase was the result of the downturn in the economy. Some members, needing more work, were willing to violate the rules, e.g., to accept wages that are below the union minimum, or to work for a nonunion employer. Other members, seeing that happen, were, in turn, more willing to point an accusing finger at those who did not abide by the rules.

Whatever the extent of the local officers' experience with disciplinary trials, their general reaction was that the conduct of the disciplinary proceedings had changed very little due to the LMRDA. However, one third conceded that they pay more attention to procedures now, specifying charges more carefully, and making certain that the accused member receives timely notification of the hearing date. Thus, while the procedures themselves may be basically unchanged, they are more conscientiously observed. Approximately two thirds of the local officers either noticed no change or had no opinion. Dissidents' views were similarly divided, one third perceiving an improvement, and two thirds either seeing no change or having no opinion.

In contrast to the experience at the local level, half of the parent body officials and two thirds of the union lawyers interviewed reported a noticeable increase in appeals from trial board decisions in recent years. They gave a number of reasons for this: the downturn of the economy, an increase in membership, a more "complaint conscious and individual-rights conscious society." All agreed that the fact that preexisting appellate procedures are now spelled out in the constitutions has made the rank and file more aware of what their rights are, and more inclined to appeal. In addition, because the procedure is part of the constitution, the member has easier access to state courts under breach of contract claims if he believes he has been unjustly disciplined.

Only one parent union reported having had fewer appeals from local decisions in recent years, and spokesmen for that union attributed that fact also to the specificity of the constitutional language. The inclusion of the language has made local officers far more conscientious in the conduct of trials.

According to two thirds of both the parent body officers and their counsel, the constitutional elaboration of appellate procedures has prompted more conscientious observance of due process over-all. Despite this, most unions reported no change in the number of reversals of local level decisions. The reason for this seems to be a heightened awareness at the parent level of the conduct of trials at the local level. Even before the enactment of the LMRDA, many parent officers watched over the total disciplinary process; they advised local officers if they thought a court might consider the result to be blackballing or whitewashing, should the member bring suit. However, they all agreed that they watch that kind of situation more carefully than they used to, because the possibility of litigation is now greater. One parent union officer, perhaps describing the extreme pre-LMRDA situation, candidly reported: "Pre-'59, we'd give the troublemaker a 'fair trial' and then we'd hang him. We don't do that anymore."

The number of union spokesmen who were willing to comment on the continued existence of blackballing and/or whitewashing in trials and appeals attests to the fact that the mere existence of detailed procedures and the pro forma observance of them does not preclude biased judgements. Local officers themselves readily admitted that they could get a favorable or adverse ruling for the accused if they were so inclined. One parent body official reported that this is equally true at his level of review. If the executive board members like the local chief officer, they will sustain whatever discipline he has imposed.

Impact of Court Cases

According to Professor Clyde Summers, the state court decisions in cases brought by disciplined members prior to 1959 "seem to have no relation to the severity of the penalty imposed, but are instead governed by the conduct which the union has sought to punish and the procedure used for determining the member's guilt."[68] With regard to judicial review of the evidence in those cases, Professor Summers went on: "The courts frequently declare that they will not reweigh the evidence before the union tribunal, but will look only to see if there is some evidence to support the finding of guilt. This language, however, is often but an apologetic prelude to a full re-evaluation of the evidence, justified by holding that the findings were 'totally unsustained.' "[69]

---

68. Summers, *The Law of Union Discipline: What the Courts Do in Fact, supra* note 2, at 179.
69. *Id.* at 185.

The federal court decisions which followed passage of the Act also looked beyond the procedures and sought to determine whether or not the punishment fit the crime. Moreover, unless the union's constitution specifically cited a particular action as subject to discipline, the member committing an act not mentioned and subsequently punished stood a good chance of having the discipline lifted by the court. For example, in the circuit court decision in *Boilermakers v. Braswell*,[70] the court, quoting from an earlier decision, asserted that "the penal provisions in union constitutions must be strictly construed."[71] The *Braswell* case involved discipline imposed on a member who struck a business agent. The court found that personal altercations were not covered in the union's disciplinary language, and thus the punitive sentence imposed on the member was unwarranted.

In a case involving identical factual circumstances within the same union, however, the Supreme Court subsequently held otherwise. In *Boilermakers v. Hardeman*,[72] where Hardeman had been disciplined for striking a union officer, the Court concluded that "[w]here . . . the union's charges make reference to specific written provisions, 101(a)(5)(A) obviously empowers the federal courts to examine those provisions and determine whether the union member had been misled or otherwise prejudiced in the presentation of his defense. But it gives courts no warrant to scrutinize the union regulations in order to determine whether particular conduct may be punished at all."[73]

The Court also held that the "written specific charges" language of Section 101(a)(5) means charges specific enough to inform the accused member of the offense he is alleged to have committed. They need not be based on particular constitutional language. Moreover, judicial review to determine whether or not a "full and fair hearing" has been accorded should be limited to a finding that "some evidence" was presented at the hearing to support the charges brought. The Court said that Section 101(a)(5) "was not intended to authorize courts to determine the scope of offense for which a union may discipline members."[74]

---

70. 388 F.2d 193 (5th Cir. 1968). See also *Vars v. International Brotherhood of Boilermakers*, 320 F.2d 576 (2d Cir. 1963); *Kelsey v. Philadelphia Local No. 8 IATSE*, 419 F.2d 491 (3d Cir. 1969).
71. 388 F.2d 193, 198 (5th Cir. 1968).
72. 401 U.S. 233 (1971).
73. *Id.* at 243.
74. *Id.* at 244.

Thus, in the *Hardeman* case, the Court quite clearly delimited the potential scope of Section 101(a)(5): the language was intended to give aggrieved members access to the courts if the procedures were deficient. It did not give courts license to go beyond that.

Approximately 60 percent of the Section 101(a)(5) cases reported in the DOL Compliance Reports required the courts to assess whether the discipline procedures in question were deficient.[75] In disciplining for nonpayment of union dues, the unions are not required to observe Section 101(a)(5) procedures at all. In such cases, the courts limit their inquiry to finding whether or not dues have in fact been paid or whether the discipline of expulsion for nonpayment was discriminatorily applied.[76]

The remaining 40 percent of the court decisions have been determinations of statutory construction, primarily concerned with whether or not the discipline involved would make the action subject to the procedural requirement of Section 101(a)(5). In order to make the decision, the courts have often had to look first to the motive behind the union's action to determine if there was evidence of possible reprisal. If there was no such suggestion, the courts have dismissed these cases.[77]

---

75. In such cases, the only question the court was asked to answer was: was the procedure used in applying discipline proper? For example, based on the language of the section, the courts have held that: the notification requirement had not been fulfilled where the union contended that notification was unnecessary because the member already knew the basis for the charges; the mere fact that the accuser was influential within the union did not mean the trial was prejudiced with regard to the requirement of a full and fair hearing; and a trial board composed of incumbent officers was not "impartial" where the accused was a candidate for office. See *Magelssen v. Local 518, Plasterers,* 240 F. Supp. 259 (W.D. Mo. 1965); *Cornelio v. District Council of Philadelphia, Carpenters,* 358 F.2d 728 (3d Cir. 1966); *Burke v. Boilermakers,* 417 F.2d 1063 (9th Cir. 1969); *Kiepura v. Local 1091, Steelworkers,* 358 F. Supp. 987 (N.D. Ill. 1973).

76. See *Burch v. IAM,* 433 F.2d 561 (5th Cir. 1970). See also *Carrasquillo v. Sindicato,* 77 L.R.R.M. 2459 (D.P.R. 1970); *Schuhardt v. Local 2834, Carpenters,* 380 F.2d 795 (10th Cir. 1967). In the latter case, a member refused to pay dues pending appeal on another disciplinary matter and was expelled for such nonpayment; the court considered his discipline appeal to be moot, consistent with both Section 101(a)(5) and the union principle that nonpayment of dues is equivalent to voluntary resignation from union membership.

77. For example, when members alleged that the union and the employer were disciplining them by not referring them to jobs, the courts denied relief on the ground that such cases were not within their jurisdiction. Similarly, when members brought suit claiming that the contract terms were a form of discipline in that they adversely affected their employment, those cases were dis-

However, when the courts have determined that the action taken by the union against the member or members seemed retributive, they have regarded it as discipline imposed in violation of the Section 101(a)(5) procedural requirements.[78]

If the cases have involved Title I sections in addition to Section 101(a)(5), the courts have, of course, taken a broader look at the issues, rather than focusing on procedures followed. We have already noted, in the discussion of Section 101(a)(2), that suits involving alleged violations of a member's free speech rights sometimes charge Section 101(a)(5) violations as well. One such case, *Semancik v. UMW District 5*,[79] directly involved the language in the constitution of a union's district organization. That

---

missed as well. In *Morrisey v. National Maritime Union* (544 F.2d 19 (2d Cir. 1976)), the court held that instigation by the union of the arrest and prosecution of a member (for trespassing and disorderly conduct because he had been distributing literature critical to the union leadership) was not "discipline" under the terms of Section 101(a)(5). In general, see *Hayes v. IBEW, Local 481*, 83 L.R.R.M. 2647 (D.C. Ind. 1973); *Martire v. Laborers*, 410 F.2d 32 (3d Cir. 1969); *Figueroa v. National Maritime Union* 342 F.2d 400 (2d Cir. 1965); *Paige v. National Maritime Union*, 63 L.R.R.M. 2505 (S.D.N.Y. 1966). But *cf. Detroy v. American Guild of Variety Artists*, 286 F.2d 75 (2d Cir. 1961), *cert. denied*, 366 U.S. 929 (1961). The courts have been criticized for the prevailing interpretation. See Christensen, *Union Discipline Under Federal Law: Institutional Dilemmas in an Industrial Democracy*, 43 N.Y.L. REV. 227 (1968).

78. For example, in *Calabrese v. United Association of Plumbers* (211 F. Supp. 609 (D.N.J. 1962)), when a parent body revoked a local's charter and issued a charter to a new local, and admitted all but the former local officers to the new organization, the action was held to be discipline equivalent to expulsion. In *Parks v. IBEW, supra* note 55, where a parent union revoked a local's charter for engaging in an unauthorized strike, the court ruled that the members had been "otherwise disciplined" under the terms of Section 609. In *Robins v. Schonfeld* (70 Lab. Cas. 13,330 (2d Cir. 1972), *aff'g* 326 F. Supp. 525,531 (S.D.N.Y. 1971)), the circuit court granted damages for lost employment where there was circumstantial evidence to sustain the claim that the plaintiff's inability to find work was proximately caused by union blacklisting subsequent to his protest of two elections. (All membership rights had been restored by stipulation.) In *Duncan v. Pennsylvania Shipbuilders* (394 F.2d 237 (4th Cir. 1968)), the plaintiff alleged that after he filed a Title IV complaint charging irregularities in his union's last election, he no longer received job referrals. The court ruled that if the union did conspire against the complainant, such conspiracy was a form of discipline covered under Section 101(a)(5). In these two cases, as well as in *Hardeman*, the plaintiffs were alleging that their inability to find work stemmed from the union's disciplinary tactics. (Duncan alleged retaliatory conspiracy; Robins alleged blacklisting. Hardeman, on the other hand, was protesting that his job loss resulted from an improper trial.)

79. 446 F.2d 144 (3d Cir. 1972).

language, which outlined the activity for which members could be disciplined, included the following provision: [A]ny member or members resorting to dishonest or questionable practices to secure the election or defeat of any candidate for district office shall be tried by the district executive board and fined, suspended, or expelled as the magnitude of the transgression may warrant." The circuit court, affirming a district court's decision, stated that this constitutional provision had been used repeatedly to infringe upon free speech rights protected under Section 101(a)(2), without any attempt on the part of the union to avoid a conflict with the provision of the LMRDA. The court noted that, had its decision adhered strictly to the finding in the *Hardeman* case, the complaint would have been outside its jurisdiction. However, it said, "the same inhibitions do not apply to actions involving free speech."[80]

The union lawyers—the only persons interviewed who commented on *Hardeman* and other related cases—found no fault whatever with the Supreme Court's decision. Indeed, they applauded the fact that it had reversed the broader reach of decisions such as that in *Braswell*. The only lawyers who commented critically on *Hardeman* were those who had argued *Hardeman*-type cases and had lost.

Removal of members from union office or staff positions. *The King decision.* Between 15 and 20 percent of all cases brought under Title I and Section 609 are brought by members who have been removed from union staff positions for exercising their rights as members under the LMRDA. The legislative history is clear that Section 101(a)(5) at least does not prohibit a union from suspending or removing a member from union office or staff positions. That section's requirement of due process in disciplinary matters protects union members only as members. It does not protect a member's status as a union officer or staff member.[81] But what of the union-employee member's other LMRDA rights, especially his right of free speech under Section 101(a)(2)? Does a union employee have a right to his job if he speaks out against the

---

80. *Id.* at 150.
81. U.S. Department of Labor, *Legislative History, supra* note 7, at 361. *Vars v. International Brotherhood of Boilermakers, supra* note 70; *Mamula v. Local 1211, Steelworkers,* 202 F. Supp. 348 (W.D. Pa. 1962); *Strauss v. International Brotherhood of Teamsters,* 179 F. Supp. 297 (E.D. Pa. 1959); *Burton v. Independent Packinghouse Workers Union,* 199 F. Supp. 138 (D. Kan. 1961).

incumbents or their policies? Or would such opposition be considered an impairment of the functioning of the union as an institution, under the Section 101(a)(2) proviso, against which the
union has a right to protect itself?

The courts have held both ways, with the circuit courts evenly
divided. On the one side, various circuit courts have held that the
discharged union employee has no rights under the LMRDA as a
staff member; that while Section 101(a)(2) accords free speech
rights to all members, including union employees, it accords no
one the "right" to union employment; that the "or otherwise discipline" language of Section 609 does not encompass discharge
from union positions; and that, as long as the dismissed employee
retains his LMRDA rights as a union member, his rights have not
been violated.[82]

But other circuit courts have held that the employee is protected with regard to his job under the LMRDA; that, regardless of
the limitations of the scope of Section 101(a)(5), Section 609 protects "any member" who exercises his Title I rights; and that,
because the language of Section 609 specifically prohibits retaliatory fines, suspensions, or expulsion, the "otherwise discipline"
phrase could only have been included to prohibit reprisal by adversely affecting a member's employment.[83]

The decision most frequently cited that argues for the latter
position is that of the Court of Appeals for the Ninth Circuit in
Grand Lodge of the IAM v. King.[84] In the *King* case, six former
appointed international representatives alleged that they had been
discharged from office because they had supported the losing candidate in the election of top union officers. The district court
found that their allegation was correct. On appeal, the circuit court
upheld the lower court, stating that nothing in the legislative history of the Act indicated that employees should not be protected
in the exercise of their rights under Sections 101(a)(1) and
101(a)(2). Further, the court held that Section 609 was specifically

---

82. E.g., *Sheridan v. Local 626, United Brotherhood of Carpenters*, 306 F.2d 152
    (3d Cir. 1962); *Martire v. Laborers, supra* note 77. See also *Sewell v. Grand
    Lodge IAM*, 445 F.2d 545 (5th Cir. 1971), *cert. denied*, 404 U.S. 1024 (1972).
83. E.g., *Grand Lodge IAM v. King*, 335 F.2d 340 (9th Cir. 1964), *cert. denied*, 379
    U.S. 920 (1964); *Salzhandler v. Caputo*, 316 F.2d 445 (2d Cir. 1963), *cert.
    denied*, 375 U.S. 946 (1963); *George v. Bricklayers Union*, 255 F. Supp. 239
    (E.D. Wis. 1966); *Retail Clerks Local 648 v. RCIA*, 299 F. Supp. 1012 (D.D.C.
    1969); *DeCampli v. Greeley*, 239 F. Supp. 749 (D.Md. 1968).
84. 335 F.2d 340 (9th Cir. 1964), *cert. denied*, 379 U.S. 920 (1964).

tailored to ensure such protection. Finally, the underlying purpose of the LMRDA is to further union democracy, and union staff members are the persons "best equipped to keep union government vigorously and effectively democratic."[85]

A subsequent circuit court decision—this time in the fifth circuit—held the other way. In *Sewell v. IAM*,[86] the court, while agreeing with the *King* decision that the "mere fact" of union employment "does not destroy . . . statutory rights," went on to say: "This conclusion does not permit an employee who accepts employment for the performance of certain specified duties to take the largesse and pay of the union, on the one hand, and, on the other, to completely subvert the purposes of his employment by engaging in activities diametrically opposed to the performance of his specified duties."[87] Whereas in *King* the court found that union employees had broad responsibilities both to the union and to the membership as a whole, in *Sewell* the court pictured their duties as solely "to promote and execute the policies of the Union President and the Executive Council at all times."[88]

Comments on the King *decision.* We received more comments from union representatives concerning the decision in the *King* case than on any other decision under the LMRDA. All but two of the unions in our sample had had problems of one kind or another with respect to staff dismissals and, except in those two organizations (in which the parent body staff had no opinions on the case), the legal counsel and top union officials were highly critical of the *King* decision. Lower level spokesmen did not necessarily agree with the top officers and their legal counsel.

Critics of the decision often made an analogy between the position of the top union executive officer vis-à-vis his staff and that of the President of the United States and his cabinet: "What those who favor the *King* decision are doing is imposing a far more stringent form of democracy on labor unions than we have within the government. It would be like expecting the President of the United States to appoint members of the opposition party to his cabinet. That would be as unworkable in unions as it is unworkable there." Nonetheless, almost half of those who were critical of

85. *Id.* at 344.
86. *Sewell v. Grand Lodge IAM*, 445 F.2d 545 (5th Cir. 1971), *cert. denied*, 404 U.S. 1024 (1972).
87. *Id.* at 550–51.
88. *Id.* at 550.

King expressed a certain ambivalence toward the rationale behind the decision: "It is against nature to require an administration to operate staffed with opposition. However, if one is serious about the notion of opposition, and the importance and healthiness of it in an organization such as a union, then appointees are really the most important source of opposition. Who sees more of the day-to-day, in-depth administration than those appointees? However, union leaders need responsible, loyal supporters and staff, and can't possibly function surrounded by dissenters."

The critics of the *King* decision fell into two categories: those who worried that if they had to retain a disloyal employee the union itself might be undermined, and those who were concerned that having to do so might impair the functioning of the organization. Those who expressed anxiety for the union per se thought in terms of confidential information that the disloyal staff member might pass on to the employer. However, none could relate an actual case in which such sabotage had been committed. Those who were more concerned with organizational stability fell into two distinct groups. In one camp were those who considered any overt opposition on the part of a union staff member to be harmful:

If your own staff isn't with you, you can't function.

Union staff members are the chief operational officers. They can't attack the leadership's policies, objectives, and principles and retain immunity from discharge.

Employees should be able to run for union office while they are so employed, but they shouldn't expect to be kept on if they don't win. There's always a risk for any loser except in labor unions. There the loser expects a built-in sinecure.

In the second camp were those who felt that only if the staff member failed to perform his duties, or to implement the union's administrative policies, would his dismissal be justified:

People should be able to run for office without reprisal. If they're doing their jobs satisfactorily, there would be no reason to fire them. Presumably, a staff member couldn't implement policies which he opposed. But that should not just be assumed. Until it is demonstrated to be the case, he is entitled to his job.

The *King* decision, however, does not pose insurmountable problems to union officers. A number of those we interviewed pointed out that the effects of the decision can be skirted. Said one parent union officer: "I would never fire anyone for political reasons. I'd find another reason." To give another example, a union lawyer told us of an appointed staff member who had supported the wrong candidate and had promptly been "dispatched to desert detail" following the election. He was then tried on entirely unrelated grounds by a union trial board and found guilty. As the spokesman indicated, "some kind of charge can be made against anyone who has been in office for a while, and the charges were found valid. But they never would have been leveled against him at all except that somebody wanted him out."

A few local union officers suggested that key staff positions should be elected posts,[89] to lessen the possibility of discharge. They added: "The top leader should have to accommodate the challenges and differences of opinion around him. It will make him more responsive and allow less chance of his being dictatorial. An elected arrangement dictates a cooperative administration." However, one local chief officer who in fact did have to accommodate himself to elected business agents strongly disagreed. The business agents were far too independent. They constantly opposed his policies, and he found himself preoccupied with in-fighting. As a consequence, union business was at a standstill. It should be noted, however, that this union officer was a self-styled "minority" chief executive. One could argue that, because his views did not reflect the wishes of the majority, he should not make unilateral policy decisions in any event.

A few union officials proposed that another way to put an end to the problem of the disloyal employee would be to prohibit all staff members from taking part in any sort of political activity. However, most other union officers disagreed with that suggestion. They argued that to institute such a prohibition could be considered a violation of the employee members' rights under Title I.[90]

---

89. While most of the court cases have involved the dismissal of appointed staff members, officers who have been removed from their elected positions have also sought and gained judicial relief. *Schonfeld v. Penza* 477 F.2d 899 (2d Cir. 1973); *Needham v. Isbister,* 84 L.R.R.M. 2105 (D. Mass. 1973); *Wood v. Dennis,* 489 F.2d 849 (7th Cir. 1973), *cert. denied,* 415 U.S. 957 (1974); *Lamb v. Local 1292 Carpenters,* 59 L.R.R.M. 2250 (E.D.N.Y. 1965).

90. In the one court case we found on this point, *Federation of Teachers v. Miesen* (82 L.R.R.M. 2091 (D.D.C. 1972)), where a provision in an agreement between the union and its national representatives prohibited the latter from engaging in intraunion political activity, and the union had discharged an employee for violating that provision, the court held that the provision was lawful. In the court's opinion, if such provision was agreed to in good faith, it was not a violation of the LMRDA.

From the employee dismissal cases that union officers and their legal counsel described to us from their own experiences, it was clear that a court decision ordering reinstatement of an employee who had been discharged because of disloyalty proved awkward to the organization concerned. For an employer to attempt to work with an employee who has openly criticized that employer or the organization's policies is, by the very nature of things, difficult. However, no matter how disturbing the court's action was in the short run, we should note that none of those who had had to accommodate themselves to such reinstatements contended that the court's action worked to the detriment of the long-range interests of the union as an institution. This is not to say that the effect of such a decision would never do permanent damage to a union's interests, but merely that among the unions studied it has not.

Sections 102 and 103—Civil Enforcement and Retention of Existing Rights

Section 102 of the LMRDA gives a complaining member the right to bring suit in the district court for the locality either in which the alleged violation occurred or in which the parent union headquarters are located. In addition, under the terms of Section 103, "[n]othing contained in this Title shall limit the rights and remedies of any member of a labor organization under any State or Federal law or before any court or under the constitution and bylaws of any labor organization." This section was added both to preserve the right of any member to enforce his union constitution as a "contract" between the member and the union in state courts, and to preserve the substantial body of law developed by the state courts prohibiting union abuses and protecting members' rights. Congress deliberately rejected arguments in favor of federal preemption in this area, opting instead to retain alternate remedies, despite possible conflict in enforcement and potential lack of uniformity.

On the basis of our interviews and reading, we have concluded that state remedies have not been preempted by Title I, except insofar as the existence of Title IV has resulted in judicial deference to DOL enforcement after an election, thus in practice preempting state remedies in that area, as well as those under Title I.[91]

---

91. See note 13, *supra*.

Section 102 specifies that the court may provide "such relief (including injunctions) as may be appropriate." The most significant question before the courts since passage of Title I has been that of determining how broadly the word "appropriate" should be construed. In particular, should that term include the awarding of attorneys' fees to the complaining member if he wins his suit? Until the 1973 Supreme Court decision in *Hall v. Cole*,[92] the circuit courts were at odds over that issue.[93] At base, the problem arose because Title I does not specifically stipulate that the court may award attorneys' fees, whereas Sections 201(c) and 501(b) of the Act do make such provision. In the *Hall* decision, the Court held that Title I's silence on that matter did not preclude a court from awarding fees. It described the litigation under Title I as of "almost infinite variety," for which the courts' discretion under Section 102 was "cast as a broad mandate to the courts to fashion 'appropriate' relief."[94] The determining factor is whether or not the bringing of the suit has been of benefit not only to the complainant, but to all members of his union. In the latter event, the awarding of attorneys' fees from union funds is warranted.

The *Hall* decision was a source of dismay to some of those interviewed; they feared that it would result in a sharp increase in the number of Title I cases. As of the close of fiscal year 1974, however, there had been no increase in the annual number of Title I cases nor in the proportion of cases in which attorneys' fees were awarded since the Supreme Court handed down its decision in 1973. Whether or not this will continue to be the case in the future is difficult to predict. However, as one lawyer observed, "with all the very able lawyers coming out of law schools and unable to find work in unions, there will be more of them representing dissidents. It won't be difficult for them to convince themselves that unions are bad—especially since some of them are."

The question remains whether or not it is realistic to assume that a member can meaningfully challenge his union by a privately brought suit, given the initial financial problems involved in retaining an attorney. Despite the *Hall* decision, that barrier is still a formidable one that constrains all but those complainants

---

92. 412 U.S. 1 (1973).
93. In favor of the award of attorneys' fees, see: *Gartner v. Soloner, supra* note 29; *Telephone Workers Local 2 v. International Brotherhood of Telephone Workers, supra* note 47. For the opposing view, see *Jacques v. Local 1418 International Longshoremen's Association*, 404 F.2d 703 (5th Cir. 1968).
94. *Hall v. Cole, supra*, n. 92 at 15.

who have very firm commitments to their cases. The magnitude of that barrier raises the question of DOL enforcement of Title I.

The Department of Labor: An Enforcement Alternative?

The DOL is not empowered to administer Title I of the LMRDA except with regard to Section 104. Nevertheless, the DOL area offices receive requests for aid from union members regarding Title I matters that fall outside Section 104. For example, they are asked what to do about unauthorized dues increases, or what recourse a member has if he is silenced when attempting to speak out at a union meeting. The agency's policy is to respond to such questions by explaining that the DOL lacks jurisdiction in such matters and by indicating what alternatives, if any, are open to the complainant. If the inquiry is by mail, the reply, also by letter, is pro forma. If the complainant phones or comes into the office, his inquiry receives more personal attention.

It is the DOL's policy not to offer an opinion as to the merits of the complaint. As one representative from a regional solicitor's office explained, "If we can't do anything, we should keep our mouths shut. Otherwise we'd jeopardize our legal effectiveness. We would be risking the possibility that the complainant would get a declaratory judgment that the DOL had said this was a Title I case, when we have no jurisdiction to say anything, much less solid evidence on which to give advice."

If a complainant expresses interest in seeking legal advice, but professes lack of funds, the DOL staff will, in general terms, describe what avenues are open to him. With a few exceptions, those interviewed said that they never recommend a particular lawyer.

One area office reported that, upon learning of a Title I complaint, the office does make an informal inquiry to the union involved. The staff members admitted that in doing so they were exceeding their actual jurisdiction, but they defended the action on the ground that informal inquiries usually resulted in remedying the matter. They contended that such inquiries do not add substantially to their over-all LMRDA-related workloads. At most, 5 percent of the total time they spend on LMRDA matters is devoted to Title I problems.

The suggestion was made by some DOL officials, as well as by some union spokesmen, that the statute should be amended to empower the agency to enforce all of Title I. Views concerning that suggestion varied widely among and between groups of interviewees.

Pros and Cons of Department of Labor Enforcement of Title I

The arguments voiced most often in favor of DOL enforcement of Title I were four:

1. The costs of bringing civil suit are too high to be borne by an individual member, and during the course of litigation that member is too vulnerable to covert, if not overt, reprisal.
2. Less educated workers are at a serious disadvantage in pursuing a civil suit. As one DOL spokesman observed: "It makes no sense to send a low-paid, perhaps illiterate, worker to a lawyer. You just know he'll never make it."
3. Title I violations are usually against individuals, as opposed to the more generalized effect of embezzlements or the improper imposition of a trusteeship. In the latter situations, groups of members are more likely to pool financial resources and offer moral support to one another.
4. Although Title I violations are usually against individuals, the benefit of successful pursuit of democratic rights redounds to the benefit of the membership as a whole. The individual willing to take on the fight deserves the support that only an agency such as the DOL can provide.

The arguments most often voiced against empowering the DOL to enforce Title I were as follows:

1. The budgetary and personnel increases that would be required for the DOL to assume the added responsibility would be too great.
2. The Title I suits that would be encouraged by agency enforcement would overtax not only the DOL but the unions as well, with officers either mired in countless frivolous suits or made ineffectual because of fear that any decisive action would provoke a suit.
3. Agency enforcement of Title I would inspire false hopes on the part of aggrieved members. As one agency representative said, "How much of an ombudsman can the executive branch of the government really be?"
4. Along the same line as the above argument, the opportunity to enlist agency aid would dampen the spirits of the "brash and relentless opposition" who *are* brash and relentless precisely because they have to do battle on their own.

Opinions of Interviewees

No group of interviewees was unanimous on the question of DOL enforcement of Title I. For example, within the DOL itself, proponents and detractors of such enforcement were found at all levels of the agency. However, as would be expected the higher up in the agency hierarchy they were, the less enthusiastic they generally were toward the idea. To many of them, the increased financial burden loomed large. On the other hand, the staff members in the area offices, the ones who have personal contact with aggrieved union members, were more likely to look with favor on the idea. While they agreed that initially their caseloads would increase substantially, they predicted that Title I complaints would taper off to a manageable level once union members realized that the DOL would not pursue frivolous complaints.

Those within the DOL who approved of the suggestion that their Title I responsibilities be broadened tended to favor a plan under which the complainant would still retain the right he now has of bringing private suit. There will always be some members who could and would want to bring private suit, they explained. Moreover, if for some reason the DOL were biased in favor of the member's union, or disliked the complaining member personally, he would still have an alternate mechanism available for redress of his grievance.

The union lawyers were evenly split on the subject, as were the union officers. The lawyers who favored agency enforcement believed (1) that the DOL understands unions better than do the courts and would be more discriminating in screening unmeritorious complaints, and (2) that the DOL is more accessible on an informal basis to unions, and the development of a cooperative continuing relationship is possible between agency and union—a situation that cannot evolve with the courts. This group did not favor giving the member the option of going to court if the DOL rejected his case. One of these lawyers also thought that DOL enforcement would be of benefit to union members. With pressure from the DOL, many cases would be handled more conscientiously by the union officers rather than being cavalierly dismissed, as they so often are now. Thus both union and aggrieved member would avoid the possibility of being involved in a lawsuit.

The union officers who favored the idea of agency enforcement contended that such a system would fill the present need to assist the rank and file members who lack the knowledge or resources to file private suit. For many, that contention was based on personal experience. They did not consider the DOL's enforcement of other sections of the Act disruptive, and felt that the added protection accorded aggrieved members outweighed any temporary disruption in any event.

On the other hand, the union lawyers and officers who did not favor the proposed DOL enforcement of Title I felt that there was already too much government interference in the internal affairs of labor unions. Most argued that instances in which rank and file members genuinely needed help in Title I suits were rare, and that giving members access to the DOL would just give the "perpetual whiner" a forum he should not have. They considered that the *Hall* decision gave adequate assistance to any member who felt his Title I rights had been violated.

Discussion

If there were evidence that the courts had not fulfilled congressional intent in enforcing Title I, a good case could be made for recommending that the DOL rather than, or in addition to, the courts enforce Title I. Such evidence was not forthcoming, however. The courts have, except in a few instances, been very solicitous in protecting individual members' Title I rights. Moreover, the impression of some union lawyers that the DOL would be a better screening mechanism than the courts suggests that members' complaints would not necessarily be given greater consideration if the DOL acted as the guardian of union members' Title I rights. Review of the cases brought under Title I indicates that, on the whole, the courts have shown sufficient understanding both of the problems and responsibilities entailed in administering a union, and of the extent of the rights of the individual rank and file member who must function within that framework.

Yet, despite the courts' mindfulness of individual rights, filing private suit remains a formidable undertaking. The *Hall* decision alleviates, but does not eliminate, the initial problem of financing such suit. An aggrieved member still either must locate a sympathetic lawyer amenable to flexible financing, or must enjoy sufficient support from his co-workers to be able to enlist their contributions. But there are still too few lawyers willing to take cases if the awarding of fees, even if the suit is successful, is not guaranteed. Moreover, co-workers, even if sympathetic, may not have sufficient funds to make a significant financial contribution, may fear reprisal for themselves, or may find resort to help outside the union family so distasteful that they may be unwilling to support the complainant no matter what the merits of his grievance may be.

Moreover, the problem of possible reprisal against the complaining member would not be lessened by empowering the DOL to enforce Title I. The member would, under normal circumstances, still be required to exhaust his internal remedies before going to the DOL, so that his identity would already have been revealed in any event.

Given the arguments above, and the lack of hard evidence that enforcement of all sections of Title I by the DOL would result in more vigilant protection of individual members' rights than they now receive, we do not recommend any changes in statutory language concerning the enforcement of Title I. However, the informal action taken by one area office we visited suggests that the DOL could make a positive contribution with regard to Title I complaints as the statute now reads. As we have reported, the staff in that office routinely inquires of the union involved as to the validity of the member's complaint; the staff members told us that, in their experience, in the majority of cases they found that the union officers had violated the complaining member's rights more through inadvertence than malice, and were quite ready to correct the matter once it was brought to their attention. By taking such action, then, that office has been able to defuse dissent quickly, quietly, and inexpensively. Inevitably there will be some instances in which the union, even when guilty of misconduct, will deny any wrongdoing, and in such cases the DOL's inquiry may have little effect. However, given the observation that the bulk of complaints stem from unintentional violations of Title I, the limited involvement that that area office engages in, if practiced by all area offices, could be of benefit to both unions and their rank and file members. Such informal contact would also enable the agency to provide other types of technical assistance in a casual and unobtrusive manner. By playing this limited, informal role in Title I complaints, the DOL area offices could thus provide service both to unions and their members, by informing both of their respective obligations and rights under Title I.

Section 105—Dissemination of Information
Concerning the Act

Section 105 of the LMRDA is not only the shortest section of the statute—"Every labor organization shall inform its members concerning the provisions of this Act"—but, judging from the blank stares that greeted inquiries concerning it, it is also the least known. When asked how their organizations had complied with this requirement, the union lawyers' responses included "printing the Act verbatim or in summary form in the union newspaper," "sending copies of it or bulletins about it to local and district officers," and "lambasting it in a newsletter." None of the unions has made a continuing effort to educate its members. Whatever they did, they did once, in 1959, and have not repeated. In the words of one union lawyer, " 'How To Sue The Union' is not a seminar topic."

Another union lawyer thought the requirement was probably unconstitutional. Still a third said he considered it a dead letter: "Since unions' constitutions and bylaws presumably are in compliance, isn't that in itself, by implication, informing the members of the provisions of the Act?" Several union lawyers defended the fact that information on the Act was not disseminated on the ground that the real dissidents will already know about the statute, or will consult attorneys or go to the NLRB which, in turn, will refer them to the DOL. One way or another, they will learn about the Act. Despite the unions' lack of diligence in this area, almost all of the union lawyers told us that they believe the members' awareness of their rights under the Act has increased tremendously over the years. "Members may not know about Landrum-Griffin per se," one commented, "but they know their rights. Landrum-Griffin is out in the open, but it's not because of the international."

Dissidents who have made use of the Act told us that they first learned of their rights either by consulting attorneys or by educating themselves, in university labor law courses. None reported learning of the LMRDA through intraunion sources.

Many members' knowledge of the Act, as many union lawyers agreed, probably derives from the publicity received by certain election cases. They cited as examples the Mineworkers' or the Steelworkers' District 31 election reruns. The highly publicized Sadlowski-McBride contest would serve as another. In addition, local and district level officers themselves often bring suits against the parent body, and their discussion and activity are a source of knowledge. The unions' constitutions, however, are not a comprehensive source of information. As noted, many of the most vital of the Title I provisions (e.g., the rights of free speech and assembly, and the four-month limit to the internal exhaustion requirement) have usually not been incorporated in the union constitutions. In any event, Section 105 has had very little impact on disseminating information concerning the LMRDA.[95]

Impact of Title I

Despite the general impression given by most union personnel that neither the unions' procedures nor the members' freedom to participate in the affairs of the union has changed qualitatively since the passage of the LMRDA, over half of the union spokesmen—officers at all levels and their counsel—agreed that individual rights are better protected now than they had been prior to passage of the Act. While, before 1959, union officers might have acknowledged that members have the right to speak freely, to challenge leaders' policies, to be accorded due process in internal trials, and even to sue the union, the existence of the Act and the members' growing awareness of it have served to remind officers that those rights can now be enforced. Of the union personnel, the officers of the parent organizations were less apt to feel this way, with only 40 percent perceiving greater protection of union members' rights. Intermediate and local level officers were more apt, with over 70 percent in agreement, to feel that individual members' Title I rights are now more fully safeguarded. Of the dissidents and their advocates, over 80% also agreed that rights are more adequately protected now, although many of them pointed out that only when members actually sued, or threatened to do so, were their officers willing to acknowledge those rights. Even with that caveat, it is noteworthy that a majority of respondents from both vantage points agreed that individual members' rights are now accorded an increased measure of protection. Their views are consistent with our own conclusion that, while some individual sections of Title I have had a greater impact than have others, over-all the effect of the Act's bill of rights has been a beneficial one.

---

95. There has been virtually no litigation under Section 105. In the one case cited in the DOL Compliance Reports in which it was raised as a tangential issue, a member argued that the union's failure to inform him of the Act's provisions was responsible for his bringing an unmeritorious suit. Therefore, the union should be assessed damages. The court answered that if the plaintiff had requested the officers to inform him of his rights, his claim might have been eliminated. The case was dismissed. *Broomer v. Schultz,* 239 F. Supp. 699 (E.D. Pa. 1965), *aff'd,* 356 F.2d 984 (3d Cir. 1966).

Chapter IV

Title III: Trusteeships

After the first year of hearings, the special Senate committee established to investigate union corruption, headed by Senator John McClellan (Arkansas), reported that its investigations had, among other things, pinpointed the fact that some unions under scrutiny had "flagrantly abused their power to place local unions under trusteeships. . . ."[1] Five major abuses by some parent organizations under investigation by the committee were found particularly troublesome:

1. Some parent bodies imposed trusteeships without a legitimate basis for doing so.
2. Some parent organizations, having legitimately imposed a trusteeship, subsequently kept their subordinate body under trusteeship for too long a time (e.g., at the time of passage of the LMRDA, seventeen United Mineworkers' districts had been in trusteeship for over twenty years, and four more for more than ten).[2]
3. The imposition and continuation of such trusteeships often went against the wishes of the rank and file members.
4. Trusteeships were at times used by the parent body as a means of looting local treasuries.
5. Some parent body officials used the votes of convention delegates from locals under trusteeship either to capture top office or to perpetuate themselves in office once elected.

Title III of the LMRDA was designed to eliminate these abuses.

Then, and since, Congress has been criticized for overreacting to the trusteeship abuses noted above. According to the critics,

---

1. "Sec. 3(h) of the *LMRDA* states: 'Trusteeship' means any receivership, trusteeship, or other method of supervision or control whereby a labor organization suspends the autonomy otherwise available to a surbordinate body under its constitution or bylaws." The quotation is from First Interim Report, S. Rep. No. 1417, 85th Cong., 2d Sess. 4 (1958) as quoted in *Union Trusteeships: Report of the Secretary of Labor to the Congress upon the Operation of Title III of the Labor-Management Reporting and Disclosure Act* (Washington, D.C.: U.S. Department of Labor, 1962), at 141.
2. Note, *Landrum-Griffin and the Trusteeship Imbroglio*, 71 YALE L. J. 1460, 1488–89 (1962).

very few unions engaged in the practices set forth above—although those few did so on a rather grand scale. Moreover, Congress gave too little recognition to the fact that parent unions have very legitimate reasons for imposing trusteeships.

Whatever the merits to this criticism, the unions have had to contend with the strictures of Title III, and therefore we turn our attention to those provisions.

Section 302, which sets forth the purposes for which a trusteeship may be imposed, was intended to rectify the first problem that the committee identified: baseless imposition of trusteeships.

Section 304(c) was inserted primarily to eliminate the second major problem the McClellan Committee hearings had focused upon: unwarranted continuation of trusteeships. Section 304(c) provides, among other things, that if the parent organization has followed its own constitution, and has held a fair hearing, a trusteeship it has imposed shall be presumed legally valid for eighteen months, "except upon clear and convincing proof that the trusteeship was not established or maintained in good faith for a purpose allowable under section 302."[3] Thereafter, the trusteeship is presumed legally invalid, and the court will order its discontinuance unless the parent body shows clear and convincing proof that its continuance is necessary for a lawful purpose.

Congress sought to eliminate the third problem, that of ignoring the wishes of the rank and file, by giving the aggrieved member or members a right to seek redress under Section 304 either by means of writing a complaint to the DOL, or by bringing "civil action in any district court of the United States having jurisdiction of the labor organization for such relief (including injunctions) as may be appropriate."

The statute provides that all written complaints to the DOL are to be treated in confidence. The reason for this is obvious; without such security, a member might not feel free to complain to the DOL, no matter how legitimate his concern, for fear of reprisal.

Under Section 306, the complainants also retain "any and all

---

3. By the terms of Sections 301(b), 301(c), and 301(d), if no report is filed, once the DOL becomes aware of the existence of an unreported trusteeship, the agency can, without a specific complaint, bring civil suit to have the report filed. Moreover, under Sections 301(c) and 301(d), a criminal suit can be filed against any person who is found willfully to have neglected to file the necessary reports, or to have filed a false one. If found guilty, the offender "shall be fined not more than $10,000 or imprisoned for not more than one year, or both."

other rights and remedies at law or in equity" until such time as the DOL files suit. At that point, the agency takes exclusive jurisdiction.

As indicated, unless the parent organization has failed to conduct a fair hearing, the complaining member faces a heavy burden of proof during the first eighteen months of the trusteeship's duration. During the course of its debates, Congress wrestled with the question of the time limits, shifting between twelve months and eighteen months, but finally decided upon eighteen months as the more reasonable length of time. Congress also vacillated back and forth on the question of the amount of evidence the complainant would have to produce within that eighteen-month period to prove that the trusteeship had been invalidly imposed. Over time, the suggested language changed from "clear and convincing proof" to "proof" and then back again. The ultimate decision to settle upon "clear and convincing proof" was deliberate. It reflected congressional desire that unions be free of outside interference during the initial eighteen months unless a clear and convincing showing could be made that the trusteeship had been imposed for invalid reasons.[4]

Thus, while Congress was concerned with trusteeships that are imposed ad infinitum or for illegitimate purposes, it also recognized that usually trusteeships are imposed for sound reasons and that, except under unusual circumstances, the parent bodies should be free of outside interference in trusteeship matters.

The fourth and fifth major problems cited, treasury looting and the packing of conventions, are dealt with under Section 303.

The DOL is empowered to use the investigatory powers vested in it under Section 601 to investigate a suspicious-looking trusteeship at any time, even without receiving a complaint from a member. However, even if such investigation were to establish that the title has been violated, the DOL can not bring suit unless a member subsequently does complain. The only exception to this limitation on the DOL involves, as previously noted, the reporting requirements of section 301.

Measuring the Impact of Title III

Table 6 outlines the data we sought to use to measure the impact of Title III. As that table shows, there are currently fewer unions

---

4. "Legislative History" in *Union Trusteeships: Report of the Secretary of Labor, supra* note 1, at 143–47.

TABLE 6. Data Used to Measure Impact of Title III

Data Sought	Issue	Findings
Number of trusteeships existing in September of 1959 and in September of 1975	Has enactment of statute caused a reduction in number of trusteeships?	September, 1959: 492* September, 1975: 303†
Number of trusteeships of duration longer than 18 months existing in September of 1959 and in September of 1975	Has enactment of statute caused a reduction in the duration of trusteeships imposed?	September, 1959: 288* September, 1975: 85†
Number of union constitutions specifying purposes and procedures for trusteeship imposition as of September of 1959 and as of September of 1975	Has statute had an effect on union constitutional language dealing with the purposes for imposing trusteeships and the procedures to be followed?	This information is not readily available for the universe through the DOL. Figures for our sample of 12 unions follow: Prior to 1959, 4 had detailed language, 7 had vague references, and 1 had nothing. Currently, 4 still retain vague language. The other 8 are quite specific, and 7 of these have adopted the Act's broad purposes language.
Private Title III suits vs. DOL-initiated suits filed since passage of statute	Title III provides that the complainant has the option of filing private suit or using the services of the DOL. Which option has been the most frequently used?	Since 1959 and through fiscal 1974, of the total of 55 court cases involving Title III, 5 were initiated by the DOL and 50 were filed privately.‡

*Note, *Landrum-Griffin and the Trusteeship Imbroglio*, 71 YALE L. J. 1460, 1522–23 (1962).
†U.S. Department of Labor.
‡DOL Compliance Reports. Of the 5 DOL-initiated suits, 2 were brought for violation of the reporting requirement.

The unions we studied represent:
      61.5% of all having subordinate bodies under trusteeship in 1959.
      67.0% of all having subordinate bodies under trusteeship at the present time.
      33.0% of all whose trusteeships were over 18 months' duration in 1959.
      51.5% of those whose trusteeships are currently over 18 months' duration.
      38.0% of those against which Title III suits have been brought.

under trusteeship than there were when the Act was passed (303 as against 492). Those figures do not tell the whole story, however; in the years immediately following the statute's enactment, there was a sharp drop in the number of active trusteeships. By November 30, 1961, only 141 had not been terminated.[5] In subsequent years, the number imposed has climbed again, although the figure has never gone as high as it stood in 1959.[6] One can conclude that the Act had an immediate effect, given the number of trusteeships that were terminated shortly after September of 1959. Moreover, the statute has had a lasting impact as well. Unions are using their powers to impose trusteeships less often than they did before Title III was enacted.

More striking still is the change in the number of trusteeships of more than an eighteen-month duration. In 1959 there were 288; as of September 15, 1975 there were only 85. Here the impact of the Act is quite unmistakable.

The third item listed in table 6 is concerned with the changes in constitutional language which were made in order to comply with the requirements of Title III. Here we have data only for our twelve sample unions. Prior to 1959, four of them had fairly detailed language in their constitutions specifying the purposes for which trusteeships could be imposed and the procedures to be followed in so doing. Seven had vague references to the practices to be followed, and the one remaining union constitution contained no reference to trusteeships whatever. Currently, four of the seven that contained vague language prior to 1959 have not revised it. The other eight presently have very detailed procedures. Of the latter, seven have adoped the statute's language in listing the purposes for which trusteeships may be imposed. More often than not the new language in those seven constitutions was taken verbatim from Section 302.

However, one should be cautious in attributing the constitutional language changes solely to Title III. Even prior to its passage, unions had begun to include at least some constitutional provisions, however vague, dealing with the imposition of trusteeships. They did so in part because of a number of court decisions requiring that there be language in a union's constitution providing

---

5. See Note, *Landrum-Griffin and the Trusteeship Imbroglio, supra* note 2, at 1525.

6. There are no good data on the number of trusteeships in existence at any time prior to September, 1959.

for the imposition of a trusteeship before such imposition would be held to be valid. Moreover, because of a trend towards increased centralization of power in the hands of the parent organizations vis-à-vis their subordinate bodies, parent unions were more ready to impose trusteeships, and began including language in their constitutions which specifically granted them that authority.[7]

The last item for which we were able to obtain data compares the number of privately brought Title III suits with the number of Title III suits filed by the DOL. Those figures reveal to what extent union members have taken advantage of the fact that they can, if they desire, use the free legal services of the DOL to bring suit against a parent organization that has imposed a trusteeship for illegal reasons rather than opting to continue the practice of filing private suit instead—the only recourse open to them before the statute's enactment. Between 1959 and June 30, 1974, fifty-five court cases involving Title III were decided. Of those, only five (or 9.9 percent) were initiated by the DOL. Such a disproportionate number of private suits could mean one of two things: either the complaining members preferred to take private action, or they found appeals to the DOL futile and therefore had to bring private suit. As we will discuss at greater length when we deal with the DOL enforcement of Title III, the latter is the predominant cause. Thus, while some language of the LMRDA may be of value to the complaining members, the option of going to the DOL on Title III matters has had little impact.

There follows a list of data which we sought but which were either unavailable or had not been compiled by the DOL or other sources:

1. The number of members in organizations under trusteeship in 1959 and at the present time
2. The stated reasons for which trusteeships are now imposed
3. The number of Title III complaints received by the DOL per annum
4. The subject matter of those complaints

It seems reasonable to assume, although it cannot be proven, that the number of union members in organizations under trusteeship was higher in 1959 than it now is, simply because there are fewer trusteeships now. However, the fact that locals have tended to grow larger in recent years weakens that assumption somewhat.

---

7. Davis, *Receivership in American Unions*, 67 Q. J. ECON. 231, 233–34 (1953).

It also seems reasonable, in at least the majority of cases, to assume that the unions that do impose trusteeships at the present time give some variation of Title III's "acceptable purposes" language as their stated reason for doing so.

Such broad assumptions cannot be made with regard to the number of Title III complaints received by the DOL each year, the nature of those complaints, or what percentage of them are found to have merit. The agency keeps no such statistics. The DOL spokesmen conversant with Title III complaints could tell us only that "very few" Title III complaints are filed each year, and that "fewer still" have merit. They also stated that complaining members' charges are usually quite vague. Most often, they said, the complainant was a local union officer who was ousted from his position when the parent organization put his local under trusteeship, "and all he's really after is to get back into office."

Because of the paucity of statistical material, heavy reliance was placed on the memories and impressions of the union officials interviewed. The vast majority of the parent body officers felt that Title III has had a favorable impact. "It is the best part of the Act," said one. "It put an end to a bad problem," reported another. Union members who have attempted to use the statute's language to lift a trusteeship imposed on their own organization, agreed: "The language is now *there*, if you want to use it." When parent bodies impose trusteeships in order to rid themselves of an irksome set of local or intermediate body officers—a practice which still continues according to many union spokesmen we interviewed—those officers or other affected rank and file members now at least have a legal framework, at the federal court level, in which to operate.[8]

Most of the union representatives told us that in their organizations the number of trusteeships had decreased considerably. In each case, they pointed to the Act as the single most important deterrent. Furthermore, not only are the parent organizations more cautious about imposing trusteeships but, once they have imposed one, they watch more closely to determine how soon it can be lifted. A number of those interviewed pointed particularly to the title's effect on the building and construction trades unions. Said one, "Those internationals used to impose a trusteeship if

8. We were also told of an instance in which the local officers asked the parent body to impose a trusteeship because they faced almost certain defeat in an upcoming election, and did not want to be removed from office. The parent organization refused, however, and the officers were subsequently defeated.

they were having *any* kind of trouble with their locals." Interestingly, it was only among the building and construction trades representatives interviewed—and only among some of them—that we encountered persons who believed that Title III constitutes too much of a deterrent upon the parent organizations. Parent bodies, they told us, have become too cautious, and move too slowly against a local that actually should be placed under trusteeship. However, in all such cases, the inhibited parent unions were involved in struggles, often of long standing, with powerful and independent-minded locals. It appeared doubtful that their reluctance to confront those locals in a power contest derived primarily from the Act. Instead, the prime motivation of these parent unions appeared to be political. As one representative of this group candidly admitted, his particular union has "a tiger by the tail" in those powerful locals, and is not quite sure how to cage it.

Furthermore, there are reasons quite apart from Title III for a reluctance to impose trusteeships. Some courts have held that the law of agency renders the parent organization suable for unlawful acts committed by its trusteed subordinate body and by the agents it appoints to administer the affairs thereof. For example, parent bodies have been held liable under Section 301 of the Taft-Hartley Act for acts of the trusteed body.[9] On the other hand, other courts have held unions liable for not imposing trusteeships when the courts found that the circumstances would have warranted such action.[10] Thus unions are currently caught on the horns of a dilemma.

Costs are an additional deterrent to the imposition of trusteeships. If the local is insolvent, the parent must pay the salary of the administrator it appoints, and must assume the local's financial obligations. Even if the local is solvent, the cost to the parent body in terms of personnel is burdensome. The administrator, most often a member of the parent organization's staff, must assume the obligation of overseeing the affairs of the local rather than perform his usual duties. Either his ordinary tasks are not performed at all during the period of the trusteeship, or other parent body staff members must assume them.

---

9. See, for example, *NLRB v. Local 542, IUOE*, 324 F.2d 447 (8th 3d Cir. 1964).
10. See, for example, *Lassiter v. Walton, L.U. 675, IUOE, and IUOE* (Cir. Ct. 17th Jud. Cir., Broward Co., Fla., December 9, 1971, Case No. 70-2824). At the time of writing, the question of damages was on appeal. See 87 L.R.R.M. 2490 (Fla. Dist. Ct. App. 1974); 92 L.R.R.M. 3711 (Fla. Sup. Ct. 1976); 96 L.R.R.M. 3040 (Fla. Sup. Ct. 1977).

Imposition of a trusteeship is, moreover, a very unpopular move—so much so that the mere threat of imposition has been used successfully to bring the local into line. Typical of the view of local union officers is the statement that "trusteeships are the worst thing that can happen to a local. It's a disgrace. It means that there is no one competent in the local to run it."

Because imposition is so unpopular, parent unions have used Title III as their excuse when imposing unwanted trusteeships. The top officers tell the members of the local that the imposition is required by the law. While those officers are stretching the law's actual reach in saying that, the resort to that subterfuge is not, in and of itself, a reprehensible act. The imposition of such trusteeships have, for example, been used quite effectively to correct financial malpractices—often sloppiness or carelessness rather than deliberate malfeasance—on the part of otherwise popular local union officers.

Officers from three parent unions reveal that in their own organizations they are now imposing more trusteeships than they did earlier. One attributed that to the fact that in some of his union's locals the members are "kicking up their heels more than they used to" and balking at ratifying contracts. As a consequence, the parent body has been putting such unruly locals under supervision. In two others, officials also pointed to "the times," but gave as additional reasons a restructuring of the organization, and the election of a new slate of top officers who are more willing to impose trusteeships than were their predecessors.

There are ways in which a parent organization can discipline an offending local other than imposing a trusteeship. One is to merge it with another local, larger and more loyal to the parent body, thus drawing the merged local's fangs. There are, of course, legitimate reasons for mergers and not every merger—nor indeed the vast majority of them—is effected for suspicious reasons. Both the DOL and the courts have held that mergers, if properly established, do not constitute trusteeships. Nonetheless, merger is a device that can be used for the wrong reasons.[11] Those we interviewed acknowledged that mergers could be used as a disciplinary measure, and knew that they had been so used in other unions, although no one—dissidents included—could point to an instance of this in their own organizations. When mergers have

---

11. See, on this point, *Union Trusteeships: Report of the Secretary of Labor, supra* note 1, at 34.

been effected in their unions, they said, it has always been for the sake of greater efficiency.

Another way a parent union can circumvent Title III is to remove a single offending officer—a power that is often specifically granted to the president of the parent body under the constitution—rather than to impose a trusteeship. In doing so, the parent organization need not even file the reports required under Section 301 of the Act. Spokesmen from one union in our sample candidly admitted to using this device. The constitutions of the rest also permit its use.

Another device described to us, but almost always in terms of "we have heard about this from a well-informed source, although we have not encountered it ourselves," is for the parent organization to impose a trusteeship for seventeen months, lift it, file the necessary terminal report with the DOL, and then, within a matter of a month or so, impose a new one. Given the DOL's failure to enforce Title III rigorously (which is discussed below), one wonders why this subterfuge, if actually used, is bothered with at all, unless it is to protect the parent organization from possible private action.

Court Interpretations of Title III

As previously indicated, the courts have held that the merger of locals does not constitute a trusteeship, if properly established.[12] In addition, they have apparently now settled an initially troublesome question concerning the interpretation of Title III: Did Congress intend the language of that title to be read as giving a union member the option of going *either* to the DOL *or* to the courts with his complaint, or of going to both? If both avenues were open, which was the member to pursue first? At first, some courts held that the member must first seek help from the DOL and only upon receiving no satisfaction there could he bring a private suit. More recently, however, the courts have held that either route is permissible under the Act, and that the member may exercise either option.[13]

---

12. See, for example, *Brewery Bottlers and Drivers Union, Local 1345 v. International Brotherhood of Teamsters*, 202 F. Supp. 464 (E.D.N.Y. 1962); *Massey v. Curry*, 46 L.R.R.M. 2140 (Ga. Sup. Ct. 1960).

13. Court decisions holding member must sue via the DOL: *Cox v. Hutcheson*, 204 F. Supp. 442 (S.D. Ind. 1962); *Rizzo v. Ammond*, 182 F. Supp. 456 (D.N.J. 1960); *Flaherty v. McDonald*, 45 L.R.R.M. 2456 (S.D. Cal. 1960). Decisions

Originally, too, the courts—here following state court precedents established prior to passage of the Act—often ruled that a parent organization could not impose a trusteeship at all unless its constitution contained specific language adequately providing for such imposition. However, at the present time, neither the DOL's interpretations nor more recent court decisions place emphasis upon constitutional language. Thus this issue has apparently also been laid to rest.[14] Since most union constitutions have such language now, it does not appear to be much of a problem in any event.[15]

The courts have settled another interpretative question as well. Section 304(c) states that, to be presumed valid during the initial eighteen-month period, the trusteeship must not only be "in conformity with the procedural requirements of [the] constitution and bylaws," but must also be "authorized or ratified after a fair hearing either before the executive board or before such other body as may be provided in accordance with [the] constitution or bylaws. . . . " Clearly, given that the trusteeship can be either "authorized" or "ratified," Congress intended that a hearing be held either before or after imposition. However, under what circumstances the hearing was to take place before, and in what situations after, the imposition was not made clear by the statute.

Local Union 13410 v. UMWA[16] appears to have settled the issue. In that case, the court held that a "hearing should, if possible be held prior to trusteeship," but went on to say:

---

holding member may sue directly: *Parks v IBEW*, 314 F.2d 886 (4th Cir. 1963), *cert. denied*, 372 U.S. 976 (1963); *Air Line Stewards and Stewardesses Association v. Transportation Workers Union*, 55 L.R.R.M. 2711 (D. N. Ill. 1963), *rev'd* on other grounds, 334 F.2d 805 (7th Cir. 1964), *cert. denied*, 379 U.S. 972 (1965); *Forline v. Helpers, Local 42*, 211 F. Supp. 315 (E.D. Pa. 1962); *Vars v. Boilermakers*, 204 F. Supp. 245 (D. Conn. 1962); *Executive Board, Local 28 IBEW v. IBEW*, 184 F. Supp. 649 (D. Md. 1960); *Hotel and Restaurant Employees' Union v. Del Valle*, 328 F.2d 885 (1st Cir. 1964); *Blue v. Carpenters*, 56 L.R.R.M. 2440 (D. Minn. 1964).

14. The DOL position is given in *Union Trusteeships: Report of the Secretary of Labor*, *supra* note 1, at 36; and in U.S. Department of Labor, Labor-Management Services Administration, Office of Labor-Management and Welfare-Pension Reports, *LMRDA Interpretative Manual*, Entry 310.200.

15. The constitutions of all unions in our sample have such language. Of the unions studied in compiling the report of the Secretary of Labor, 61.8 percent had constitutions containing such language before passage of the Act. By May, 1962, the figure had risen to 67.2 percent. *Union Trusteeships: Report of the Secretary of Labor*, *supra* note 1, at 97, 99.

16. 475 F.2d 906 (D.C. Cir. 1973).

There is no absolute requirement that a hearing be held prior to imposition, since the statute states that a hearing may either "approve or ratify" the trusteeship. The possibility of "ratification" implies that under some circumstances a hearing may occur after a trusteeship is imposed. We can imagine extreme emergencies that might compel action without prior notice and hearing. Even in such an emergency situation, however, a hearing date should be set when the trusteeship was imposed and held shortly thereafter.[17]

In *Hodgson v. United Mine Workers of America,* [18] the Court of Appeals for the District of Columbia, relying heavily on the Supreme Court decision in *Trbovich v. United Mine Workers,*[19] reversed an earlier lower court decision denying complaining members the right to intervene in a Title III suit brought by the DOL. In the *Hodgson* case, the circuit court expressly granted the members that right on the ground that "without intervention neither they nor other union members would have a voice in fashioning the relief to be afforded. . . . "[20]

Title III is silent on the question of whether or not a member must exhaust his internal remedies before bringing suit. Thus, that question, too, came before the courts. Some early decisions stated that the member must first exhaust the internal remedies. More recently, however, the courts have held that he need not.[21]

In summary, Congress intended the courts to interpret the broad language of Title III.[22] Over time, and with due consideration for both complainants and their unions, they have been doing just that.

---

17. *Id.* at 914–15. Emphasis is in the original.

18. 473 F.2d 118 (D.C. Cir. 1972).

19. *Trbovich v. United Mine Workers,* 404 U.S. 528 (1972). This case is discussed more fully in chapters 1 and 2, dealing with Title IV.

20. 473 F.2d 118, 126 (D.C. Cir. 1972), at 126.

21. For an early case, holding that the member must exhaust internal remedies, see *Chicago Federation of Musicians, Local 10 v. American Federation of Musicians* (57 L.R.R.M. 2227 (N.D. Ill. 1964)). For more recent cases, holding that the member need not exhaust internal remedies, see *Carpenters v. Brown* (343 F.2d 872 (10th Cir. 1965)); *Purcell v. Keane* (406 F.2d 1195 (3d Cir. 1969)); *Sabolsky v. Budzanowski* (457 F.2d 1245 (3d Cir. 1970)).

22. U.S. Department of Labor, Office of the Solicitor, *Legislative History of the Labor-Management Reporting and Disclosure Act of 1959, Titles I—VI* (Washington, D.C.: U.S. Department of Labor, 1964), at 640.

Administration and Enforcement of Title III by the
Department of Labor

The analysis that follows is rather critical of the DOL enforcement of Title III. Because it is critical, we should like to stress that, in writing it, we were aware of the budgetary constraints and consequent shortage of personnel that the agency faces. In many instances, the DOL has no choice but to set priorities and, in doing so, may have to give less emphasis to certain assigned tasks than some observers might wish.

According to the DOL's own statement, the emphasis of the agency with regard to the Act is upon voluntary compliance:

> Voluntary compliance is encouraged by providing unions with a better understanding of the law through publishing interpretative materials and supplying advice on how the law applies in practice. Unions unintentionally or unwittingly violating the law are given technical assistance to permit them to voluntarily comply with the law, but the corrupt elements in the labor-management field, which the law was primarily intended to reach, are dealt with forcefully.[23]

It is difficult to determine how often the DOL has been successful in carrying out that policy in its enforcement of Title III. In the first four Compliance Reports, the number of cases of voluntary compliance with the provisions of Title III is given. Those Compliance Reports, however, do not differentiate between those unions which, once the Section 301 requirement to file a trusteeship report was called to their attention, voluntarily complied, and those organizations which responded to the DOL's questioning of the legitimacy of the trusteeships themselves by voluntarily lifting them. That distinction is important because compelling compliance with the reporting requirement was initially a substantial problem.[24]

The Compliance Reports issued subsequent to that for fiscal 1962–1963 no longer give figures of any kind for voluntary compliance under Title III. Nor, according to DOL spokesmen, are figures on trusteeship investigations kept in such manner that that information could easily be extracted. On the contrary, they told us, it would entail a rather major effort to break out the relevant statistical

---

23. *Union Trusteeships: Report of the Secretary of Labor, supra* note 1, at 25–26. The emphasis on voluntary compliance is stressed year after year in the annual DOL Compliance Reports.
24. *Union Trusteeships: Report of the Secretary of Labor, supra* note 1, at 109.

data. As previously indicated, the total number of complaints received under Title III is also no longer recorded separately. Instead, it is included only as a part of the tabular compilation of "Basic Investigations" contained in the Compliance Reports.

If the DOL finds a Title III complaint to have merit, it is agency policy to inform the parent body concerned that this determination has been made and that, unless some satisfactory arrangement can be made that points to the lifting of the trusteeship, the DOL will file suit. The "arrangements" agreed to vary, and can range from the instance where the parent organization agrees to lift the trusteeship as soon as the members of the supervised body have held elections and new officers have been installed, to the case where the parent body agrees to give leadership training to selected members of the unit under trusteeship, presumably with the idea that when elections are eventually held the members will have a skilled pool of candidates from which to draw. We have examples of both instances.

One statistic we found raises the question whether the agency's previously quoted statement that it deals forcefully with allegedly corrupt elements applies to Title III matters. As indicated in table 6 and noted there in the text, of the fifty-five cases decided between 1959 and June 30, 1974, only five were initiated by the DOL, and two of those concerned violations of the reporting requirements, rather than a questioning of the validity of the trusteeship itself. One of the remaining three was the celebrated Mineworkers' trusteeship case, which took over seven years from the time the complaint was first filed until the decision was handed down.[25] In the opinion in that case, the judge took special note of the time lag and pointed out that a private suit,[26] also involving a Mineworker's trusteeship, required less than a year to be heard and decided.[27] Spokesmen at the DOL admit that complaining members are more likely to take private action than to come to the agency because the former route is surer and faster. This may account for the fact that the DOL receives "very few" complaints.

Although the DOL now uses a computer to keep track of the

---

25. That suit was being handled by the Department of Justice rather than by the DOL solicitor's office. Thus, after December 15, 1964, it was no longer the DOL's full responsibility.

26. *Monborne v. UMWA District 2*, 342 F. Supp. 718 (W. D. Pa. 1971).

27. See the judge's comment in *Hodgson v. UMWA* (473 F.2d 118, 130 (D.C. Cir. 1972)).

annual financial reports required under Title II, it does not do so with respect to the reports required under Title III. Thus the agency has no quick method for determining whether or not the parent organization is filing Title III reports on time, nor can it routinely check on trusteeships that have existed for over eighteen months.

We were told by one member of the national office that the DOL does keep watch over "suspicious-looking" trusteeships— presumably those imposed by unions with suspicious past records. On the basis of information supplied by other national office personnel, however, it appears that the trusteeship reports are accepted with so little scrutiny that even if the report gives no reason whatever for the imposition of the trusteeship,[28] no action is taken.

Enforcement of Title III at the area office level is minimal. When we asked area office staff members what percentage of the total time consumed by LMRDA matters is spent on Title III problems, the answers they gave ranged from a low of zero to a high of 10 percent. Upon reflection, the person who had given us the 10 percent figure decided that the figure was probably too high. Typically, the reason given for inactivity was stated in terms such as: "You can't make a case the way the law is written, so why bother?" Some area office staff told us that they do make a preliminary investigation if the complainant persists. However, they warn the complaining member that during the first eighteen months, the burden of proof is a substantial one. One area office is more active than the others with regard to trusteeship matters. Yet even in that office, the personnel do nothing after eighteen months if no member complains. "We could inquire and investigate without a complaint after eighteen months," they told us, "but Washington low-keys trusteeships, so why bother?"[29]

Entry 353.100 of the *LMRDA Interpretative Manual* specifically states: "If the Secretary has received a complaint alleging violation of Title III before the end of the 18 month period of presumptive validity, he may take enforcement action after the

---

28. This practice is not new. See, for example, Levitan, *Union Trusteeships: The Federal Law and an Inventory*, 11 LAB. L. J. 1067, 1079 (1960); and *Union Trusteeships: Report of the Secretary of Labor, supra* note 1, at 167 n.2. The latter states that almost 10 percent of the reports filed by that time gave no reason whatever for imposition.

29. The attitude of the national office was also cited as the reason for not pursuing Title III cases in two other area offices we visited.

expiration of the 18 month period without a new complaint. . . . "[30]
Yet, tickler files are not routinely kept to reactivate complaints
that are received during the initial eighteen-month period. On the
other hand, in some area offices, if the staff knows of the existence
of a trusteeship in their jurisdiction—and in the case of the more
visible unions in their area they do know—they will always make
an informal inquiry once the eighteen months have elapsed. One
union lawyer said that he can expect a telephone call from the
area office one week after the eighteen months are up. The union
he represents, while large and thus clearly visible, is almost
wholly devoid of a "suspicious" past.

Union lawyers we interviewed often expressed the wish that
the DOL would disclose the decision it makes in Title III cases,
i.e., the determinations it makes as to the validity or invalidity of a
complaint, and the reasons therefor. The DOL does not now normally make such decisions public, although the law appears per-
missive in that regard.[31]

The lawyers' desire for firmer guidelines is a very reasonable
one. Of the labor unions in this country, the great majority is not
corrupt and is willing to obey the law. There is thus much merit
to the argument that unions are entitled to guidance from the
DOL. We can find no justification for the DOL's current policy
of not making the rationale behind its decisions public. If the
underlying cause is that the decisions may vary from day to day,
depending on who is in office and other vagaries—and we were
given that explanation by two national office spokesmen—then
we simply cannot agree that that is sufficient grounds. Another
DOL official gave a more cogent explanation. In his view, making public those decisions and their underlying reasons might do
a disservice to the unions involved, in terms of adverse publicity
or further internal disruption. However, that possibility could be
avoided if the agency issued its statements in terms of *Case A,
Case B*, etc., thus providing anonymity to the particular organizations involved. We believe such a policy should be instituted.

A substantial number of DOL personnel charged with administering the Act, both in the national office and in the field, be-

---

30. U.S. Department of Labor, *LMRDA Interpretative Manual,* Entry 353.100.

31. See also AFL-CIO Maritime Trades Department, *A Report After Eight Years of
the Landrum-Griffin Act* (Washington, D.C.: AFL-CIO, 1967), at 17; and Note,
Landrum-Griffin and the Trusteeship Imbroglio, supra note 2, at 1491–92.

lieved that they had done too little to enforce Title III adequately, and that they should have been doing more. Despite the fact that private suits have been the major vehicle used to lift trusteeships, bringing such action remains a formidable undertaking. One agency representative noted: "We should be doing more simply because the individual's bringing suit is usually a joke."

Over-all, one must say that the impact of the enforcement of Title III by the DOL has been less than Congress intended.[32] Having made that statement, we reiterate again that we are aware that the DOL has a genuine problem in attempting to carry out all the duties assigned to it under the Act. It is understandable that member complaints with regard to the imposition of a trusteeship are given low priority, since the individual has the alternative of filing a private suit in a Title III case, whereas he must rely exclusively on the DOL when filing an election complaint under Title IV. Moreover, in our own study, we found that the overwhelming majority of parent unions that have imposed trusteeships have done so for quite legitimate reasons. Thus, those charged with administering Title III are not closing their eyes to a myriad of horrendous situations; far from that. Nevertheless, if one looks at the court cases involving Title III that we have mentioned, it is worthy of note that, of the fifty-five cases decided between 1959 and fiscal 1974, twenty-five resulted in a court order that the trusteeship be lifted. Moreover, of the five dissidents we interviewed who had approached the DOL with a Title III complaint and been turned away, all but one won the cases that they themselves subsequently brought.[33] In that one exception, the mere filing of the suit triggered action on the part of the parent organization to lift the trusteeship. Thus, when the case reached court, the judge, aware that elections were already scheduled, dismissed the case. Even in that instance, then, it was the member's own action that resulted in the lifting of the trusteeship. That fact, coupled with the information that better than 45 percent of the privately brought suits were successful, is in itself some indication that closer scrutiny of trusteeship complaints by the DOL is warranted.

---

32. For additional criticism of DOL enforcement, see Note, *Landrum-Griffin and the Trusteeship Imbroglio, supra* note 2, at 1492–97.

33. A less clear-cut case is *McDonald v. Oliver*, 400 F. Supp. 660 (S. D. Miss. 1974); *aff'd* 525 F.2d 1217 (5th Cir., 1976); *cert. denied*, 429 U.S. 817 (1976).

Suggested Changes in Statutory Language

The Eighteen-Month Presumption

Almost everyone we interviewed within the DOL, as well as union members who have sought to lift trusteeships imposed upon their own local unions, strongly criticized the eighteen-month presumption of trusteeship validity. To their minds, the present language puts too heavy a burden on the complainant during that initial period. These critics would much prefer no heavy burden, or one which would be lightened after three to six months. Moreover, they wish that the DOL could file suit, if warranted, without waiting for a member complaint. According to one dissident, despite the fact that the DOL does not divulge the name of the complainant, the parent body usually knows his identity in any event and he then becomes "a marked man." He explained that this fact deters all but the most insistent from complaining at all.

A number of those interviewed who take the position that the eighteen-month period is too long suggested that after three months—or at most six—the parent body should routinely be required to justify imposition of the trusteeship. Some suggested that the parent body go before the DOL at the close of the three or six months. Others proposed that the union seek court sanction instead, on the ground that the courts traditionally have been the source of relief concerning improperly imposed trusteeships and that, in any event, the investigation of a trusteeship's validity is "too hot a potato" to be left to the discretion of the DOL. If the parent body could not make a prima-facie case to the DOL, or to the courts, the agency or court should immediately challenge imposition and do so as speedily as possible. Some proponents of that plan told us that a change in statutory language would be necessary in order to impose time limits on Title III investigations similar to those imposed on the DOL with regard to Title IV union election complaints. Others, however, said that a language change was not necessary. All that is required is for the DOL to seek summary judgment, as the complaining members did in *Monborne v. UMWA, District 2*,[34] or to find some other mechanism for speeding up the procedure. (*Monborne* was the Mineworkers' trusteeship case mentioned earlier that was decided in less than a year after the complaint was brought.)

One lawyer who has represented both unions and dissident members made a novel proposal. He suggested that the complain-

---

34. 342 F. Supp. 718 (W.D. Pa. 1971).

ant should be empowered to go to federal district court with the understanding that the court would give the DOL thirty days to make its own investigation and make recommendations to the court before the judge issued his opinion. The findings of the DOL would not be binding on the court. However, if the agency agreed that the complaint was legitimate, it would join forces with the complainant in bringing suit. According to this plan, the complainant could go into court as soon as the trusteeship was established and the necessary hearing was held.

The great majority of union representatives interviewed had strong arguments against shortening the eighteen-month period of presumption. Unions impose trusteeships only with the greatest reluctance, they said. When unions do, they have legitimate reasons for doing so, and always lift trusteeships as quickly as possible: "The trustee [the parent body's representative] is the first who wants out." The eighteen-month presumption represents the legislative intent at the time the Act was passed, and no valid reason has, arisen since to justify either shortening or eliminating that. These representatives also noted that the proposal described above is much like the amendment which Senator Thomas Dodd (Connecticut) proposed in 1959, and which Congress rejected.[35] Moreover, they said, if complainants were empowered to protest immediately upon imposition, the union would be subjected to a multiplicity of frivolous suits. Congress set the eighteen-month period to avoid just that.

One very telling comment came from a man who was a member of a dissident group that had succeeded in ousting the former leaders and is now itself in power: "I used to think eighteen months was too long. Now I consider it quite reasonable, as long as the trusteeship is imposed for a valid reason. And if it isn't, the hell-bent international wouldn't need eighteen months—they could wreck things in three."

As for the argument that shortening the period of presumption would prevent the parent body from looting the local's treasury, a former dissident in a different union retorted: "Who needs eighteen months? If that's what I wanted to do, I could do it in one day, by writing one check." He also added that if a parent body were to impose trusteeships for illicit reasons very often, the word would spread quickly, and the top officials of that union would be out of office following the next election. However, the Mine-

---

35. The Dodd amendment is described in detail in Note, *Landrum-Griffin and the Trusteeship Imbroglio, supa* note 2, at 1502–03 n. 228.

workers' seemingly endless trusteeships—though not characteristic of trusteeships generally—are too clear a counterexample for his statement to be accepted without qualification.

Congress purposely made the decision to presume that a trusteeship was validly imposed for the initial eighteen-month period unless there was "clear and convincing" proof to the contrary. Most trusteeships are imposed for valid reasons and there are sufficient deterrents to prolonging them so that, to subject unions to suits immediately after imposition, would all too often be unwarranted and could result in needless litigation.

As we see it, the underlying problem is not the eighteen-month limitation. It is, rather, that even if a member were to protest to the DOL, either before or after the expiration of the eighteen months, the chances are too slim that the agency would act.

The Language of Section 302

Another criticism often leveled at the Title III language is that the reasons for imposing trusteeship, as listed in Section 302, are far too broad. Here the critics point particularly to "for the purpose of . . . restoring democratic procedures, or otherwise carrying out the legitimate objects of such labor organizations." If that language is coupled with the provisions in union constitutions which spell out the general objectives of the organization (usually in very sweeping language), the result is "dangerous," according to one interviewee, and "a real stickler" according to another. The implication in both instances is that the two documents read together give great leeway to a parent organization to impose a trusteeship at any time and for whatever reasons it chooses.

On the other hand, some union lawyers told us that the language is not broad enough. They would prefer it if the Act spelled out under what circumstances a trusteeship would be invalid, rather than listing the circumstances in which it is presumed valid. In the 1962 report on trusteeships, the DOL stated:

> The Department has decided that if in fact a trusteeship is established and administered for at least one of the purposes enumerated in Section 302 of the Act, the validity of the trusteeship will not be affected merely because it may have been designed to accomplish other purposes not specified in the statute. These other purposes, however, must not include any of the prohibited activities specified in Section 303(a).[36]

---

36. *Union Trusteeships: Report of the Secretary of Labor, supra* note 1, at 36–37.

Later in the same report, the DOL also commented that "the extreme breadth of [the standards set forth in Section 302] makes it very difficult for the Department to establish a violation of these provisions of 302."[37] Given the above statements and the poor quality of the DOL's enforcement of Title III, one is led to wonder what the basis for the lawyers' complaint concerning the language of Section 302, as now written, can possibly be.

Those who perceive the language of Section 302 as being very broad are quite right. It is very broad, and was intended to be. Congress wanted to express its will in rather nebulous language and have the courts and the DOL make specific interpretations of it.[38] The courts are in the process of interpreting the language of Title III, and nothing is to be gained by halting that process.

Moreover, if one looks closely at the language of Section 301, it is evident that Title III presently directs the parent body to supply the DOL with a detailed statement of the reason or reasons for establishing or continuing a trusteeship. In addition, the legislative history of the Act makes clear that Congress intended those statements to be detailed.[39] Thus, to the extent that the DOL is content if the parent union simply checks one or more boxes on the reporting form—or, worse yet, none at all—the agency is ignoring congressional intent. We believe that, rather than changing the language of the title, more careful enforcement of it as now written would carry out legislative intent and would, in addition, go a long way towards silencing the criticism leveled at the DOL's current administration of Title III.

There is one additional suggestion: While Section 305 required a report from the DOL to Congress concerning Title III only after an initial three-year period, it would be instructive if the DOL were to issue at least one additional report. The 1962 document was published before a number of the unions covered had held any post-LMRDA conventions and, more important, less than a year after the standardized reporting forms for trusteeships had been issued for the first time. Therefore, the statistics on constitutional language changes are incomplete, and the data on trusteeships are uneven. The DOL itself noted that the report was issued

---

37. *Id.* at 118.
38. U.S. Department of Labor, *Legislative History, supra* note 22.
39. See, for example, Senator Ervin's remarks, in U.S. Department of Labor, *Legislative History, supra* note 22, at 668.

before the effect of Title III could be fully measured.[40] Thus, if the purpose of inserting Section 305 was to ensure that Congress be fully informed as to the operation of Title III—and the section itself makes that intent quite clear—then that purpose has not been fulfilled. It would seem appropriate at this time to correct that deficiency by issuing a supplemental report on this subject to the Congress.

Impact of Title III

Despite our critical comments concerning the DOL's current enforcement of Title III, we believe that the enactment of the title has had a beneficial impact. Once Title III was promulgated, trusteeships of long standing were lifted, and language was added to union constitutions specifying allowable purposes for trusteeship impositions and outlining the procedures to be followed. Unions have become more cautious than they previously were in imposing such trusteeships, and quicker to lift them. Moreover, the courts are in the process of clarifying the language of Title III, as Congress intended.

An additional question occurred to us: Given that DOL enforcement of Title III is not vigorous, why has the title's enactment had such a salutary effect? We believe one reason to be that the intent of Title III is clearer and simpler to comply with than those of Titles I, IV, and V, and that unions therefore find it easier to obey. Moreover, the vigorous enforcement by the DOL of the Title IV election provisions has probably also played its part. On the basis of our interviews, we have concluded that a parent union officer is now less quick to impose controls over a recalcitrant subordinate unit without a readily defensible reason. His knowledge that the price of hasty action might be defeat in the next election stays his hand.

---

40. *Union Trusteeships: Report of the Secretary of Labor, supra* note 1, at 21 and (for deficiencies in reports received by the DOL) 28 *et seq.*

Chapter V

Titles II and V: Financial Reporting and Fiduciary Responsibility

The main concern in this study has been with sections of the LMRDA other than Titles II and V. Nevertheless, the survey returns showed that these two sections of the Act were often the ones that were uppermost in the minds of rank and file union members. Moreover, the union representatives reached through personal interview supplied a great deal of interesting and useful information concerning those two titles, and we therefore decided to include this chapter. Those reporting were primarily interested in DOL enforcement, although there were also numerous comments concerning the impact of the titles themselves on the internal operation of labor unions. We will therefore discuss both the enforcement and impact of Titles II and V.

Enforcement of Titles II and V

The DOL's enforcement of that portion of Title II which requires that unions file annual financial reports, and its administration of the segments of Title V which deal with the fiduciary responsibility of union officers, are interrelated. Both titles are concerned with union finances; the first with the prompt and accurate reporting of income and expenditures, and the second with the way in which union funds are expended. Moreover, the annual reports filed as a Title II requirement can furnish members or the DOL with information that leads to Title V suits.[1] As indicated earlier, if a member believes that his Section 201(c) right to inspect the union's financial records has been violated, his only recourse is to the courts. Moreover, the DOL does not enforce Section 501(a),

---

1. The annual financial reports are filed on Form LM-2 or Form LM-3, the latter being a simplified version of the former, required of unions with less than $30,000 in annual receipts. (Unions in trusteeship all file LM-2's, no matter what their annual receipts.)

which covers financial mishandling, except insofar as its Section 601 investigative authority permits. Again, the complaining member or members must file private suit. The Justice Department investigates Section 501(c) allegations of embezzlement unless the violation complained of also includes the charge that a false report was filed. In the latter instance, which is normally the case, the DOL conducts the inquiry.

All DOL area office personnel told us that, next to Title IV election matters, they spend the most time on investigations arising under Titles II and V. Estimates ranged from a low of 20 percent to a high of 40 percent of the total time spent on LMRDA-related assignments. The area offices receive computer printouts from the national office, listing which unions in the particular area have been found to have filed deficient financial reports or none at all; the area offices are expected to contact the unions listed and seek compliance with the requirements of the Act. Area office staff explained that a major reason that unions file incomplete or late reports is that new financial officers have been installed in those organizations who either do not know that those reports are to be filed or do not know how to fill them out. At times, the new officers are reluctant to file reports because the records kept by their predecessors are inadequate, and they would prefer not to run the risk of being held liable for filing an inaccurate report. In such cases, the area office member who contacts them offers technical assistance to the newcomers, often going to union headquarters to help them fill out the reports.

If the original DOL inquiry does not prod the responsible union officer into sending in the required report, the organization is contacted again. If that is to no avail, the director of the area office sends a letter to the local union, with a copy to the parent organization. The parent organization is notified so that it has an opportunity to assist in persuading its local to comply. The letter states that, unless the union files its report within a specified time, the area office will turn the case over to the solicitor's office. According to DOL officials, the contacts and letter together reduce the number of unions having delinquent financial reports to an average of 5 percent annually.[2]

If the letter produces no report within the time specified, the area office still may delay sending the case on to the solicitor's

---

2. The DOL records do not currently indicate how often the same unions are repeatedly delinquent in filing. However, we have been told that a system is being devised that will make it possible to retrieve that information as well.

office if there is reason to believe that the union is making a sincere effort to comply. Even when the case is sent on to the Solicitor, and the Solicitor turns the case over to the Department of Justice with the recommendation that a suit be filed, the press of work of more critical importance often precludes the U.S. attorney from taking quick action. Parent union officials told us that in some cases neglectful locals have failed to file, been contacted by the area office, and received its follow-up letter year after year without suit being brought. In time, the officers of such a local come to consider the DOL's actions as a meaningless ritual, and nothing the parent union does to persuade them to comply can change their minds. DOL spokesmen, both in the area offices and at the national office level, admitted that that situation does arise, but stated that they have no control over what happens once they have passed the case on to the solicitor's office. Said one, "the whole thing is nothing but an exercise in futility."

Another agency spokesman reported that even when a case does go to court, and the financial officer fails to respond to the judge's order that the report be produced, the agency official is nevertheless reluctant to press contempt-of-court charges if the local is a small one. (The vast majority of delinquencies occur among the small units.) His hesitancy is based on the fact that if the financial officer is found guilty, the local union will have a difficult time cajoling anyone else to take his place. Therefore, rather than press charges, the DOL official just keeps prodding the incumbent until he finally produces the report.

Prior to filing either a Form LM-2 or LM-3 annual report, a newly formed labor organization is required by Title II to file a Form LM-1, on which it states the name of the organization, its address, the names and titles of the officers, and the fees and dues required of members. In addition, the report must contain either detailed statements of provisions and procedures designed to comply with the Act (e.g., how expenditures are authorized, under what circumstances members are disciplined, how elections are conducted) or, if those provisions are set forth in the organization's constitution or bylaws, a copy of that document and references to the pertinent sections thereof are required instead. Subsequent changes in the information supplied on the LM-1's are to be filed on LM-1A forms to be included when the organization files its annual financial report, although that provision is often ignored.[3]

---

3. On February 15, 1977, the *LMRDA Interpretative Manual* was amended so that a subordinate labor organization is no longer required to file a form LM-

From what we were told by those we interviewed, including DOL officials, some labor organizations have never filed even the LM-1's, far less the required financial reports. The local union officers and three dissidents who found that the organizations they were interested in had never filed LM-1's simply shrugged it off as "still another bureaucratic goof-up" and did nothing further. Six others, primarily union lawyers and advocates for dissidents, reported that they did inform DOL officials that the records they were seeking were lacking, but said that nothing had been done to correct the matter. They went on to comment that they found it incomprehensible that the DOL national office does not develop some sort of system to keep current on which organizations should submit those records. Even requiring a parent union to inform the national office of newly chartered locals would be a step in the right direction. One legal scholar pointed to the first part of Section 208 as empowering the DOL to require that parent unions submit lists of all subordinate bodies subject to the Act:

> The Secretary shall have authority to issue, amend, and rescind rules and regulations prescribing the form and publication of reports required to be filed under this title and such other reasonable rules and regulations (including rules prescribing reports concerning trusts in which a labor organization is interested) *as he may find necessary to prevent the circumvention* or evasion of such reporting requirements. . . . [Emphasis added.]

Moreover, all those who have tried to use such records as are available at the national office told us that they are "in impossible condition."

The DOL officials at the national office are aware of these complaints and readily admit that many of them are valid. They told us that they have recently streamlined the procedure for keeping current concerning organizations which are delinquent in reporting, but they themselves recognize that that is just one step forward. As to other complaints, they told us that they do from

---

1A for a reporting period in which a change in constitution or bylaw language was made, so long as the parent organization has "filed the required number of copies of the amended constitution and bylaws with [the DOL, and provided] that there have been no changes in the practices described in the latest statements submitted with the subordinate labor organization's Form LM-1 or LM-1A, and that there have been no changes in any additional constitution, bylaws or other governing rules adopted by the subordinate labor organization." U.S. Department of Labor, Labor-Management Services Administration, Notice No. 15–77 (February 15, 1977).

time to time happen upon a labor union that has never filed any report, although that situation is increasingly rare; that they do not have up-to-date information on new labor organizations; and that they do not do all they could with the reports they do get. These officials are troubled by these deficiencies, but they do not have the manpower to do anything about them.

As to the Section 208 language quoted above, we were told that the DOL has interpreted it as limiting the agency to requiring only those items listed in Section 201(a). If that interpretation is accurate (and it has never been tested), then an amendment to the statute would be necessary before the agency could require the parent unions to furnish lists of its subordinate units.

Because so little activity of any consequence results from the inspection of the financial reports, five local union officers and two parent body officials suggested to us that the reporting requirement, especially for the small unions, could well be eliminated. However, the rest of the parent organization officials interviewed claimed that imposing reporting requirements had had a beneficial effect over-all. Moreover, in situations where the reporting requirement did work a real hardship, DOL representatives are said to have been quite receptive to bending the enforcement requirements to fit the circumstances.

Section 203

Spokesmen from approximately one third of the unions in our sample leveled criticism at the DOL for paying so little heed to the provisions of Section 203, particularly with regard to the requirement that employers must report contributions they have made to their employees or others (such as labor consultants) for the purpose of impeding union organizing drives or of undermining the effectiveness of the union they bargain with. The section also includes a requirement that these labor consultants and others receiving such contributions from employers must also report them. The critics contend that these requirements, virtually the only ones in the Act aimed at the antiunion employer and those who aid him, were just thrown in to appease the unions; the provisions were never intended to be enforced, nor have they been. As one union lawyer reported: "I've tried to get the DOL to do something to get consultants to file. I've sent them NLRB affidavits verifying that a certain employer had a labor consultant talk to his employees in an antiunion way, and have asked for copies of the Title II reports listing such 'consultation.' The DOL didn't even answer."

The consensus of DOL officials at all levels is that the agency does very little to enforce Section 203. However, they point out that to expect an employee who has accepted money from an employer to report that he has been paid to take a stand against a union—little short of a bribe—is rather ridiculous. Moreover, Section 204, which exempts attorney-client communications from the Section 203 reporting requirements, in itself makes Section 203 difficult to enforce because many labor consultants are also lawyers. In addition, the courts have held that even if the National Labor Relations Board has brought suit against an employer for committing an unfair labor practice in an area involving the kind of activity covered in Section 203 and has won the case, the DOL cannot use the decision in that case to force the employer to comply with the reporting requirement. Two court decisions have held that, instead, the agency must bring suit on its own initiative.[4] Moreover, two members of the national office staff contended that once a National Labor Relations Board suit has been brought and the employer found guilty, it would be fruitless and needlessly costly for the DOL to bring its own suit. The union is already on notice, has proof of the employer's wrongdoing, and need not rely on a financial report filed with the DOL that will only confirm the evidence it already has. Two other national office staff members disagree. They argue that the Board has jurisdiction only if the unfair labor practice involves a direct threat to the worker's employment, e.g., "You'll be fired if you join the union." The Board has no authority if the activity involves other means of persuasion. From an investigative point of view, no matter how the language of Section 203 is worded— and the DOL would like the Section to state more precisely the nature of the activity to be reported—these staff members told us that the provision will always be a "killer." Employers can argue, and have, that they were merely exercising their rights of free speech. The employer can also plead that reporting such expenditures amounts to self-incrimination.

While the reasons given by agency officials for their inactivity with regard to Section 203 may have merit, there has been so little litigation brought under that section that it is hard to predict what the courts generally would hold if more suits were brought.

---

4. In support of their position, DOL personnel cite *Wirtz v. Ken-Lee, Inc.* (369 F.2d 393 (5th Cir. 1966)), and *Wirtz v. National Welders Supply Company* (254 F. Supp. 62 (W.D.N.C. 1966)).

Spot Audits

Of greatest concern to union spokesmen with regard to the enforcement of Title II and portions of Title V is the DOL national office policy of requesting area offices to conduct a specified number of spot audits every year.[5] In such audits of union books, the DOL uses its Section 601 authority to investigate without prior complaint from a member. The national office's ideal would be to send area office personnel out to audit randomly the books of 0.5 percent of all locals filing LM-3's, 5 percent of all locals and intermediate bodies filing LM-2's, and 20 percent of all parent organizations every year. Actually, that ideal is never realized, and the unions that are randomly audited therefore appear suspect. This is doubly true because some unions are not actually selected at random, but are instead pinpointed because there is suspicion of financial mishandling. This adds to the discomfort of those organizations which are randomly selected, since they are being classed with those that are not above suspicion.

The national office recognizes that it cannot put its full program into operation, but nevertheless assigns each area office a quota of spot audits to be met each year. In fact, area office personnel rarely can manage to meet even those limited demands. If they had the resources, the area office directors would like to meet the quota and even expand the spot audit program to come closer to the ideal figure, on the ground that "there's a lot of hanky-panky going on that we aren't uncovering." The majority of the compliance officers, however, shrink from the very idea of trying to audit the records of a parent union. They regard it as "an impossible task." Moreover, they doubt their own qualifications to do an adequate review of any union's books, since they lack the requisite accounting skills.

In the beginning, the spot audits were conducted whenever area office personnel had the time to make the investigations. Now, however, the DOL has a policy of not conducting an audit of a union's financial records when a union is about to hold an election or when contract negotiations are taking place. While about 80 percent of the local officers now shrug off the spot audit as a mere nuisance, the other 20 percent we talked to still find the experience a disconcerting one. Even those who are not overly disturbed by the spot audits told us that they would much prefer it

---

5. Some personnel in the national office prefer the term "field audits." However, the term we have used was more common among those interviewed.

if, upon completion of an investigation which uncovered no wrongdoing, the DOL would issue a statement indicating that nothing of an irregular nature had been found. One national office DOL spokesman disagreed, saying that if such a statement were issued, more suspicions would be raised, and the members would simply assume that the union officer responsible for keeping the financial records "got away with it." The rest, all area office personnel, told us that if the union officers request such a statement and the area office receives the approval of the national office, the statement will be issued. The national office approval is required, they explained, because of past experience. They told of an instance where the DOL had completed its investigation, had uncovered no wrongdoing, and had issued the requested statement, and then six months later, the FBI received another complaint from two members of the same union concerning misuse of funds by its officers, conducted its own investigation of the records, and found that the officers had mishandled the funds. The union, as it happened, kept two sets of books. As a result of this and similar experiences, the DOL is wary of issuing "clean record" statements. Rather than raising suspicion, those statements could assuage members' concerns or discourage them from challenging genuine wrongdoing.

If the DOL finds in the course of a spot audit that the financial officer's activities are in violation of Section 501(a), the agency then conforms to the requirements of Section 601, under the authority of which it made the investigation, and informs the "interested" parties. Who these parties are depends on the circumstances. The DOL will reveal its findings to other officials of the local union involved, or to officials of the parent organization, in order to give them an opportunity to correct the situation themselves. If it appears that the other local officers already know of the matter (usually because they too were involved in the malpractice), and if the parent union, for political reasons, is reluctant to act, the DOL has at times, we were told, informed other members of the local union so that they would have a basis upon which to file private suit.

One gray area that spot audits have sometimes uncovered troubled seven of those interviewed, labor union officials and DOL personnel alike. That is the practice of "double-dipping," i.e., seeking reimbursement from two sources for carrying out one activity. One example would be the case where the local union officer bills the parent union and his own local for the same travel expenses. Another would be where the officer requests reimbursement from his union for work time lost while carrying out union business when, in fact, he had worked and received wages from his employer. More complex yet is the case where the officer had actually been on union business during the course of his regular shift and been reimbursed by the union but had, on the same day, also worked for his employer on another shift and been compensated. What kind of Title V violation does double-dipping constitute? The answer was that it varies according to the particular circumstance. One has to look at the double-dipper's intent, at whether or not "he was being a pig about it," in order to determine which section of Title V is applicable, Section 501(a) or Section 501(c). It may well be that neither is, in the sense that the union is knowingly making a lost time payment for what is actually a political debt—a way of reimbursing the election committee, for example. If the double-dipper was "just plain greedy"—in one case recounted to us, the man made more money charging the union for lost time than he earned at his job—then the DOL would file Section 501(c) embezzlement and false reporting charges. If the amounts taken were small, on the other hand, the DOL would consider the violation a Section 501(a) case and tell the complaining members to file private suit to recover the funds. We were also told—this time by two local union officers—of a case that involved an officer who had worked both for the union and the company on the same day. In that instance, the complaining member had gone to the Department of Justice rather than to the DOL, and after an FBI investigation, the U.S. attorney had filed Section 501(c) charges. Those who recounted this case felt strongly that the Justice Department had overreacted to what they considered to be at most a minor infraction. We do not know whether this is regular Justice Department practice or an isolated instance, but the DOL's policy in these cases—to consider such activities as Section 501(a) violations—strikes us as the more reasonable one.

On the other hand, a labor lawyer representing a local union told us of instances in which, to his mind, it was the DOL that had overreacted. He mentioned cases in which, upon hearing the complaint and without making any kind of investigation, the DOL determined that the infraction amounted to embezzlement and turned the matter over to the Justice Department. The ensuing FBI investigation had thrown the local union into a panic and thoroughly discredited the officers. It would have been much less frightening, he felt, it the DOL had conducted the investigation under the guise of a spot audit. (Again, these may be isolated instances. He was the only one who mentioned them.)

Section 501(c)

Three members of the DOL national office staff told us that spot audits uncover approximately 8 percent of the Section 501(c) embezzlement cases processed by the DOL or Justice Department. The rest are the result of statements made in the reports of bonding companies or of tips from local officers, from members, or from the parent union. Area office directors said that of the tips, those from the parent union, though not the most numerous, are the most reliable. The parent union knows that a problem exists, but prefers to turn the evidence over to the DOL rather than take action itself. Information from members or local officers has proven less valuable. More often than not, the complainant is planning to run against the incumbents and wants to use the DOL investigation as a campaign issue. If there had been any substance to the complaint, the other officers and members ordinarily would have settled the matter quietly by pressuring the offender to resign. A large majority of the actionable Section 501(c) violations, then, has been uncovered because a particular parent union considered it politically wise to enlist the aid of an outside agency to bring the case to light.

Should the Department of Labor Enforce Section 501(a)?

The suggestion was made by lawyers representing five parent unions that, rather than requiring a member to file private suit, the LMRDA should be amended to empower the DOL to bring suit to enforce Section 501(a). According to the advocates of that amendment, one of the most important goals Congress had in mind in passing the Act was to safeguard union funds. Yet the members, lacking special investigative skills, might not be able to uncover financial malpractices even if they suspected their existence. Moreover, even if they knew of them, either from their own observations or as the result of a DOL spot audit, they might not have the funds to file suit. One lawyer pointed out that, under the 1974 law regulating union pension funds, the DOL is empowered to bring suit against a fund trustee who has mishandled union pension funds, and that those trustees are usually also union officers. Why police the same people one way under the new law and another way under the LMRDA? In almost every instance, the proponents of DOL enforcement of Section 501(a) suggested that the member should retain the option of filing private suit, rather than using the services of the DOL, if he prefers to. That way, if a group of members collected sufficient funds to go to court themselves and won the case, they not only would be doing their union a service but, according to the provisions of Section 501(b),[6] they could also be reimbursed for their legal and other expenses.

Not every proponent of the change favored granting both options. Two of the five lawyers would prefer that the DOL be given exclusive enforcement powers. Their reasoning is that the DOL would weed out the frivolous complaints, some of which the courts, wrongly in their opinion, have considered meritorious. However, the lawyers representing four other unions in our sample disagreed strongly with that proposal, primarily on the ground that the government is already too much involved in union affairs. As far as they are concerned, the DOL uses the investigative authority it already has for the wrong reasons. Said one: "Some of the cases read to me like income tax cases, where they are investigating one thing when they really want to get a guy on something else. Give a little power to somebody with not much brains and that power may well be used wrongly." The lawyers representing the remaining three unions offered no opinion.

Union officers were solidly opposed to the idea of enabling the DOL to enforce Section 501(a). In their eyes, it would "open the door to witch hunts," and the DOL "might be inclined to use the term 'fiduciary responsibility' as an investigative umbrella." Moreover, whether or not an officer is handling union money wisely is a matter of judgment. What if he made what he considered to be a perfectly sound investment, but the DOL thought differently? Even if the investment had been unwise, if he made it in good faith and with the union's best interests in mind, should he be punished for doing what corporate directors do on a daily basis with impunity?

The DOL spokesmen themselves were not overly enthusiastic about the idea of assuming the enforcement responsibility:

Should we be the judges of whether or not they should spend union money to give each member a Christmas turkey?

What if the majority of the members know their money is

---

6. Section 501(b) generally sets forth the procedures to be followed in bringing a Section 501(a) suit.

being spent unwisely and don't care? Should we play the white knight under such circumstances?

We have enough trouble trying to figure out what "adequate safeguards" means in a Title IV situation without getting involved in that mess.

Some also feared that even if the member were given the option of going to court on his own rather than using the DOL's investigatory skills, the majority of the complaints would end up with the DOL. The agency has enough to do already.

Given that the DOL, while it cannot file suit under Section 501(a), can nevertheless investigate Section 501(a) complaints using its Section 601 powers and make the results known, and that, armed with those results, a member can go to court and, if he wins, be reimbursed, we do not think that a change in the statutory language to give the member an additional avenue of relief is necessary.

Impact of Titles II and V

Much of the effect of Titles II and V of the LMRDA is not visible in the language of union constitutions. However, Title V's bonding requirements have now been incorporated into those documents where they were often silent or nonspecific before. In addition, in the union constitutions we studied, the provisions detailing the purposes for which the organizations were established have been broadened to encompass all possible goals. That was done to make sure that all the kinds of expenditures a financial officer is likely to make could be interpreted as serving the objectives of the organization as listed in its constitution, thus reducing the likelihood that such officers could be charged with having violated the fiduciary obligation to the union and its members.[7]

According to a substantial majority of those we interviewed, the reporting requirements of Title II have had a favorable impact, particularly on the record keeping of local unions. Parent organizations kept good records of income and expenditure prior to the Act's passage, but many local unions did not. Now, as one local officer phrased it, "we have a much better set of checks and balances."

---

7. See, for example *Bernard W. McNamara v. Robert Johnston*, 522 F.2d 1157 (7th Cir. 1975), *cert. denied*, 425 U.S. 911 (1976).

When the Act was first passed, many local financial officers had no idea of what records they were to keep, or what information they were to include on the reporting forms. In this area, they were quite willing to request technical assistance from the DOL to learn what to do. Parent unions, too, were inundated with letters and phone calls from their locals, seeking help. In response, those unions prepared and mailed out sample reports and instructive memoranda. Their staffs also conducted educational sessions throughout the country, and visited local union offices that required special assistance. Parent bodies continue to provide these services whenever a newcomer is elected to serve as financial officer of a local. Despite these aids, top union officials from four unions contended that in small local unions, where the financial officer serves in that capacity on a part-time basis, it has become difficult to find candidates willing to run for that office. The work required in keeping the financial records in order is too time consuming, and the potential for liability is too great. If the small local can afford to, it hires a full-time bookkeeper, or pays an accountant a fee to handle the record-keeping chores and to fill out the annual reports required under Title II. If this is not possible, the staff of the parent union (or, less frequently, the intermediate body) often assumes responsibility for keeping the books and filling out the necessary papers. In such cases, the increased workload to the parent body means either that the staff members who are assisting those locals have had to neglect other duties or, more commonly, that the parent organization has had to hire additional staff. To avoid this situation, the parent organization often encourages small locals to merge with one or more others, or to increase dues to cover bookkeeping costs.

Union officials were quick to point out, however, that the reporting requirements of the LMRDA were not the sole reason for urging mergers or local dues increases. Larger locals are more efficient. They can afford to pay the salaries of full-time staff to police contracts more effectively and serve the members' needs more adequately. Thus, the consolidation of small locals into larger units may well have taken place in any event. Moreover, other legislation, such as the 1974 pension reform law and other statutes requiring more careful record keeping, has also played a role in causing locals to consolidate.[8]

8. For a short period prior to passage of the LMRDA, unions were required to keep more careful records because of provisions in the Welfare and Pension Plan Disclosure Act, but none of our interviewees mentioned that statute as a problem.

About 50 percent of the local union officers reported that the Title II reporting requirements and the Section 201(c) provision that officers must make financial records available to members have made the rank and file more knowledgeable concerning union finances.[9] That same 50 percent stated that since passage of the Act there has been a substantial increase in the number of inquiries they receive concerning individual expenses they have authorized. In their unions, members are often aware that the Act gives them the right to see the organization's financial records, although they rarely exercise it. Those who do are usually planning to run against the incumbents in the next election, and are hopeful that a perusal of the records will uncover a useful campaign issue. Sharp questioning of the financial reports distributed at union meetings often is also so motivated. In contrast, the other 50 percent of the local union officers in the sample said that they never have been questioned about financial matters and still are not. They were often quite wistful in relating that information to us, particularly if they had made an especially lucrative investment that they would have been eager to expound in detail—if only members had asked.

The officers told us that opposition candidates often go to the DOL area office to request copies of the reporting forms on file there, to check the figures on those reports against those made available to them at local headquarters. Again, their hope is that they will find a discrepancy that they can use during the course of their campaigns. Opposition candidates are not the only ones who attempt to make use of the reports on file in the DOL offices. The DOL spokesmen told us that employers and rival unions also ask for those reports, and have a particular interest in the figures giving officers' salaries and expense reimbursements. If those figures are high, they are publicized. The reports are also useful to nonunion reform groups. For example, according to Trevor Armbrister, author of *Act of Vengeance*, the LM-2's filed by the United Mineworkers were virtually the sole source of Ralph Nader's information concerning that union's financial malpractices.[10]

---

9. In *Conley v. Steelworkers, Local 1014* (549 F.2d 1122 (7th Cir. 1977)), the court held that if a member has just cause to look at his union's financial records, he has the further right to make copies of them.

10. Trevor Armbrister, *Act of Vengeance* (New York: E. P. Dutton & Co., Inc., 1975), at 57.

Rank and File Members' Views on Title II

Of all aspects of the statute investigated in the survey question-naires, rank and file members were least knowledgeable about their right to look at their union's financial records. Only 66 percent said they did have a right to do so; slightly over 11 percent said they did not; and the other 22 percent said they did not know whether they did or not (appendix G, table 14).

We found this fact somewhat surprising. Not only did a large proportion of the union officers interviewed believe that the members knew they had that right, but the rank and file survey respondents who had specific knowledge of the Act frequently singled out the right to see their union's financial records, together with union officers' fiduciary obligations and the filing of the reports required under Title II, as being the most important tenets of the Act. Moreover, if the members did know their rights under the statute, a number of them considered the impact of Title II greater than that of Title IV: twice as many thought the Act had made it easier to inspect the books as believed the Act had made it less difficult to become a union officer (appendix G, table 22). Nevertheless, even among those respondents, only one third felt that the Act had made inspection of financial records easier, and over half said the Act had made no difference at all.

The majority of the respondents who said that they could not look at their union's books, or that there had been a time when they had wanted to but did not, gave the standard reasons: their own inactivity, or the futility of doing so (30 percent and 28 percent, respectively). Again, specific deterrents—the absence of a right, or denial of access to the books—figured much less prominently (appendix G, table 21).

Interviewees' Opinions of Impact of Title V

The assessment of Title V's impact by those interviewed was less specific than their views on the effectiveness of Title II. When the Act was first passed, the bonding provisions applicable to officers and staff responsible for union finances were a major source of complaint. As originally enacted, Section 502, which specifies that any union official or employee who handles funds or other union property must be bonded, stated that such person was to "be bonded for the faithful discharge of his duties." That language was so broad that surety companies charged extremely high rates in order to protect themselves. Union protests against those costs were vehement and effective: in September of 1965, Congress amended Section 502. As it now reads, the union official or employee "shall be bonded to provide protection against loss by reason of acts of fraud or dishonesty on his part directly or through connivance with others." Surety company charges dropped considerably as a consequence of that language change.

On the whole, the union representatives interviewed found the impact of Title V beneficial. Said one: "It's the strongest point in the Act. When handling money is involved, there is the greatest potential for corruption and for destroying a union. Titles II and V are the only really punitive sections of the statute and they have worked well." These representatives believe that Title V has made most union officials more conscientious and responsible in handling union funds, and has deterred the potential but timid wrongdoer. The determined culprits, however, are as elusive as ever. They stated that they could cite specific examples to prove the last assertion, and in a few instances they even did so.

Virtually all of the parent union officers told us that if their own auditors find something in a local union's financial records that looks suspicious and the sums involved are substantial, they will often inform the DOL and let that agency look into the matter. That saves the parent organization the time and cost of extensive investigation, as well as possible political embarrassment. If the discrepancy is minor, the union prefers to look into the matter on its own, and thereby avoid possible bad publicity. Moreover, when the local officer has been guilty of misappropriating small amounts, there may be extenuating circumstances, such as unforeseen medical expenses, and it would be needlessly cruel to expose the local officer's misdeeds. Whatever the reason, if the amount taken is not large, it makes more sense to the parent union to ask the officer to resign and reimburse the local's treasury as soon as he is financially able to do so than to file charges that would lead to a prison sentence. There is a good deal of logic to that. From his jail cell, the guilty officer can hardly be expected to repay his debt to the union.

Section 504. One section of Title V that does not involve union finances was viewed critically by some of those we interviewed. That is Section 504 ("Prohibition Against Certain Persons Holding Union Office"). By its terms, any person who has been convicted of "robbery, bribery, extortion, embezzlement, grand larceny, burglary, arson, violation of narcotics laws, murder, rape, assault with intent to kill, assault which inflicts grievous bodily injury, or a violation of Title II or III [failure to file, or willfully filing a false, report] of this Act, or conspiracy to commit any such crimes" cannot, without special dispensation from the United States Parole Commission, be a union officer for five years after such conviction, or imprisonment therefor.

Until the 1965 decision in *U.S. v. Brown*,[11] no member or former member of the Communist Party could hold union office until he had terminated that membership for five years. Since then, there has been no legal prohibition against such persons being officers, but in practice most union constitutions state that membership in that party is sufficient grounds for not admitting a person into the union or, if such affiliation is later discovered, for expelling him—thus automatically excluding him from holding office in any event.

Two critics of the language of Section 504 suggested that the list of prohibited activities should be broadened, either to include specific items (e.g., jury tampering and mail fraud), or to encompass all felonies.[12] Two others believe the list should be narrowed. The inclusion of narcotics law violations struck some as too stringent. Moreover, "assault which inflicts grievous bodily injury" can be read to include fist fights and thus, these critics charged, it has no relevance to trade unionists: "You're not administering ladies' croquet." Two additional interviewees thought Section 504 should be deleted from the Act altogether:

Take it out. Let them vote for whoever they want to.

Whatever the guy's done should be a campaign issue.

It's too punitive. What assertive trade unionist, particularly among some minority groups, hasn't been charged with at least one of those crimes by the time he's thirty-five?

All of the proposals for changes or deletion of Section 504 came from either union lawyers or DOL officials. None were made by local union officers or dissidents. Moreover, since our primary focus in this study has been on sections other than Titles II and V, we made no effort to seek out persons who may have been prevented from holding union office because of the provi-

---

11. 381 U.S. 437 (1965).

12. One court has held that the listing is already broader than it might appear, finding that the listing of offenses was meant to be "generic and inclusive, rather than specific and exclusive." *Illario v. Frawley*, 426 F. Supp. 1132 (D.N.J. 1977).

sions of Section 504. We therefore make no recommendations with regard to that section of the Act.

Except for Section 504, which was subject to some criticism as outlined above, the reporting and disclosure provisions of Title II and the restraints imposed by Title V on the handling of union funds were viewed favorably by those interviewed. They claimed that financial records are better kept, that union monies are handled more carefully, and that Titles II and V have had a deterrent effect on at least some potential wrongdoers. Moreover, members have a better idea of how their dues are being spent.

While the public availability of the union financial reports may at times serve as an embarrassment if the information contained in them is publicized in an unfair or sensational manner, the adverse effect is more than offset by the fact that public access to that information has usually served a useful and beneficial purpose.

Chapter VI

Enforcement by the Department of Labor

The following quotation, made by an advocate for dissidents, reflects the thinking of the majority of those interviewed concerning DOL enforcement of the LMRDA:

> If I ever had to choose between good language and good enforcement, I'll take the latter. Now that's obviously not a good equation, but it's the way I really feel about it because I've seen, in the many years around here, I've seen bureaucrats that could wreck good clear language, and I've seen bureaucrats that could make sense out of bad language. That's why I feel the way I do about it.

They stressed that "the Act is paper; the people who enforce it are what make it." It is because there is so much truth in what they said that we have stressed the enforcement of the individual titles as we dealt with them, and why we do so again here.

Enforcement of Title I by the DOL currently is limited to Section 104, which requires that, upon request, a union make available a copy of its latest collective bargaining agreement to any employee affected by that agreement. That requirement has caused no enforcement problems, as far as we could determine. However, the administration of Titles II and V has been more troublesome. Spot audits, the incompleteness of the reporting records, and the lack of activity with regard to the employer/labor consultant reporting requirements are among the criticisms leveled most frequently.

As to Title III, most union representatives reported that they believe the level of enforcement is adequate. A few others, as well as the dissidents and their advocates, deplored the fact that so little is done by the DOL to determine whether a trusteeship has been validly imposed. Even after the eighteen-month period has elapsed, when the burden of proof falls more heavily on the union to prove that continuation of the trusteeship is necessary, the DOL does almost nothing other than to make a routine inquiry of the parent organization, if that.

We have also discussed the use by the DOL of its Section 601 investigatory powers, and the question whether it has the authority to invoke those powers in a pre-election setting. We have concluded that it does, but that the agency's current cautious policy of using those powers very infrequently is warranted.

Enforcement of Title IV—the election provisions of the Act—came in for the greatest amount of critical comment. Dissidents and their advocates believe that the DOL does too little, whereas many union officials reported that the agency interferes too much.

That dichotomy of viewpoint was generally true with regard to remarks concerning the enforcement of the Act as a whole. If a complaining member thought his rights under any section of the Act had been violated, he usually felt that the DOL gave short shrift to his complaint. To the dissidents, the existence of the Act was the important thing. In theory, the DOL should have helped, but the dissidents claimed that, in practice, they had to do everything themselves. The DOL is doing nothing to enforce the Act, as far as they are concerned. Many union officials disagree—the DOL is doing something to enforce the statute. The problem is not inaction but rather the wrong action. Enforcement is "supertechnical," petty, and superficial. Those in charge harass the honest union officer, and sidestep their real responsibility, to root out the dangerous and corrupt. There, according to these critics, the DOL moves too slowly; witness the Mineworkers' case and the long-awaited investigation of the Teamsters' Central States Pension Fund.[1] Or, again according to the critics, they move not at all; witness the elections that are still stolen, the records that are still falsified, the embezzlements that the critics themselves uncover, and the trusteeships that are still wrongfully imposed and continued, unquestioned, for years.

To about 35 percent of the agency's critics, the culprits are the area office personnel, particularly those who carry out the actual investigations. They are usually young, inexperienced, and untrained. They cannot read financial records well enough to catch falsifications, and cannot investigate elections meaningfully. Moreover, they are totally unfamiliar with trade union practices. That is why they pounce on bookkeeping errors, concentrate on techni-

---

1. DOL spokesmen counter that, as previously noted, the Mineworkers' case was turned over to the Justice Department in mid-December of 1964. As to the Teamsters' investigation, there was some question whether the conduct involved constituted a Title V violation. When the DOL did begin its investigation of the Teamsters' pension fund, it did so under the pension reform law, not the LMRDA.

calities, and bewilder the union members. That is also why the clever crook can so easily elude them.

To approximately 45 percent of the detractors, the DOL's top policy makers are at fault. These men are political appointees, ever mindful of who contributes to campaign funds. No matter how thoroughly the field offices do their jobs, if their recommendations might result in action that would be politically harmful, their advice goes unheeded. Furthermore, some of the top policy makers are identified with a particular union or group of unions, based on past relationships. In such a case, "you can't expect an honest count. A conflict of interest can't be avoided."

The other 20 percent of the critics place the blame not on individuals in the DOL but on the role into which they are forced in trying to administer the Act. As one advocate for dissidents described it, the DOL has a contradictory assignment:

> On the one hand it's supposed to get along with all the labor officials, cooperate with them, etc., in the name of the public's interest in preserving industrial peace. On the other hand, they are supposed to support the rights of men in a union who are trying to throw those same labor officials out. It can't possibly fulfill those two assignments because in its role as a protector of union democracy, the DOL is in the most sensitive area of internal union relations. For a member to criticize his union is an unpardonable crime. You could do anything else—criticize them outside—but to threaten them inside their own base of power is absolutely intolerable. That is the root of all their strength, influence, everything. So, the DOL simply cannot do the job.

Let us consider the three alleged roots of the problems with enforcement: the area office personnel; the top DOL policy makers; and the dual role the agency must play.

Area Office Personnel

Well over half of the labor spokesmen interviewed who had come in contact with area office personnel spoke quite favorably of them. Adjectives such as "conscientious," "helpful," and "fair" were common. Indeed, the majority considered them much better than their Washington-based superiors in terms of understanding the internal workings of a labor union and in attempting to deal with problems realistically. According to these spokesmen, too many of the national office staff "don't know if they're dealing with a labor union or the national zoo." Moreover, they contended, the DOL staff who are "close to the top" try to impress the top officials by making the politically expedient decision, rather than enforcing the Act honestly. The area office personnel, on the other hand, were frequently described as much less political and far more professional.

Nevertheless, there were a few who much preferred the national office personnel. One labor lawyer told us that he dealt with area office people as little as possible on the ground that "it's only at the highest levels that you can get any kind of frank discussion of your case: where you stand, what alternatives might be available to you, and what they plan to do."

Those who view the area office personnel unfavorably do so because they consider the people who do the actual initial investigations, the compliance officers, to be too young, inexperienced, and untrained, and without any comprehension of how a trade union actually functions. In checking on this with area office directors, we were told that it is practice in all offices that when a person is hired as a compliance officer he receives on-the-job training from more experienced personnel. During that training period, he is given only simple assignments (e.g., contacting unions whose financial reports were not received on time) and is always accompanied by a seasoned compliance officer when he is assigned to his initial election investigations. During his training period, he is also sent to a week-long seminar on the labor movement given by institutions such as the University of Wisconsin or Cornell University, as well as to one of the two-week training sessions which the DOL conducts in various parts of the country, designed to develop investigative skills and interview techniques. Each area office also has an extensive library containing material concerning the American labor movement, with which the new employee is expected to become familiar. He does not, however, receive special instruction on how to read union financial records. He is expected to develop that skill during the course of his on-the-job training period. How well a compliance officer is trained and the attitude he develops toward the labor movement depend in large measure on the caliber and outlook of the area office director under whom he serves. Personalities and conscientiousness differ, of course, but two knowledgeable and experienced national office staff members reported that the outlook of any area office director depends at least to some extent on his personal reaction to the national office's rejection of his recommendations. Some directors become apathetic and require only the minimum of effort from then on. Others shrug off rejections as "part of the job," do not take them personally, and continue the work of the office at the same pace as before. Still others become hyperactive. One DOL national office spokesman noted that the differences in levels of activity among the area offices were especially apparent during the course of the investigation of the Mineworkers' election. The reports, sent in for review by the national office from the various area offices involved, differed significantly in quality and thoroughness.

We can only conclude from the foregoing that both those who reported good experience with the area office staff and those who reported incompetence at that level are probably right.

Department of Labor Policy Makers

The first question that arises in this section is who *are* the real makers of DOL policy: those who hold their positions through political appointment, or the career civil servants at the national office who report to the appointees? We asked that question of a half dozen long-time DOL officials, past and present, and a dozen additional close observers, primarily labor lawyers, who have been concerned with the enforcement of the LMRDA since the law was passed and who thus have seen how it has operated under various administrations. We chose these individuals not only because of their long experience, but also because they appeared to us to be unusually perceptive, knowledgeable, and candid. The over-all conclusion of those "DOL-watchers," was that the everyday decisions are left to career civil servants. Key decisions, on the other hand, are made by the Solicitor and the Assistant Secretary for Labor-Management Relations. In an unusually sensitive situation (e.g., the Jennings-Carey election), the Secretary of Labor himself might become involved—but only then. Ordinarily, according to the DOL-watchers, the Assistant Secretary, with the advice of the Solicitor, is the really key figure. Indeed, in their experience, it is when a new Assistant Secretary has been installed that major policy changes have taken place.

If the DOL-watchers' assessment is accurate, then the question of whether or not partisan politics enters into the decision-making process becomes relevant. Depending on how much influence political considerations do, in fact, have, that factor might also have some bearing on the argument that a complaining member should have the right to file private suit even if he already has access to the services of the DOL. In a circumstance where the administration in the White House is beholden to the complaining member's union, that member's chances of seeing justice done might be greater if he did not need to rely exclusively on the DOL.

We again turned to the DOL-watchers to ask whether key decisions were politically motivated and, if so, how great an influence partisan politics exerted. They all contended that political considerations played a part. As one union lawyer said, "The White House can stop an investigation if it wants to. Big contributors can get 'a fix.'" The Nixon-Fitzsimmons relationship was the one most often cited. However, when we asked for specific examples of cases that had been buried because of political considerations alone, they could not supply us with any. There were always other factors involved in those cases that could have influenced the final decision.

Thus, all that can be said is that it is widely believed that partisan politics do play a role in key decisions reached by top DOL policy makers. However, no hard evidence in support of that allegation was cited. One would think that politics could play only a limited role—favorable treatment for political reasons to a union or unions can only be given as long as it does not violate the law or alienate other potential contributors and voters.

What of the allegation that past associations with certain unions have an influence on DOL policy makers? Do the top officials play favorites? Here the record appears to be mixed. We were told, and given specifics in this case, that some DOL officials have lent a more favorable ear to union officials with whom, through former contacts, they had established a warm personal relationship than they did to officials of other unions. It was alleged both by the DOL-watchers and various DOL staff members at all levels that some DOL executives went so far as to "pass the word" to area office personnel to "go easy" on their pet organizations. Yet when the cases in the annual Compliance Reports were checked, the pet unions named to us were ordinarily the recipients of some share of the investigations that took place while their alleged special guardian was in office. At least, then, if there were a "go easy" policy, it did not mean "don't go at all." Here again, political expediency dictates that favoritism, if it exists, can be displayed only up to a point. Thereafter, it becomes a political liability.

The Dual Role of the Department of Labor

As previously noted, some of those interviewed said that, as regards enforcement of the LMRDA, the DOL is in an untenable position. It must foster the cause of industrial peace by promoting the stability of labor organizations while, at the same time, it is charged with protecting the individual member's right to challenge the authority of his union if it believes those rights have been abridged. In carrying out the latter assignment, the DOL runs the risk that the member's challenge may cause instability within the union. In other words, the DOL is being asked to do two things, and those two things may come into conflict. Four DOL spokesmen in the national office agreed that the two tasks were incompatible; being both the intermediary between management and labor and the union policeman is unfeasible. Moreover, it is true, according to them, that some decisions have been made for political reasons, but the worst thing about the situation is that more are considered to have been so motivated than actually have been. Carrying out the two conflicting functions has often led to unfounded suspicion.

A third of the labor union spokesmen in the sample saw no conflict of interest. Such a perception presumes that the DOL acts as labor's ally and, as one said, "that hasn't been true since [former Secretary of Labor Frances] Perkins." To them, the DOL has forgotten its role as the keeper of industrial peace. Many dissidents and their advocates, on the other hand, believed that that is the only role the DOL remembers. Over half of those went further and contended that the DOL should not try to play both parts. It should concentrate solely on protecting individual rights. Unions are now big business and can look after themselves.

Still, 20 percent of those we interviewed did believe that the DOL has two incompatible functions. Because it does, and because of the political pressures that inevitably flow from trying to fulfill both, over two thirds of these respondents thought that the Act should be administered elsewhere, or that at least additional safeguards should be imposed. One parent union officer, for example, suggested creating a national public review board, a neutral body that could oversee the DOL's decisions and take corrective action where necessary. In his view, the board appointments should be for life, "to get politics out of it." Others, primarily advocates for dissidents, suggested placing the administration of the Act with another existing agency, such as the Department of

Justice or the National Labor Relations Board. Four national office
DOL officials said that they wished that Congress had created an
entirely new government agency, autonomous of any existing one,
whose only charge would have been to administer the LMRDA. If
that had happened, they would not be in the difficult position in
which they now sometimes find themselves. Given a separate
agency for the LMRDA, the DOL could be more receptive to
unions' suggestions, as it theoretically should be. The new agency, on the other hand, could have pursued enforcement of the Act
single-mindedly, devoting its entire attention to protecting members' rights. These observers went on to say, however, that by now
the creation of such an agency is highly unlikely. The public has
become weary of the myriad of government agencies with which
they must already contend. One national office DOL official who
at one time had thought a separate agency should administer the
Act stated that, upon reflection, he had changed his mind. He has
concluded that a new agency, without the expertise and knowledge concerning labor relations that the DOL has, would end up
being an investigatory agency because it would not know what
else to be. In that event, unions really would be harassed.

Another idea suggested, primarily by union lawyers, was that
either the language of the current Act be amended or new legislation be enacted setting forth minimum standards that unions
should follow to comply with the Act's intent; and if the unions
followed those guidelines and, in addition, created their own public review boards to ensure that the new minimum standards were
met, the DOL would no longer have jurisdiction over them. The
complaining member would go to the public review board instead. Appeals from the decisions of such boards would be subject
to judicial review or—an idea proposed by a parent union officer—
to review by a national "super" public review board appointed by
the government. Appointments to the unions' public review
boards would be for fixed terms, to ensure that an irate union
president could not discharge the board members if their decisions displeased him. The proponents of this idea pointed out that
unions should welcome such legislation because it would give
them a choice between regulating themselves or continuing to be
regulated by the government. If they opted for their own boards,
it could save the time and cost involved in the investigations and
litigation initiated by the DOL.

Aside from the original proponents of the super review board,
the interviewees to whom we mentioned the proposal showed

little enthusiasm for it. It would just be another superstructure. Moreover, how could one be assured that a national public review board would remain neutral? Would its members not be as subject to political pressure as the DOL now is?

As to the idea of giving unions the option of accepting basic standards and, concurrently, establishing their own public review boards, the reaction was generally negative. One union lawyer thought that the idea would help the image of those unions which did create their own boards—"especially with liberals and Congressmen." Another said it might pressure some unions, whose disciplinary procedures are shams, into making those procedures meaningful. But it would not be helpful for most unions. It would just represent a further loss of control over their own internal affairs.

The whole concept that labor unions require public review boards came under fire. Why single out labor unions as the only organizations in this country in need of perpetual parole boards? Moreover, a tyrannical or corrupt union leader could easily select a complacent board that would serve only as window dressing and to rubber stamp the leader's actions. That would leave the members of those unions that really require policing even more vulnerable than they are now.

Even the few parent union officers who personally would like the idea of establishing such a board in their own unions said that the members of their organizations would never stand for it. The members believe that their own union's legal staff represents too much outside interference as it is. They would be appalled at the thought of what they termed "yet another bunch of funny-looking Washington lawyers" having a voice in their affairs.

The proposal to move enforcement of the Act to another existing agency also fell on deaf ears. The vast majority of those who expressed any opinion could see no advantage to such a transfer. The Justice Department knows too little about trade union problems; the National Labor Relations Board is overloaded as it is. One union lawyer with past experience on the Board staff was emphatic that the Act should not be enforced by that agency: "I wouldn't let the NLRB administer my *house!*" Despite its faults, they contended, the DOL still has the most expertise. A change could only be for the worse.

We agree with those who contended that the establishing of a new government agency either to act as the DOL's conscience or to replace the DOL as the administrator of the LMRDA is politically unfeasible. Moreover, the courts have already in effect assumed the role of guardian of the DOL's morals, so that an additional agency of that nature is unnecessary. We see no advantage, and the possibility of some disadvantage, to transferring the administration of the Act to another existing agency.

As to the idea of basic standards coupled with a public review board, we have already indicated, in the course of our discussion of Title IV, that we favor the establishment of basic standards and guidelines for the conduct of elections. Thus we can hardly quarrel with that part of the proposal. We do, however, see merit in the argument that the leaders in those unions which really require outside scrutiny could use a pliable public review board as a screen to hide behind. The only way to prevent that situation from occurring would be to establish a new government agency to assume the role of general public review board watchdog, or to assign that task to an existing agency, such as the DOL. Thus, if the aim of the proposal to have unions establish their own review boards is to have less government interference in the internal affairs of unions, that purpose would not necessarily be served.

A Conflict of Interest?

How strongly is a conflict of interest felt by any but the highest DOL policy makers? To find out, we asked the career civil servants both in Washington and in the field how they viewed their role in enforcing the LMRDA. We found that the staff members in the national office were conscious that their dual function could cause a conflict, whereas those in the field saw the two roles as going hand-in-hand.

It would be natural that the national office personnel would view the question of dual responsibility in terms of conflict, since they would be more aware that the two roles do now often clash. They would have firsthand knowledge of the political or other pressures exerted on top officials in given situations and would have watched those officials try to cope with the attendant problems. In the field, the people know that those problems and pressures do exist, but they know it only remotely. Their concern is with promoting union democracy and, as they view it, thereby increasing labor-management harmony. Typical of their attitude was the statement made by one area office director: "Everything I do is based on the theory that improving democracy strengthens the union, by legitimizing the leadership and dissolving factions. Companies don't know with whom to deal as representatives of the members if there is noisy, unresolved factionalism."

In only one area office we visited did the compliance officers appear to view their role solely in terms of the protection of the rights of the rank and file members. They were aware of, and followed, the DOL policy of not auditing a union's books just before an election or during contract negotiations, but had never thought about why that policy existed. When we asked about the role of the DOL in promoting labor-management peace, it was clear that the idea of that function had never occurred to them before. Upon reflection, they decided that they knew only their "own little niche" in a much larger picture. In every other field office we visited, however, everyone interviewed recognized the broader aspects of their assignments.

The DOL officials thus stress their neutrality. They don't keep records on the outcome of supervised reruns because they do not care who wins. They identify with neither the incumbent nor his opposition. Their concern is that the members be able to exercise their rights freely, not who wins or loses. They feel a responsibility to "help the little guy who can't help himself, who has no place to go." At the same time, if that little guy turns out to be, as one compliance officer said, "a grouser who is trying to use the DOL to get at his union, I have no patience with him."

Those in the field were asked if they thought they currently have enough staff to do a thorough job and, if not, what they would do differently if they did have additional personnel. As noted, the area office directors stated that they would use added staff in the investigation of elections and to do more spot audits. Many have a further desire to implement a stronger technical assistance program, especially in connection with union elections. They perceive the need for such a program, much as we do. Most election problems, except for outright fraud, could, in their opinion, be avoided if unions knew how to establish better election procedures. The technical violations the DOL finds are of just enough magnitude at the present time to raise the suspicions of the opposition. If such violations could be eliminated or at least reduced, unions could avoid most of the election protests and reruns they now must cope with. This, in turn, would serve to fulfill the DOL's other function, that of promoting industrial peace.

Moreover, if the agency also were to give technical assistance to members and officers so that they understood both their rights and their obligations under Title I, the agency would discharge its obligation both to the unions and to the individual members more fully.

In summary, what currently may appear to be a conflict to top DOL policy makers could well be resolved, or at least minimized over time, if the agency would share its expertise more widely.

Chapter VII

Over-all Impact of the Act

This chapter first concentrates on the impact of the enactment of the statute—i.e., what has the existence of the Act meant, in and of itself, in terms of the internal operation of labor unions? We follow that evaluation with a special section on a topic which we wish to highlight: our findings concerning the effect of the Act on the collective bargaining process.

Opinions of Interviewees

Almost every union spokesman in the sample claimed that the Act has made his organization more expensive to administer, with a consequent need to increase individual members' dues. Many cited the increased expenses the unions now have—legal fees, accountants' fees, mailing charges, election rerun costs. All parent unions engaged lawyers prior to passage of the Act, as did many intermediate bodies, but they now have a much larger legal staff than they did before 1959. Except for the largest of the local unions, which also retained counsel before the LMRDA, most locals had much less need for legal assistance than they now do. If they required help in the past, they could usually count on receiving it from the parent union's lawyers. Now, only the smallest of the locals contacted do not retain the services of counsel. The same pattern is discernible with regard to engaging accountants.

Nevertheless, while these spokesmen pointed to the increased need for specialists' advice, they placed only part of the blame on LMRDA. The Taft-Hartley Act (particularly since the *Vaca v. Sipes* decision[1],) the Welfare and Pension Plan Disclosure Act, the civil rights legislation, and the 1974 union pension fund reform law contributed substantially too.

The cost of mailing out election notices has been previously mentioned as constituting a particularly onerous burden for the small local union on a very limited budget. The financial drain of rerunning an election however, falls equally upon large and small unions—the larger the organization, the higher the cost. One local

---

1.   386 U.S. 171 (1967).

officer whose union uses an accounting firm to oversee its elections explained that the cost of hiring that firm is more than offset by the savings made, in terms of money and internal stability, in that it spares the union the costs and headaches of a rerun. He also added, however, that if an election required rerunning, "so be it." The extra costs would then be justified.

Each section of the statute has had the effect of sharpening and clarifying the unions' constitutional language and of making officers more cautious about observing the intent behind the provisions. This same claim, with regard to the officers' increased caution, was made by many with regard to the Act as a whole. One parent union officer remarked: "Over-all, it has caused unions to be more careful. It has underscored the officers' responsibility towards the members in terms of procedures, money handling, and lines of behavior."

In addition, according to a few interviewees, the statute has changed the relationship between parent union and subordinate bodies. Whether that change, from the parent union's vantage point, was good or bad varied with the union. In unions in which parent union officials had earlier been autocratic in dealing with their locals, those officials now feel somewhat frustrated because they must be more responsive to local challenges to their authority. Moreover, in such unions, if the top officials oversee contract negotiations, they also feel greater pressure to drive a hard bargain than they once did. On the other hand, in some unions the balance of power has shifted in the other direction. In those, local union leaders formerly paid slight heed to the advice offered by parent union officials. Now they willingly and quickly seek guidance from the parent union in order not to run afoul of the law. Moreover, such local union officers are more conscientious in processing their members' grievances than they once were, knowing that they must be so in order to remain in office.

To approximately 20 percent of the parent union officers and their counsel, the local leaders' increased responsiveness to the members has had an adverse influence in that the responsiveness amounts to immobilization on the part of some marginal local union leaders: "They're paranoid—afraid to move." Virtually everyone we spoke to, pointing specifically to the well-publicized activities of the International Brotherhood of Teamsters, believed that in an organization as powerful and—in their view—potentially dangerous as that one, the leadership, at whatever level, has been affected very little by the statute. Yet even that union, they conceded, has had to develop internal appellate procedures to protect itself against members' complaints to the DOL or the courts.

One knowledgeable academician, while conceding that "old-time bosses have to be more wary of the shrewd dissident than they used to be," still believes that the Act "does not really disturb what goes on within unions, as a practical matter." To him, if the statute had had a meaningful impact, "you'd see more public-review-board type organizations being established by the unions. They'd really try to clean house themselves, rather than have the DOL intervene—and they haven't." He also stated that the law was not really designed to give a meaningful voice to the individual worker, and that he does not believe it has. Over-all, he thought the Act's impact had been slight.

The individual worker would agree only up to a point. Everyone we interviewed who has either sought to challenge entrenched leaders by opposing them in an election or by exposing internal corruption, or who has closely observed others making such an attempt, agreed on one point: the Act itself has meant nothing, unless a member has been willing to use the mechanisms it provides. "It has enabled those who care to lay the groundwork. Once you make a start somewhere it builds. You establish the principle for the next guy and it makes it a little easier each time. So eventually it will have an impact." The Act, then, created a climate favorable to those who wished to assert themselves. But the willingness to do so still remains an act of courage:

> By and large, for the average, run-of-the-mill, poor bastard in the shop who has a grievance, the Act doesn't mean too much, because he can't afford to hire a lawyer and the Labor Department generally tries to get rid of him. What the Act has done is, where you have an absolutely terrific guy who has something on the ball and is able to use it and fight his way tooth and nail—a really sharp shooter—he is able to survive. Or, if he does not survive, he is able to give them a damn good fight for their money. And they will think twice about the next guy like that.

Each title has generally had a favorable impact on the internal structure and operation of the labor unions covered and the same holds true of the Act's over-all effect. The enactment of the statute did not cause a revolution, by any means, but then in most unions a revolution was uncalled for.

In the overwhelming majority of the unions studied, the changes made to comply with the Act were important and have led to more democratic procedures within those organizations, but the changes were not dramatic. Even in the few unions in which substantial reforms were called for, a certain amount of progress has been made, and the Act is now there if the members of those unions wish to implement further changes.

The single most important impact of the Act arises from the fact that it exists. It serves as the legal foundation upon which an aggrieved member can build. It does, however, still require that a member have the courage to do so.

The Impact of the Act on Collective Bargaining

It is sometimes contended that the LMRDA has impeded responsible collective bargaining. For example, in describing the increased frequency with which union members have, since the 1960s, been refusing to ratify contracts, an article in the July, 1975, issue of *Fortune* noted that if union leaders were "too timid or statesmanlike" in bargaining, "they faced the danger of soon ceasing to be union leaders. Unions were now required to be more democratic: the Landrum-Griffin Act, passed in 1959, had mandated certain minimum standards for elections and was increasingly invoked by the losers in crooked elections (they could get redress from the Labor Department.)"[2]

In an earlier article in the January 10, 1971, issue of the *Los Angeles Times*, the employers the reporter had interviewed had said much the same thing. Employers generally had favored passage of the Act because they thought irresponsible union leaders had too much power over the rank and file. It was because of those omnipotent leaders, they believed, that they were faced with unreasonable contract demands and unnecessary strikes. They thus favored the idea that unions be more democratic because leaders would then have to be more responsive to the members' real desires and be more tractable. Now, however, the article went on, employers are complaining that unions are too democratic. It is now the rank and file members who are unreasonable and, because of the Act, the leaders are afraid to stand up to them for fear that, if they do, they will lose the next election. Therefore, the article concludes, employers can no longer count on the union officers to persuade the members to accept the contract terms that

---

2. Irwin Ross, "How to Tell When the Unions Will be Tough," *Fortune* (July 1975), at 102.

they and those leaders have mutually agreed upon.[3] Note that implicit in the employers' yearning for the "bad old days" is the assumption that in those days the union leaders did not need to worry about the outcome of the next election—they knew they could always steal it if necessary.

The majority of those who criticize the effect of the Act on collective bargaining indicated that it has made the officers too responsive to the will of the membership because they fear the outcome of the next election if they are not. But some laid the blame on court interpretations of the provisions of Title I, particularly those dealing with free speech rights. In these critics' minds, the courts have stripped the officers of the power to deal effectively with the machinations of a vocal dissident minority.[4]

Interestingly enough, the *Los Angeles Times* article and the *Fortune* piece make the employers' reaction to the Act appear too monolithic, at least when viewed in comparison with the answers we received from a sample of management representatives. Approximately 80 percent of those who had an opinion did not see the Act as a major factor, or indeed even a contributing one, except tangentially, to account for the increased number of times that members refuse to ratify the contract terms. The allegation that the Act has somehow had an adverse influence on collective bargaining, they said, was at best overinflated and actually just served as a useful crutch for labor leaders. The Act could have a tangential effect, however, in that union officers had been making this charge against it for so long that they now believe the allegation themselves. The other 20 percent of the management representatives contacted did see the Act as the culprit, but when pressed to give some evidence or examples to substantiate that claim, they could not do so.

We asked the eighty-four practitioners interviewed—those actually involved in negotiations—whether or not they thought the Act had had any impact, for good or ill, on the collective bargaining process.[5] To our surprise, almost 50 percent of them had

3. Harry Bernstein, "Union Democracy: A Vigorous Activism," *Los Angeles Times* (January 10, 1971), Sec. G, at 1–2.
4. National Commission for Industrial Peace (David L. Cole, chairman), *Report and Recommendations* (Washington, D.C.: Executive Office of the President, 1975) at 9. The commission noted the results of a tripartite study made in 1969 by lawyers conversant with the construction industry which also focused upon Title I's adverse impact on collective bargaining.
5. We posed this question to all persons interviewed, but are concerned here with only the responses of those who are actually involved in the collective bargaining process.

thought so little about the question that they were unwilling to venture an opinion. Of those who had a firm view on the matter, just over 45 percent thought the Act had had an effect on collective bargaining relationships, and just under 55 percent thought it had had none.

The fact that just under 50 percent of the practitioners had not thought about the question sufficiently to want to venture a firm opinion may be significant in itself. (That figure, incidentally, includes a small group—12 percent of the total responses—who answered "maybe.") It is telling that so high a percentage of those directly involved in the collective bargaining process had not pondered the question before. One could conclude that to most of them, at least, the Act's impact must have been minimal.

Of the 45 percent who thought the Act had had an impact, the majority believed that its influence had been adverse, though, interestingly enough, almost a third of them believed its effect had been favorable. There follows a summary of the opinions of those who thought the Act had affected the collective bargaining process adversely:

> Just under 31 percent put at least some blame on the *Salzhandler* decision, although they also usually added that fear of losing the next union election was an additional factor. (This view was also expressed by 20 percent of the "maybe-and-if-so-adverse" group.)

> The rest of the practitioners who thought the Act's effect detrimental put the blame squarely on Title IV. To almost 40 percent of them, fear of losing the next election was the major factor in making officers too responsive to the rank and file, and consequently less statesmanlike during contract negotiations.

> Approximately 30 percent of the respondents in this group, all local union officers, while agreeing that fear of losing elections was a key factor, placed primary blame for the adverse effect on the fact that the Act limited local officers to three-year terms. Because of such short terms, one said, "I'm running all the time. Contract changes that might be beneficial in the long run just aren't made because they'd be campaign fodder before the benefit became evident." Said another, "Because of [the three-year limit], we're too conscious of elections. You'd better believe you've got your eye on the election. If a contract is coming up in a unit with 500 members in it, boy, you try your damnedest to satisfy them. It's 'hey, guys, what do you want?' "

The 30 percent of responding practitioners who considered the Act's impact on collective bargaining to have been a favorable one thought in terms of increased officer responsiveness to the wishes of the members they serve, and considered that to be a point in the Act's favor. One parent union lawyer summed up that point of view very well when he said:

> If what is meant is that Landrum-Griffin has created a climate whereby workers get the idea that somehow they have a right to vote on things, that is fine. That is what the labor movement is all about. And if it inhibits some officers and they feel they are inhibited or that the deals they make won't be ratified because the workers get the idea that they have some rights, that's too bad about 'em.

An advocate for dissidents made an interesting additional point:

> One of the issues raised by union lawyers in some of these cases has been the argument that if you enforce the Act you will bring about more militant labor bosses. In some respects there may be merit in that. They are talking about unions in which you might find this, unions in which the membership has a plug stuck over it; that is, where there has been rage and frustration building up over a long time. If you can keep that rage and frustration bottled up and continue to keep the union tractable for the employer, sooner or later that rage has got to come out of there. I should think that from the point of view of some policy maker who wouldn't want unions to be militant, he still would have to conclude that it is better to have that rage express itself by democracy within the union than to wait until the whole thing blows up. A crooked union doesn't really help anybody.

A management representative said virtually the same thing, although he was talking specifically about the current upheaval in the Mineworkers' union. The long years of autocratic rule, in his view, are largely responsible for the present leadership's problems.

As to the point that the local union officers made with regard to shorter terms, one parent union official argued that shorter terms were for the good: "More frequent elections make for more responsible officers, and therefore probably more responsible collective bargaining." This argument was partially echoed by a local union officer who did not want to venture an opinion on the effect of the Act on collective bargaining. He, like the other local union officers cited, wanted a longer term—four years rather than three—but he stressed that legislatively-mandated limits were imperative. Without them, a popular officer could persuade his constituency to vote for a change in the bylaws that would permit him to stay in office for life. This, he felt, would be clearly wrong.

The 55 percent of the responding practitioners who were willing to make a flat statement that the Act had had no impact whatever on collective bargaining strongly disagreed with the argument that it made union officers less responsible during contract negotiations for fear their members would reject the contract terms they had negotiated. Their views are best summarized by the following quotations:

> Either an officer is responsible or he isn't—and that's always been true.
>
> I don't even understand the argument. If the contract is no good, why should the membership be forced to accept it?
>
> That's a cop-out for employers.
>
> That's the union's conventional wisdom. It doesn't mean a damned thing.

The most frequent response was some variation of the first quotation—a capable officer would be able to cope with whatever protests might arise, and always had been.

All agreed that it seemed more difficult to sell a contract now than it once had been, but they attributed that to other factors— "general economic and political unrest," "the general atmosphere," "the antiestablishment tenor of the times." Or, as one put it, "the Act didn't make the times; it's a product of them."

In summary, then, it appears from the practitioners' responses that the fear that the Act would impede responsible collective bargaining has been at best exaggerated.[6] To bolster the argument that the existence of the statute has had such an effect, it would be necessary to demonstrate that there has been more unrest and dissatisfaction within American labor unions than, say, on the college campuses or within other economic and political organizations of this nation which have no such legislation covering them. A quick perusal of the daily newspapers clearly shows that to be a difficult task.

This being the case, why did the employers interviewed by *Fortune* and the *Los Angeles Times* express such criticism of the Act's impact on collective bargaining, and why has that criticism

---

6. On this point, see also Odewahn & Krislov, *Contract Rejections: Testing the Explanatory Hypothesis*, XII INDUS. REL. 289, 294 (1973).

so often been expressed by other management representatives? One management representative to whom we posed that question suggested that those employers, as well as labor leaders critical of the Act's impact on collective bargaining, are engaging in unwarranted nostalgia. They are now claiming that they could once win approval of contract terms less favorable to the rank and file than those that members now reject. In fact, he said, that has never been true.

An academician had a different explanation. In his view, the employer representatives probably do see a short-run relationship between bargaining difficulties, increases in contract rejection, and the Act. Employers find it easier to deal with an authoritarian organization than with a democratic one. Authoritarian unions, like dictatorial governments, make decisions quickly and, when they find it convenient, stick to them. Democratic unions—again like their government counterparts—are slow to make decisions, move ahead by fits and starts, and at times even appear to behave irrationally. Truly democratic organizations are thus more difficult to deal with, at least in the short run. What the employers are really faced with are the intangible problems always inherent in negotiating with democratic institutions. In the long run, however, a labor movement that is both responsive and responsible strikes a balance that is in the best interests of employer, union, and member alike.

Epilogue

Throughout this study, we have indicated what criticisms were leveled at the LMRDA in terms of its effectiveness in fostering internal union democracy. Such criticism focused on the statutory language of the Act itself, as interpreted either by the courts or the DOL, as well as on the nature of the enforcement of the Act by the DOL. In a number of instances, amendments to the statute were suggested as a means of correcting alleged inadequacies. In the course of this work, we have summarized the arguments for and against each of those suggested amendments and have stated our own opinions with regard to them. In the main, we have concluded that the suggested changes in language are either unnecessary or unwise. Either the present language of the statute already appears to permit what its critics believe it does not, or the suggested amendment, in our opinion, would not serve the purpose of safeguarding individual members' rights any more adequately than they are now protected.

However, in two instances we have concluded that if Congress were to determine that it should make changes in the language of the statute, strong consideration should be given to two amendments that were proposed. The first would broaden the Act's coverage to include all public employee organizations. The second would give opposition candidates the right not only to inspect the union's membership list but to possess the list itself.

Other recommendations we made to the DOL were intended to correct deficiencies in DOL enforcement practices and procedures in its role as chief administrator of the Act as now written. Some of them relate to what can be classified as housekeeping matters, such as the need for closer agency scrutiny of financial and other records received and more diligent efforts to communicate effectively with those who seek guidance, both within and outside the agency. Others would have the DOL place greater emphasis on offering technical assistance to union representatives, as well as to individual rank and file members.

Subsequent to the filing of our report with the DOL, some procedural changes were made in conformity with our recommendations; other changes are planned, once time and money permit. For example, a recent change in DOL policy encourages agency personnel in certain instances to play a larger role in serving in an advisory capacity and observing procedures prior to a parent union election. This new policy provides at least a partial remedy for a deficiency in enforcement policy that we focused upon, and should help to prevent the necessity of rerunning parent union elections where the violations involve technicalities rather than malicious intent. The Secretary of Labor has created a permanent unit within the Labor-Management Services Administration to provide such technical assistance to union officials charged with the conduct of major union elections, when such officials request its help. That unit's work should reduce costs both to unions and to the public.

One additional suggestion was made, stating that the issuance of a supplement to the 1962 report to the Congress with regard to the effectiveness of Title III would be in order. The agency rejected that recommendation, however, on the ground that such a report could be issued only at congressional request.

Appendices

Labor-Management Reporting and Disclosure Act of 1959, As Amended

[Revised text[1] showing in bold face new or amended language provided by Public Law 89—216, as enacted September 29, 1965, 79 Stat. 888]

AN ACT

ɔ provide for the reporting and disclosure of certain financial transactions and administrative practices of labor organizations and employers, to prevent abuses in the administration of trusteeships by labor organizations, to provide standards with respect to the election of officers of labor organizations, and for other purposes.

ℰ it enacted by the Senate and House of Representatives of the United States of America in Congress assembled, That this Act may be cited as the "Labor-Management Reporting and Disclosure Act of 1959."

---

[1]Public Law 257, 86th Cong. (73 Stat. 519–546), as amended by Public Law 216, 89th Cong. (79 Stat. 888). This revised text has been prepared by the U.S. Department of Labor.

AUGUST 1976

TABLE OF CONTENTS

Labor-Management Reporting and Disclosure Act of 1959, As Amended

Sec. 2. Findings and policy
Sec. 3. Definitions

Title I. Bill of rights of union members

Sec. 101(a)(1). Equal rights
Sec. 101(a)(2). Freedom of speech and assembly
Sec. 101(a)(3). Dues, initiation fees and assessments
Sec. 101(a)(4). Protection of right to sue
Sec. 101(a)(5). Safeguards against improper disciplinary action
Sec. 102. Civil enforcement
Sec. 103. Retention of existing rights
Sec. 104. Rights to copies of collective bargaining agreements
Sec. 105. Information as to the Act

Title II. Reporting requirements

Sec. 201. Report of labor organizations
Sec. 202. Report of union officers and employees
Sec. 203. Report of employers; labor-relations consultants
Sec. 204. Attorney-client privilege
Sec. 205. Reports made public information
Sec. 206. Retention of records
Sec. 207. Effective date
Sec. 208. Rules and regulations
Sec. 209. Criminal provisions
Sec. 210. Civil enforcement
Sec. 211. Surety company reports

Title III. Trusteeships

Sec. 301. Reports
Sec. 302. Purposes for a valid trusteeship
Sec. 303. Unlawful acts under trusteeship
Sec. 304. Enforcement
Sec. 305. Report to Congress
Sec. 306. Complaint by Secretary

Title IV. Elections

Sec. 401. Office terms; elections procedures
Sec. 402. Enforcement
Sec. 403. Application of other laws
Sec. 404. Effective date

Title V. Safeguards for labor organizatio

Sec. 501. Fiduciary responsibility of uni officers
Sec. 502. Bonding
Sec. 503. Loans; payment of fines
Sec. 504. Prohibition against holding office
Sec. 505. Amendment of Sec. 302, Ta Hartley Act

Title VI. Miscellaneous provisions

Sec. 601. Investigations
Sec. 602. Extortionate picketing
Sec. 603. Retention of rights under other Fe eral and State laws
Sec. 604. Effect on State laws
Sec. 605. Service of process
Sec. 606. Administrative procedure act
Sec. 607. Other agencies and departments
Sec. 608. Criminal contempt
Sec. 609. Prohibition of certain union dis pline
Sec. 610. Deprivation of rights by violence
Sec. 611. Separability provisions

Title VII. Amendments to Taft-Hartle Act

Sec. 701. Federal-State jurisdiction
Sec. 702. Economic strikers
Sec. 703. Vacancy in General Counsel's Off
Sec. 704. Boycotts and recognition picketin
Sec. 705. Building and construction industr
Sec. 706. Priority in case handling
Sec. 707. Effective date of amendments

Declaration of Findings, Purposes, and Policy
(29 U.S.C. 401)

73 Stat. 519.

SEC. 2. (a) The Congress finds that, in the public interest, it continues to be the responsibility of the Federal Government to protect employees' rights to organize, choose their own representatives, bargain collectively, and otherwise engage in concerted activities for their mutual aid or protection; that the relations between employers and labor organizations and the millions of workers they represent have a substantial impact on the commerce of the Nation; and that in order to accomplish the objective of a free flow of commerce it is essential that labor organizations, employers, and their officials adhere to the highest standards of responsibility and ethical conduct in administering the affairs of their organizations, particularly as they affect labor-management relations.

(b) The Congress further finds, from recent investigations in the labor and management fields, that there have been a number of instances of breach of trust, corruption, disregard of the rights of individual employees, and other failures to observe high standards of responsibility and ethical conduct which require further and supplementary legislation that will afford necessary protection of the rights and interests of employees and the public generally as they relate to the activities of labor organizations, employers, labor relations consultants, and their officers and representatives.

(c) The Congress, therefore, further finds and declares that the enactment of this Act is necessary to eliminate or prevent improper practices on the part of labor organizations, employers, labor relations consultants, and their officers and representatives which distort and defeat the policies of the Labor Management Relations Act, 1947, as amended, and the Railway Labor Act, as amended, and have the tendency or necessary effect of burdening or obstructing commerce by (1) impairing the efficiency, safety, or operation of the instrumentalities of commerce; (2) occurring in the current of commerce; (3) materially affecting, restraining, or controlling the flow of raw materials or manufactured or processed goods into or from the channels of commerce, or the prices of such materials or goods in commerce; or (4) causing diminution of employment and wages in such volume as substantially to impair or disrupt the market for goods flowing into or from the channels of commerce.

61 Stat. 136;
29 U.S.C. 141.
44 Stat. 577;
45 U.S.C. 151.

Definitions
(29 U.S.C. 402)

73 Stat. 520.

SEC. 3. For the purposes of titles I, II, III, IV, V (except section 505), and VI of this Act—

(a) "Commerce" means trade, traffic, commerce, transportation, transmission, or communication among the several States or between any State and any place outside thereof.

(b) "State" includes any State of the United States, the District of Columbia, Puerto Rico, the Virgin Islands, American Samoa, Guam, Wake Island, the Canal Zone, and Outer Continental Shelf lands defined in the Outer Continental Shelf Lands Act (43 U.S.C. 1331–1343).

67 Stat. 462.

(c) "Industry affecting commerce" means any activity, business, or industry in commerce or in which a labor dispute would hinder or obstruct commerce or the free flow of commerce and includes any activity or industry "affecting commerce" within the meaning of the Labor Management Relations Act, 1947, as amended, or the Railway Labor Act, as amended.

(d) "Person" includes one or more individuals, labor organizations, partnerships, associations, corporations, legal representatives, mutual companies, joint-stock companies, trusts, unincorporated organizations, trustees, trustees in bankruptcy, or receivers.

(e) "Employer" means any employer or any group or association of employers engaged in an industry affecting commerce (1) which is, with respect to employees engaged in an industry affecting commerce, an employer within the meaning of any law of the United States relating to the employment of any employees or (2) which may deal with any labor organization concerning grievances, labor disputes, wages, rates of pay, hours of employment, or conditions of work, and includes any person acting directly or indirectly as an employer or as an agent of an employer in relation to an employee but does not include the United States or any corporation wholly owned by the Government of the United States or any State or political subdivision thereof.

(f) "Employee" means any individual employed by an employer, and includes any individual whose work has ceased as a consequence of, or in connection with, any current labor dispute or because of any unfair labor practice or because of exclusion or expulsion from a labor organization in any manner or for any reason inconsistent with the requirements of this Act.

(g) "Labor dispute" includes any controversy concerning terms, tenure, or conditions of employment, or concerning the association or representation of persons in negotiating, fixing, maintaining, changing, or seeking to arrange terms or conditions of employment, regardless of whether the disputants stand in the proximate relation of employer and employee.

(h) "Trusteeship" means any receivership, trusteeship, or other method of supervision or control whereby a labor organization suspends the autonomy otherwise available to a subordinate body under its constitution or bylaws.

(i) "Labor organization" means a labor organization engaged in an industry affecting commerce and includes any organization of any kind, any agency, or employee representation committee, group, association, or plan so engaged in which employees participate and which exists for the purpose, in whole or in part, of dealing with employers concerning grievances, labor disputes, wages, rates of pay, hours, or other terms or conditions of employment, and any conference, general committee, joint or system board, or joint council so engaged which is subordinate to a national or international labor organization, other than a State or local central body.

73 Stat. 521.

(j) A labor organization shall be deemed to be engaged in an industry affecting commerce if it—

61 Stat. 136;
29 U.S.C. 167.
44 Stat. 577;
45 U.S.C. 151.

(1) is the certified representative of employees under the provisions of the National Labor Relations Act, as amended, or the Railway Labor Act, as amended; or

(2) although not certified, is a national or international labor organization or a local labor organization recognized or acting as the representative of employees of an employer or employers engaged in an industry affecting commerce; or

(3) has chartered a local labor organization or subsidiary body which is representing or actively seeking to represent employees of employers within the meaning of paragraph (1) or (2); or

(4) has been chartered by a labor organization representing or actively seeking to represent employees within the meaning of paragraph (1) or

(2) as the local or subordinate body through which such employees may enjoy membership or become affiliated with such labor organization; or

(5) is a conference, general committee, joint or system board, or joint council, subordinate to a national or international labor organization, which includes a labor organization engaged in an industry affecting commerce within the meaning of any of the preceding paragraphs of this subsection, other than a State or local central body.

(k) "Secret ballot" means the expression by ballot, voting machine, or otherwise, but in no event by proxy, of a choice with respect to any election or vote taken upon any matter, which is cast in such a manner that the person expressing such choice cannot be identified with the choice expressed.

(l) "Trust in which a labor organization is interested" means a trust or other fund or organization (1) which was created or established by a labor organization, or one or more of the trustees or one or more members of the governing body of which is selected or appointed by a labor organization, and (2) a primary purpose of which is to provide benefits for the members of such labor organization or their beneficiaries.

(m) "Labor relations consultant" means any person who, for compensation, advises or represents an employer, employer organization, or labor organization concerning employee organizing, concerted activities, or collective bargaining activities.

(n) "Officer" means any constitutional officer, any person authorized to perform the functions of president, vice president, secretary, treasurer, or other executive functions of a labor organization, and any member of its executive board or similar governing body.

(o) "Member" or "member in good standing", when used in reference to a labor organization, includes any person who has fulfilled the requirements for membership in such organization, and who neither has voluntarily withdrawn from membership nor has been expelled or suspended from membership after appropriate proceedings consistent with lawful provisions of the constitution and bylaws of such organization.

(p) "Secretary" means the Secretary of Labor.

(q) "Officer, agent, shop steward, or other representative", when used with respect to a labor organization, includes elected officials and key administrative personnel, whether elected or appointed (such as business agents, heads of departments or major units, and organizers who exercise substantial independent authority), but does not include salaried nonsupervisory professional staff, stenographic, and service personnel.

(r) "District court of the United States" means a United States district court 73 Stat. 522. and a United States court of any place subject to the jurisdiction of the United States.

TITLE I—BILL OF RIGHTS OF MEMBERS OF LABOR ORGANIZATIONS

Bill of Rights
(29 U.S.C. 411)

Sec. 101. (a)(1) Equal Rights.—Every member of a labor organization shall have equal rights and privileges within such organization to nominate candidates, to vote in elections or referendums of the labor organization, to attend membership meetings and to participate in the deliberations and voting upon the business of such meetings, subject to reasonable rules and regulations in such organization's constitution and bylaws.

(2) FREEDOM OF SPEECH AND ASSEMBLY.—Every member of any labor organization shall have the right to meet and assemble freely with other members; and to express any views, arguments, or opinions; and to express at meetings of the labor organization his views, upon candidates in an election of the labor organization or upon any business properly before the meeting, subject to the organization's established and reasonable rules pertaining to the conduct of meetings: *Provided*, That nothing herein shall be construed to impair the right of a labor organization to adopt and enforce reasonable rules as to the responsibility of every member toward the organization as an institution and to his refraining from conduct that would interfere with its performance of its legal or contractual obligations.

(3) DUES, INITIATION FEES, AND ASSESSMENTS.—Except in the case of a federation of national or international labor organizations, the rates of dues and initiation fees payable by members of any labor organization in effect on the date of enactment of this Act shall not be increased, and no general or special assessment shall be levied upon such members, except—

(A) in the case of a local organization, (i) by majority vote by secret ballot of the members in good standing voting at a general or special membership meeting, after reasonable notice of the intention to vote upon such question, or (ii) by majority vote of the members in good standing voting in a membership referendum conducted by secret ballot; or

(B) in the case of a labor organization, other than a local labor organization or a federation of national or international labor organizations, (i) by majority vote of the delegates voting at a regular convention, or at a special convention of such labor organization held upon not less than thirty days' written notice to the principal office of each local or constituent labor organization entitled to such notice, or (ii) by majority vote of the members in good standing of such labor organization voting in a membership referendum conducted by secret ballot, or (iii) by majority vote of the members of the executive board or similar governing body of such labor organization, pursuant to express authority contained in the constitution and bylaws of such labor organization: *Provided*, That such action on the part of the executive board or similar governing body shall be effective only until the next regular convention of such labor organization.

(4) PROTECTION OF THE RIGHT TO SUE.—No labor organization shall limit the right of any member thereof to institute an action in any court, or in a proceeding before any administrative agency, irrespective of whether or not the labor organization or its officers are named as defendants or respondents in such action or proceeding, or the right of any member of a labor organization to appear as a witness in any judicial, administrative, or legislative proceeding, or to petition any legislature or to communicate with any legislator: *Provided*, That any such member may be required to exhaust reasonable hearing procedures (but not to exceed a four-month lapse of time) within such organization, before instituting legal or administrative proceedings against such organizations or any officer thereof: *And provided further*, That no interested employer or employer association shall directly or indirectly finance, encourage, or participate in, except as a party, any such action, proceeding, appearance, or petition.

(5) SAFEGUARDS AGAINST IMPROPER DISCIPLINARY ACTION.—No member of any labor organization may be fined, suspended, expelled, or otherwise disciplined except for nonpayment of dues by such organization or by any officer thereof unless such member has been (A) served with written specific charges; (B) given a reasonable time to prepare his defense; (C) afforded a full and fair hearing.

73 Stat. 523.

(b) Any provision of the constitution and bylaws of any labor organization which is inconsistent with the provisions of this section shall be of no force or effect.

Civil Enforcement
(29 U.S.C. 412)

SEC. 102. Any person whose rights secured by the provisions of this title have been infringed by any violation of this title may bring a civil action in a district court of the United States for such relief (including injunctions) as may be appropriate. Any such action against a labor organization shall be brought in the district court of the United States for the district where the alleged violation occurred, or where the principal office of such labor organization is located.

Retention of Existing Rights
(29 U.S.C. 413)

SEC. 103. Nothing contained in this title shall limit the rights and remedies of any member of a labor organization under any State or Federal law or before any court or other tribunal, or under the constitution and bylaws of any labor organization.

Right to Copies of Collective Bargaining Agreements
(29 U.S.C. 414)

SEC. 104. It shall be the duty of the secretary or corresponding principal officer of each labor organization, in the case of a local labor organization, to forward a copy of each collective bargaining agreement made by such labor organization with any employer to any employee who requests such a copy and whose rights as such employee are directly affected by such agreement, and in the case of a labor organization other than a local labor organization, to forward a copy of any such agreement to each constituent unit which has members directly affected by such agreement; and such officer shall maintain at the principal office of the labor organization of which he is an officer copies of any such agreement made or received by such labor organization, which copies shall be available for inspection by any member or by any employee whose rights are affected by such agreement. The provisions of section 210 shall be applicable in the enforcement of this section.

Information as to Act
(29 U.S.C. 415)

SEC. 105. Every labor organization shall inform its members concerning the provisions of this Act.

TITLE II—REPORTING BY LABOR ORGANIZATIONS, OFFICERS AND EMPLOYEES OF LABOR ORGANIZATIONS, AND EMPLOYERS
73 Stat. 524.

Report of Labor Organizations
(29 U.S.C. 431)

SEC. 201. (a) Every labor organization shall adopt a constitution and bylaws and shall file a copy thereof with the Secretary, together with a report, signed by its president and secretary or corresponding principal officers, containing the following information—

(1) the name of the labor organization, its mailing address, and any other address at which it maintains its principal office or at which it keeps the records referred to in this title;

(2) the name and title of each of its officers;

(3) the initiation fee or fees required from a new or transferred member and fees for work permits required by the reporting labor organization;

(4) the regular dues or fees of other periodic payments required to remain a member of the reporting labor organization; and

(5) detailed statements, or references to specific provisions of documents filed under this subsection which contain such statements, showing the provisions made and procedures followed with respect to each of the following: (A) qualifications for or restrictions on membership, (B) levying of assessments, (C) participation in insurance or other benefit plans, (D) authorization for disbursement of funds of the labor organization, (E) audit of financial transactions of the labor organization, (F) the calling of regular and special meetings, (G) the selection of officers and stewards and of any representatives to other bodies composed of labor organizations' representatives, with a specific statement of the manner in which each officer was elected, appointed, or otherwise selected, (H) discipline or removal of officers or agents for breaches of their trust, (I) imposition of fines, suspensions, and expulsions of members, including the grounds for such action and any provision made for notice, hearing, judgment on the evidence, and appeal procedures, (J) authorization for bargaining demands, (K) ratification of contract terms, (L) authorization for strikes, and (M) issuance of work permits. Any change in the information required by this subsection shall be reported to the Secretary at the time the reporting labor organization files with the Secretary the annual financial report required by subsection (b).

(b) Every labor organization shall file annually with the Secretary a financial report signed by its president and treasurer or corresponding principal officers containing the following information in such detail as may be necessary accurately to disclose its financial condition and operations for its preceding fiscal year—

(1) assets and liabilities at the beginning and end of the fiscal year;

(2) receipts of any kind and the sources thereof;

(3) salary, allowances, and other direct or indirect disbursements (including reimbursed expenses) to each officer and also to each employee who, during such fiscal year, received more than $10,000 in the aggregate from such labor organization and any other labor organization affiliated with it or with which it is affiliated, or which is affiliated with the same national or international labor organization;

(4) direct and indirect loans made to any officer, employee, or member, which aggregated more than $250 during the fiscal year, together with a statement of the purpose, security, if any, and arrangements for repayment;

73 Stat. 525.   (5) direct and indirect loans to any business enterprise, together with a statement of the purpose, security, if any, and arrangements for repayment; and

(6) other disbursements made by it including the purposes thereof; all in such categories as the Secretary may prescribe.

(c) Every labor organization required to submit a report under this title shall make available the information required to be contained in such report to all of its members, and every such labor organization and its officers shall be under a duty enforceable at the suit of any member of such organization in any State court of competent jurisdiction or in the district court of the United States for the district in which such labor organization maintains its principal office, to permit such member for just cause to examine any books, records, and accounts necessary to verify such report. The court in such action may, in its discretion, in addition to any judgment awarded to the plaintiff or plaintiffs, allow a reasonable attorney's fee to be paid by the defendant, and costs of the action.

(d) Subsections (f), (g), and (h) of section 9 of the National Labor Relations Act, as amended, are hereby repealed. 61 Stat. 143; 29 U.S.C. 159.

(e) Clause (i) of section 8(a)(3) of the National Labor Relations Act, as amended, is amended by striking out the following: "and has at the time the agreement was made or within the preceding twelve months received from the Board a notice of compliance with sections 9 (f), (g), (h)". 29 U.S.C. 158.

Report of Officers and Employees of Labor Organizations
(29 U.S.C. 432)

SEC. 202. (a) Every officer of a labor organization and every employee of a labor organization (other than an employee performing exclusively clerical or custodial services) shall file with the Secretary a signed report listing and describing for his preceding fiscal year—

(1) any stock, bond, security, or other interest, legal or equitable, which he or his spouse or minor child directly or indirectly held in, and any income or any other benefit with monetary value (including reimbursed expenses) which he or his spouse or minor child derived directly or indirectly from, an employer whose employees such labor organization represents or is actively seeking to represent, except payments and other benefits received as a bona fide employee of such employer;

(2) any transaction in which he or his spouse or minor child engaged, directly or indirectly, involving any stock, bond, security, or loan to or from, or other legal or equitable interest in the business of an employer whose employees such labor organization represents or is actively seeking to represent;

(3) any stock, bond, security, or other interest, legal or equitable, which he or his spouse or minor child directly or indirectly held in, and any income or any other benefit with monetary value (including reimbursed expenses) which he or his spouse or minor child directly or indirectly derived from, any business a substantial part of which consists of buying from, selling or leasing to, or otherwise dealing with, the business of an employer whose employees such labor organization represents or is actively seeking to represent;

(4) any stock, bond, security, or other interest, legal or equitable, which he or his spouse or minor child directly or indirectly held in, and any income or any other benefit with monetary value (including reimbursed expenses) which he or his spouse or minor child directly or indirectly derived from, a business any part of which consists of buying from, or selling or leasing directly or indirectly to, or otherwise dealing with such labor organization; 73 Stat. 526.

(5) any direct or indirect business transaction or arrangement between him or his spouse or minor child and any employer whose employees his organization represents or is actively seeking to represent, except work performed and payments and benefits received as a bona fide employee of such employer and except purchases and sales of goods or services in the regular course of business at prices generally available to any employee of such employer; and

(6) any payment of money or other thing of value (including reimbursed expenses) which he or his spouse or minor child received directly or indirectly from any employer or any person who acts as a labor relations consultant to an employer, except payments of the kinds referred to in section

302(c) of the Labor Management Relations Act, 1947, as amended.

(b) The provisions of paragraphs (1), (2), (3), (4), and (5) of subsection (a) shall not be construed to require any such officer or employee to report his bona fide investments in securities traded on a securities exchange registered as a national securities exchange under the Securities Exchange Act of 1934, in shares in an investment company registered under the Investment Company Act of 1940, or in securities of a public utility holding company registered under the Public Utility Holding Company Act of 1935, or to report any income derived therefrom.

48 Stat. 881;
15 U.S.C. 78a
54 Stat. 789;
15 U.S.C. 80a–51.
49 Stat. 803;
15 U.S.C. 79.

(c) Nothing contained in this section shall be construed to require any officer or employee of a labor organization to file a report under subsection (a) unless he or his spouse or minor child holds or has held an interest, has received income or any other benefit with monetary value or a loan, or has engaged in a transaction described therein.

Report of Employers
(29 U.S.C. 433)

SEC. 203. (a) Every employer who in any fiscal year made—

(1) any payment or loan, direct or indirect, of money or other thing of value (including reimbursed expenses), or any promise or agreement therefor, to any labor organization or officer, agent, shop steward, or other representative of a labor organization, or employee of any labor organization, except (A) payments or loans made by any national or State bank, credit union, insurance company, savings and loan association or other credit institution and (B) payments of the kind referred to in section 302(c) of the Labor Management Relations Act, 1947, as amended;

(2) any payment (including reimbursed expenses) to any of his employees, or any group or committee of such employees, for the purpose of causing such employee or group or committee of employees to persuade other employees to exercise or not to exercise, or as the manner of exercising, the right to organize and bargain collectively through representatives of their own choosing unless such payments were contemporaneously or previously disclosed to such other employees;

(3) any expenditure, during the fiscal year, where an object thereof, directly or indirectly, is to interfere with, restrain, or coerce employees in the exercise of the right to organize and bargain collectively through representatives of their own choosing, or is to obtain information concerning the activities of employees or a labor organization in connection with a labor dispute involving such employer, except for use solely in conjunction with an administrative or arbitral proceeding or a criminal or civil judicial proceeding;

73 Stat. 527.

(4) any agreement or arrangement with a labor relations consultant or other independent contractor or organization pursuant to which such person undertakes activities where an object thereof, directly or indirectly, is to persuade employees to exercise or not to exercise, or persuade employees as to the manner of exercising, the right to organize and bargain collectively through representatives of their own choosing, or undertakes to supply such employer with information concerning the activities of employees or a labor organization in connection with a labor dispute involving such employer, except information for use solely in conjunction with an administrative or arbitral proceeding or a criminal or civil judicial proceeding; or

(5) any payment (including reimbursed expenses) pursuant to an agreement or arrangement described in subdivision (4);

shall file with the Secretary a report, in a form prescribed by him, signed by its president and treasurer or corresponding principal officers showing in detail the date and amount of each such payment, loan, promise, agreement, or arrangement and the name, address, and position, if any, in any firm or labor organization of the person to whom it was made and a full explanation of the circumstances of all such payments, including the terms of any agreement or understanding pursuant to which they were made.

(b) Every person who pursuant to any agreement or arrangement with an employer undertakes activities where an object thereof is, directly or indirectly—

(1) to persuade employees to exercise or not to exercise, or persuade employees as to the manner of exercising, the right to organize and bargain collectively through representatives of their own choosing; or

(2) to supply an employer with information concerning the activities of employees or a labor organization in connection with a labor dispute involving such employer, except information for use solely in conjunction with an administrative or arbitral proceeding or a criminal or civil judicial proceeding;

shall file within thirty days after entering into such agreement or arrangement a report with the Secretary, signed by its president and treasurer or corresponding principal officers, containing the name under which such person is engaged in doing business and the address of its principal office, and a detailed statement of the terms and conditions of such agreement or arrangement. Every such person shall file annually, with respect to each fiscal year during which payments were made as a result of such an agreement or arrangement, a report with the Secretary, signed by its president and treasurer or corresponding principal officers, containing a statement (A) of its receipts of any kind from employers on account of labor relations advice or services, designating the sources thereof, and (B) of its disbursements of any kind, in connection with such services and the purposes thereof. In each such case such information shall be set forth in such categories as the Secretary may prescribe.

(c) Nothing in this section shall be construed to require any employer or other person to file a report covering the services of such person by reason of his giving or agreeing to give advice to such employer or representing or agreeing to represent such employer before any court, administrative agency, or tribunal of arbitration or engaging or agreeing to engage in collective bargaining on behalf of such employer with respect to wages, hours, or other terms or conditions of employment or the negotiation of an agreement or any question arising thereunder.

(d) Nothing contained in this section shall be construed to require an em- 73 Stat. 528. ployer to file a report under subsection (a) unless he has made an expenditure, payment, loan, agreement, or arrangement of the kind described therein. Nothing contained in this section shall be construed to require any other person to file a report under subsection (b) unless he was a party to an agreement or arrangement of the kind described therein.

(e) Nothing contained in this section shall be construed to require any regular officer, supervisor, or employee of an employer to file a report in connection with services rendered to such employer nor shall any employer be required to file a report covering expenditures made to any regular officer, supervisor, or employee of an employer as compensation for service as a regular officer, supervisor, or employee of such employer.

(f) Nothing contained in this section shall be construed as an amendment to, or modification of the rights protected by, section 8(c) of the National Labor Relations Act, as amended. 29 U.S.C. 158.

29 U.S.C. 157.

(g) The term "interfere with, restrain, or coerce" as used in this section means interference, restraint, and coercion which, if done with respect to the exercise of rights guaranteed in section 7 of the National Labor Relations Act, as amended, would, under section 8(a) of such Act, constitute an unfair labor practice.

Attorney-Client Communications Exempted
(29 U.S.C. 434)

SEC. 204. Nothing contained in this Act shall be construed to require an attorney who is a member in good standing of the bar of any State, to include in any report required to be filed pursuant to the provisions of this Act any information which was lawfully communicated to such attorney by any of his clients in the course of a legitimate attorney-client relationship.

Reports Made Public Information
(29 U.S.C. 435)

SEC. 205. (a)[2] The contents of the reports and documents filed with the Secretary pursuant to sections 201, 202, **203, and 211** shall be public information, and the Secretary may publish any information and data which he obtains pursuant to the provisions of this title. The Secretary may use the information and data for statistical and research purposes, and compile and publish such studies, analyses, reports, and surveys based thereon as he may deem appropriate.

(b)[3] The Secretary shall by regulation make reasonable provision for the inspection and examination, on the request of any person, of the information and data contained in any report or other document filed with him pursuant to section 201, 202, **203, or 211.**

(c)[4] The Secretary shall by regulation provide for the furnishing by the Department of Labor of copies of reports or other documents filed with the Secretary pursuant to this title, upon payment of a charge based upon the cost of the service. The Secretary shall make available without payment of a charge, or require any person to furnish, to such State agency as is designated by law or by the Governor of the State in which such person has his principal place of business or headquarters, upon request of the Governor of such State, copies of any reports and documents filed by such person with the Secretary pursuant to section 201, 202, **203, or 211,** or of information and data contained therein. No person shall be required by reason of any law of any State to furnish to any officer or agency of such State any information included in a report filed by such person with the Secretary pursuant to the provisions of this title, if a copy of such report, or of the portion thereof containing such information, is furnished to such officer or agency. All moneys received in payment of such charges fixed by the Secretary pursuant to this subsection shall be deposited in the general fund of the Treasury.

73 Stat. 529.

---

[2]Prior to amendment by section 2(a) of Public Law 89-216, the first sentence of section 205(a) read as follows: "Sec. 205. (a) The contents of the reports and documents filed with the Secretary pursuant to sections 201, 202, and 203 shall be public information, and the Secretary may publish any information and data which he obtains pursuant to the provisions of this title."

[3]Prior to amendment by section 2(b) of Public Law 89-216, section 205(b) read as follows: "(b) The Secretary shall by regulation make reasonable provision for the inspection and examination, on the request of any person, of the information and data contained in any report or other document filed with him pursuant to section 201, 202, or 203."

[4]Prior to amendment by section 2(c) of Public Law 89-216, the second sentence of section 205(c) read as follows: "The Secretary shall make available without payment of a charge, or require any person to furnish, to such State agency as is designated by law or by the Governor of the State in which such person has his principal place of business or headquarters, upon request of the Governor of such State, copies of any reports and documents filed by such person with the Secretary pursuant to section 201, 202, or 203, or of information and data contained therein."

Retention of Records
(29 U.S.C. 436)

Sec. 206. Every person required to file any report under this title shall maintain records on the matters required to be reported which will provide in sufficient detail the necessary basic information and data from which the documents filed with the Secretary may be verified, explained or clarified, and checked for accuracy and completeness, and shall include vouchers, worksheets, receipts, and applicable resolutions, and shall keep such records available for examination for a period of not less than five years after the filing of the documents based on the information which they contain.

Effective Date
(29 U.S.C. 437)

Sec. 207. (a) Each labor organization shall file the initial report required under section 201(a) within ninety days after the date on which it first becomes subject to this Act.

(b)[5] Each person required to file a report under section 201(b), 202, 203(a), **the second sentence of section 203(b), or section 211** shall file such report within ninety days after the end of each of its fiscal years; except that where such person is subject to section 201(b), 202, 203(a), **the second sentence of section 203(b), or section 211,** as the case may be, for only a portion of such a fiscal year (because the date of enactment of this Act occurs during such person's fiscal year or such person becomes subject to this Act during its fiscal year) such person may consider that portion as the entire fiscal year in making such report.

Rules and Regulations
(29 U.S.C. 438)

Sec. 208. The Secretary shall have authority to issue, amend, and rescind rules and regulations prescribing the form and publication of reports required to be filed under this title and such other reasonable rules and regulations (including rules prescribing reports concerning trusts in which a labor organization is interested) as he may find necessary to prevent the circumvention or evasion of such reporting requirements. In exercising his power under this section the Secretary shall prescribe by general rule simplified reports for labor organizations or employers for whom he finds that by virtue of their size a detailed report would be unduly burdensome, but the Secretary may revoke such provision for simplified forms of any labor organization or employer if he determines, after such investigation as he deems proper and due notice and opportunity for a hearing, that the purposes of this section would be served thereby.

Criminal Provisions
(29 U.S.C. 439)

Sec. 209. (a) Any person who willfully violates this title shall be fined not more than $10,000 or imprisoned for not more than one year, or both.

(b) Any person who makes a false statement or representation of a material fact, knowing it to be false, or who knowingly fails to disclose a material fact, in any document, report, or other information required under the provisions of this

---

[5]Prior to amendment by section 2(d) of Public Law 89-216, section 207(b) read as follows: "(b) Each person required to file a report under section 201(b), 202, 203(a), or the second sentence of 203(b) shall file such report within ninety days after the end of each of its fiscal years; except that where such person is subject to section 201(b), 202, 203(a), or the second sentence of 203(b), as the case may be, for only a portion of such a fiscal year (because the date of enactment of this Act occurs during such person's fiscal year or such person becomes subject to this Act during its fiscal year) such person may consider that portion as the entire fiscal year in making such report."

title shall be fined not more than $10,000 or imprisoned for not more than one year, or both.

(c) Any person who willfully makes a false entry in or willfully conceals, withholds, or destroys any books, records, reports, or statements required to be kept by any provision of this title shall be fined not more than $10,000 or imprisoned for not more than one year, or both.

(d) Each individual required to sign reports under sections 201 and 203 shall be personally responsible for the filing of such reports and for any statement contained therein which he knows to be false.

Civil Enforcement
(29 U.S.C. 440)

SEC. 210. Whenever it shall appear that any person has violated or is about to violate any of the provisions of this title, the Secretary may bring a civil action for such relief (including injunctions) as may be appropriate. Any such action may be brought in the district court of the United States where the violation occurred or, at the option of the parties, in the United States District Court for the District of Columbia.

Surety Company Reports [6]
(29 U.S.C. 441)

Sec. 211. Each surety company which issues any bond required by this Act or the Welfare and Pension Plans Disclosure Act shall file annually with the Secretary, with respect to each fiscal year during which any such bond was in force, a report, in such form and detail as he may prescribe by regulation, filed by the president and treasurer or corresponding principal officers of the surety company, describing its bond experience under each such Act, including information as to the premiums received, total claims paid, amounts recovered by way of subrogation, administrative and legal expenses and such related data and information as the Secretary shall determine to be necessary in the public interest and to carry out the policy of the Act. Notwithstanding the foregoing, if the Secretary finds that any such specific information cannot be practicably ascertained or would be uninformative, the Secretary may modify or waive the requirement for such information.

TITLE III—TRUSTEESHIPS

Reports
(29 U.S.C. 461)

SEC. 301. (a) Every labor organization which has or assumes trusteeship over any subordinate labor organization shall file with the Secretary within thirty days after the date of the enactment of this Act or the imposition of any such trusteeship, and semiannually thereafter, a report, signed by its president and treasurer or corresponding principal officers, as well as by the trustees of such subordinate labor organization, containing the following information: (1) the name and address of the subordinate organization; (2) the date of establishing the trusteeship; (3) a detailed statement of the reason or reasons for establishing or continuing the trusteeship; and (4) the nature and extent of participation by the membership of the subordinate organization in the selection of delegates to represent such organization in regular or special conventions or other policy-determining bodies and in the election of officers of the labor organization which has assumed trusteeship over such subordinate organization. The initial report

---

[6]Section 211 was added by section 3 of Public Law 89-216 (79 Stat. 888).

73 Stat. 530.

72 Stat. 997;
29 U.S.C. 301 note.

shall also include a full and complete account of the financial condition of such subordinate organization as of the time trusteeship was assumed over it. During the continuance of a trusteeship the labor organization which has assumed trusteeship over a subordinate labor organization shall file on behalf of the subordinate labor organization the annual financial report required by section 201(b) signed by the president and treasurer or corresponding principal officers of the labor organization which has assumed such trusteeship and the trustees of the subordinate labor organization.

(b) The provisions of section 201(c), 205, 206, 208, and 210 shall be applicable to reports filed under this title.

(c) Any person who willfully violates this section shall be fined not more than $10,000 or imprisoned for not more than one year, or both.

(d) Any person who makes a false statement or representation of a material fact, knowing it to be false, or who knowingly fails to disclose a material fact, in any report required under the provisions of this section or willfully makes any false entry in or willfully withholds, conceals, or destroys any documents, books, records, reports, or statements upon which such report is based, shall be fined not more than $10,000 or imprisoned for not more than one year, or both.

(e) Each individual required to sign a report under this section shall be personally responsible for the filing of such report and for any statement contained therein which he knows to be false.

Purposes for Which a Trusteeship May Be Established
(29 U.S.C. 462)

73 Stat. 531.

SEC. 302. Trusteeships shall be established and administered by a labor organization over a subordinate body only in accordance with the constitution and bylaws of the organization which has assumed trusteeship over the subordinate body and for the purpose of correcting corruption or financial malpractice, assuring the performance of collective bargaining agreements or other duties of a bargaining representative, restoring democratic procedures, or otherwise carrying out the legitimate objects of such labor organization.

Unlawful Acts Relating to Labor Organization Under Trusteeship
(29 U.S.C. 463)

SEC. 303. (a) During any period when a subordinate body of a labor organization is in trusteeship, it shall be unlawful (1) to count the vote of delegates from such body in any convention or election of officers of the labor organization unless the delegates have been chosen by secret ballot in an election in which all the members in good standing of such subordinate body were eligible to participate or (2) to transfer to such organization any current receipts or other funds of the subordinate body except the normal per capita tax and assessments payable by subordinate bodies not in trusteeship: *Provided*, That nothing herein contained shall prevent the distribution of the assets of a labor organization in accordance with its constitution and bylaws upon the bona fide dissolution thereof.

(b) Any person who willfully violates this section shall be fined not more than $10,000 or imprisoned for not more than one year, or both.

Enforcement
(29 U.S.C. 464)

SEC. 304. (a) Upon the written complaint of any member or subordinate body of a labor organization alleging that such organization has violated the provisions of this title (except section 301) the Secretary shall investigate the complaint and if the Secretary finds probable cause to believe that such violation has occurred and has not been remedied he shall, without disclosing the identity of the complainant, bring a civil action in any district court of the United States having jurisdiction of the labor organization for such relief (including injunctions) as may be appropriate. Any member or subordinate body of a labor organization affected by any violation of this title (except section 301) may bring a civil action in any district court of the United States having jurisdiction of the labor organization for such relief (including injunctions) as may be appropriate.

(b) For the purpose of actions under this section, district courts of the United States shall be deemed to have jurisdiction of a labor organization (1) in the district in which the principal office of such labor organization is located, or (2) in any district in which its duly authorized officers or agents are engaged in conducting the affairs of the trusteeship.

(c) In any proceeding pursuant to this section a trusteeship established by a labor organization in conformity with the procedural requirements of its constitution and bylaws and authorized or ratified after a fair hearing either before the executive board or before such other body as may be provided in accordance with its constitution or bylaws shall be presumed valid for a period of eighteen months from the date of its establishment and shall not be subject to attack during such period except upon clear and convincing proof that the trusteeship was not established or maintained in good faith for a purpose allowable under section 302. After the expiration of eighteen months the trusteeship shall be presumed invalid in any such proceeding and its discontinuance shall be decreed unless the labor organization shall show by clear and convincing proof that the continuation of the trusteeship is necessary for a purpose allowable under section 302. In the latter event the court may dismiss the complaint or retain jurisdiction of the cause on such conditions and for such period as it deems appropriate.

73 Stat. 532.

Report to Congress
(29 U.S.C. 465)

SEC. 305. The Secretary shall submit to the Congress at the expiration of three years from the date of enactment of this Act a report upon the operation of this title.

Complaint by Secretary
(29 U.S.C. 466)

SEC. 306. The rights and remedies provided by this title shall be in addition to any and all other rights and remedies at law or in equity: *Provided*, That upon the filing of a complaint by the Secretary the jurisdiction of the district court over such trusteeship shall be exclusive and the final judgment shall be res judicata.

TITLE IV—ELECTIONS

Terms of Office; Election Procedures
(29 U.S.C. 481).

SEC. 401. (a) Every national or international labor organization, except a federation of national or international labor organizations, shall elect its officers not less often than once every five years either by secret ballot among the members in good standing or at a convention of delegates chosen by secret ballot.

(b) Every local labor organization shall elect its officers not less often than once every three years by secret ballot among the members in good standing.

(c) Every national or international labor organization, except a federation of national or international labor organizations, and every local labor organization, and its officers, shall be under a duty, enforceable at the suit of any bona fide candidate for office in such labor organization in the district court of the United States in which such labor organization maintains its principal office, to comply with all reasonable requests of any candidate to distribute by mail or otherwise at the candidate's expense campaign literature in aid of such person's candidacy to all members in good standing of such labor organization and to refrain from discrimination in favor of or against any candidate with respect to the use of lists of members, and whenever such labor organizations or its officers authorize the distribution by mail or otherwise to members of campaign literature on behalf of any candidate or of the labor organization itself with reference to such election, similar distribution at the request of any other bona fide candidate shall be made by such labor organization and its officers, with equal treatment as to the expense of such distribution. Every bona fide candidate shall have the right, once within 30 days prior to an election of a labor organization in which he is a candidate, to inspect a list containing the names and last known addresses of all members of the labor organization who are subject to a collective bargaining agreement requiring membership therein as a condition of employment, which list shall be maintained and kept at the principal office of such labor organization by a designated official thereof. Adequate safeguards to insure a fair election shall be provided, including the right of any candidate to have an observer at the polls and at the counting of the ballots.

(d) Officers of intermediate bodies, such as general committees, system boards, joint boards, or joint councils, shall be elected not less often than once every four years by secret ballot among the members in good standing or by labor organization officers representative of such members who have been elected by secret ballot. 73 Stat. 533.

(e) In any election required by this section which is to be held by secret ballot a reasonable opportunity shall be given for the nomination of candidates and every member in good standing shall be eligible to be a candidate and to hold office (subject to section 504 and to reasonable qualifications uniformly imposed) and shall have the right to vote for or otherwise support the candidate or candidates of his choice, without being subject to penalty, discipline, or improper interference or reprisal of any kind by such organization or any member thereof. Not less than fifteen days prior to the election notice thereof shall be mailed to each member at his last known home address. Each member in good standing shall be entitled to one vote. No member whose dues have been withheld by his employer for payment to such organization pursuant to his voluntary authorization provided for in a collective bargaining agreement shall be declared ineligible to vote or be a candidate for office in such organization by reason of alleged delay or default in the payment of dues. The votes cast by members of each local labor organization shall be counted, and the results published, separately. The election officials designated in the constitution and bylaws or the secretary, if no other official is designated, shall preserve for one year the ballots and all other records pertaining to the election. The election shall be conducted in accordance with the constitution and bylaws of such organization insofar as they are not inconsistent with the provisions of this title.

(f) When officers are chosen by a convention of delegates elected by secret ballot, the convention shall be conducted in accordance with the constitution and bylaws of the labor organization insofar as they are not inconsistent with the provisions of this title. The officials designated in the constitution and bylaws or the secretary, if no other is designated, shall preserve for one year the credentials of the delegates and all minutes and other records of the convention pertaining to the election of officers.

(g) No moneys received by any labor organization by way of dues, assessment, or similar levy, and no moneys of an employer shall be contributed or applied to promote the candidacy of any person in an election subject to the provisions of this title. Such moneys of a labor organization may be utilized for notices, factual statements of issues not involving candidates, and other expenses necessary for the holding of an election.

(h) If the Secretary, upon application of any member of a local labor organization, finds after hearing in accordance with the Administrative Procedure Act that the constitution and bylaws of such labor organization do not provide an adequate procedure for the removal of an elected officer guilty of serious misconduct, such officer may be removed, for cause shown and after notice and hearing, by the members in good standing voting in a secret ballot conducted by the officers of such labor organization in accordance with its constitution and bylaws insofar as they are not inconsistent with the provisions of this title.

(i) The Secretary shall promulgate rules and regulations prescribing mimimum standards and procedures for determining the adequacy of the removal procedures to which reference is made in subsection (h).

73 Stat. 534.

Enforcement
(29 U.S.C. 482)

SEC. 402. (a) A member of a labor organization—

(1) who has exhausted the remedies available under the constitution and bylaws of such organization and of any parent body, or

(2) who has invoked such available remedies without obtaining a final decision within three calendar months after their invocation,

may file a complaint with the Secretary within one calendar month thereafter alleging the violation of any provision of section 401 (including violation of the constitution and bylaws of the labor organization pertaining to the election and removal of officers). The challenged election shall be presumed valid pending a final decision thereon (as hereinafter provided) and in the interim the affairs of the organization shall be conducted by the officers elected or in such other manner as its constitution and bylaws may provide.

(b) The Secretary shall investigate such complaint and, if he finds probable cause to believe that a violation of this title has occurred and has not been remedied, he shall, within sixty days after the filing of such complaint, bring a civil action against the labor organization as an entity in the district court of the the United States in which such labor organization maintains its principal office to set aside the invalid election, if any, and to direct the conduct of an election or hearing and vote upon the removal of officers under the supervision of the Secretary and in accordance with the provisions of this title and such rules and regulations as the Secretary may prescribe. The court shall have power to take such action as it deems proper to preserve the assets of the labor organization.

(c) If, upon a preponderance of the evidence after a trial upon the merits, the court finds—

(1) that an election has not been held within the time prescribed by section 401, or

(2) that the violation of section 401 may have affected the outcome of an election,

the court shall declare the election, if any, to be void and direct the conduct of a new election under supervision of the Secretary and, so far as lawful and practicable, in conformity with the constitution and bylaws of the labor organization. The Secretary shall promptly certify to the court the names of the persons elected, and the court shall thereupon enter a decree declaring such persons to be the officers of the labor oganization. If the proceeding is for the removal of officers pursuant to subsection (h) of section 401, the Secretary shall certify the results of the vote and the court shall enter a decree declaring whether such persons have been removed as officers of the labor organization.

(d) An order directing an election, dismissing a complaint, or designating elected officers of a labor organization shall be appealable in the same manner as the final judgment in a civil action, but an order directing an election shall not be stayed pending appeal.

Application of Other Laws
(29 U.S.C. 483)

SEC. 403. No labor organization shall be required by law to conduct elections of officers with greater frequency or in a different form or manner than is required by its own constitution or bylaws, except as otherwise provided by this title. Existing rights and remedies to enforce the constitution and bylaws of a labor organization with respect to elections prior to the conduct thereof shall not be affected by the provisions of this title. The remedy provided by this title for challenging an election already conducted shall be exclusive.

Effective Date
(29 U.S.C. 484)

73 Stat. 535.

SEC. 404. The provisions of this title shall become applicable—

(1) ninety days after the date of enactment of this Act in the case of a labor organization whose constitution and bylaws can lawfully be modified or amended by action of its constitutional officers or governing body, or

(2) where such modification can only be made by a constitutional convention of the labor organization, not later than the next constitutional convention of such labor organization after the date of enactment of this Act, or one year after such date, whichever is sooner. If no such convention is held within such one-year period, the executive board or similar governing body empowered to act for such labor organization between conventions is empowered to make such interim constitutional changes as are necessary to carry out the provisions of this title.

TITLE V—SAFEGUARDS FOR LABOR ORGANIZATIONS

Fiduciary Responsibility of Officers of Labor Organizations
(29 U.S.C. 501)

SEC. 501. (a) The officers, agents, shop stewards, and other representatives of a labor organization occupy positions of trust in relation to such organization and its members as a group. It is, therefore, the duty of each such person, taking into account the special problems and functions of a labor organization, to hold its money and property solely for the benefit of the organization and its members and to manage, invest, and expend the same in accordance with its constitution and bylaws and any resolutions of the governing bodies adopted thereunder, to refrain from dealing with such organization as an adverse party or in behalf of an adverse party in any matter connected with his duties and from holding or acquiring any pecuniary or personal interest which conflicts with the interests of such organization, and to account to the organization for any profit received by him in whatever capacity in connection with transactions conducted by him or under his direction on behalf of the organization. A general exculpatory provision in the constitution and bylaws of such a labor organization or a general exculpatory resolution of a governing body purporting to relieve any such person of liability for breach of the duties declared by this section shall be void as against public policy.

(b) When any officer, agent, shop steward, or representative of any labor organization is alleged to have violated the duties declared in subsection (a) and the labor organization or its governing board or officers refuse or fail to sue or recover damages or secure an accounting or other appropriate relief within a reasonable time after being requested to do so by any member of the labor organization, such member may sue such officer,.agent, shop steward, or representative in any district court of the United States or in any State court of competent jurisdiction to recover damages or secure an accounting or other appropriate relief for the benefit of the labor organization. No such proceeding shall be brought except upon leave of the court obtained upon verified application and for good cause shown which application may be made ex parte. The trial judge may allot a reasonable part of the recovery in any action under this subsection to pay the fees of counsel prosecuting the suit at the instance of the member of the labor organization and to compensate such member for any expenses necessarily paid or incurred by him in connection with the litigation.

73 Stat. 536.

(c) Any person who embezzles, steals, or unlawfully and willfully abstracts or converts to his own use, or the use of another, any of the moneys, funds, securities, property, or other assets of a labor organization of which he is an officer, or by which he is employed, directly or indirectly, shall be fined not more than $10,000 or imprisoned for not more than five years, or both.

Bonding
(29 U.S.C. 502)

SEC. 502. (a)[7] Every officer, agent, shop steward, or other representative or employee of any labor organization (other than a labor organization whose property and annual financial receipts do not exceed $5,000 in value), or of a trust in which a labor organization is interested, who handles funds or other property thereof shall be bonded **to provide protection against loss by reason of acts of fraud or dishonesty on his part directly or through connivance with others.** The bond of each such person shall be fixed at the beginning of the organization's fiscal year and shall be in an amount not less than 10 per centum of the funds handled by him and his predecessor or predecessors, if any, during the preceding fiscal year, but in no case more than $500,000. If the labor organization or the trust in which a labor organization is interested does not have a preceding fiscal year, the amount of the bond shall be, in the case of a local labor organization, not less than $1,000, and in the case of any other labor organization or of a trust in which a labor organization is interested, not less than $10,000. Such bonds shall be individual or schedule in form, and shall have a corporate surety company as surety thereon. Any person who is not covered by such bonds shall not be permitted to receive, handle, disburse, or otherwise exercise custody or control of the funds or other property of a labor organization or of a trust in which a labor organization is interested. No such bond shall be placed through an agent or broker or with a surety company in which any labor organization or any officer, agent, shop steward, or other representative of a labor organization has any direct or indirect interest. Such surety company shall be a corporate surety which holds a grant of authority from the Secretary of the Treasury under the Act of July 30,

---

[7]Prior to amendment by section 1 of Public Law 89-216, the first sentence of section 502(a) read as follows: "Sec. 502(a) Every officer, agent, shop steward, or other representative or employee of any labor organization (other than a labor organization whose property and annual financial receipts do not exceed $5,000 in value), or of a trust in which a labor organization is interested, who handles funds or other property thererof shall be bonded for the faithful discharge of his duties." Section 1 of Public Law 89-216 also added the proviso at the end of section 502(a).

1947 (6 U.S.C. 6–13), as an acceptable surety on Federal bonds: *Provided,* That [61 Stat. 648.] when in the opinion of the Secretary a labor organization has made other bonding arrangements which would provide the protection required by this section at comparable cost or less, he may exempt such labor organization from placing a bond through a surety company holding such grant of authority.

(b) Any person who willfully violates this section shall be fined not more than $10,000 or imprisoned for not more than one year, or both.

Making of Loans; Payment of Fines
(29 U.S.C. 503)

Sec. 503. (a) No labor organization shall make directly or indirectly any loan or loans to any officer or employee of such organization which results in a total indebtedness on the part of such officer or employee to the labor organization in excess of $2,000.

(b) No labor organization or employer shall directly or indirectly pay the fine of any officer or employee convicted of any willful violation of this Act.

(c) Any person who willfully violates this section shall be fined not more than $5,000 or imprisoned for not more than one year, or both.

Prohibition Against Certain Persons Holding Office
(29 U.S.C. 504)

Sec. 504. (a) No person who is or has been a member of the Communist Party [8] or who has been convicted of, or served any part of a prison term resulting from his conviction of, robbery, bribery, extortion, embezzlement, grand larceny, burglary, arson, violation of narcotics laws, murder, rape, assault with intent to kill, assault which inflicts grievous bodily injury, or a violation of title II or III of [73 Stat. 537.] this Act, or conspiracy to commit any such crimes, shall serve—

(1) as an officer, director, trustee, member of any executive board or similar governing body, business agent, manager, organizer, or other employee (other than as an employee performing exclusively clerical or custodial duties) of any labor organization, or

(2) as a labor relations consultant to a person engaged in an industry or activity affecting commerce, or as an officer, director, agent, or employee (other than as an employee performing exclusively clerical or custodial duties) of any group or association of employers dealing with any labor organization,

during or for five years after the termination of his membership in the Communist Party,[8] or for five years after such conviction or after the end of such imprisonment, unless prior to the end of such five-year period, in the case of a person so convicted or imprisoned, (A) his citizenship rights, having been revoked as a result of such conviction, have been fully restored, or (B) the Board of Parole of the United States Department of Justice determines that such person's service in any capacity referred to in clause (1) or (2) would not be contrary to the purposes of this Act. Prior to making any such determination the Board shall hold an administrative hearing and shall give notice of such proceeding by certified mail to the State, county, and Federal prosecuting officials in the jurisdiction or jurisdictions in which such person was convicted. The Board's determination in any such proceeding shall be final. No labor organization or officer thereof shall knowingly permit any person to assume or hold any office or paid position in violation of this subsection.

(b) Any person who willfully violates this section shall be fined not more than $10,000 or imprisoned for not more than one year, or both.

---

[8]The U.S. Supreme Court, on June 7, 1965, held unconstitutional as a bill of attainder the section 504 provision which imposes criminal sanctions on Communist Party members for holding union office (*U.S.* v. *Brown,* 381 U.S. 437, 85 S. Ct. 1707).

(c) For the purposes of this section, any person shall be deemed to have been "convicted" and under the disability of "conviction" from the date of the judgment of the trial court or the date of the final sustaining of such judgment on appeal, whichever is the later event, regardless of whether such conviction occurred before or after the date of enactment of this Act.

Amendment to Section 302, Labor Management Relations Act, 1947

29 U.S.C. 186.

SEC. 505. Subsections (a), (b), and (c) of section 302 of the Labor Management Relations Act, 1947, as amended, are amended to read as follows:

"SEC. 302. (a) It shall be unlawful for any employer or association of employers or any person who acts as a labor relations expert, adviser, or consultant to an employer or who acts in the interest of an employer to pay, lend, or deliver, or agree to pay, lend, or deliver, any money or other thing of value—

"(1) to any representative of any of his employees who are employed in an industry affecting commerce; or

"(2) to any labor organization, or any officer or employee thereof, which represents, seeks to represent, or would admit to membership, any of the employees of such employer who are employed in an industry affecting commerce; or

"(3) to any employee or group or committee of employees of such employer employed in an industry affecting commerce in excess of their normal compensation for the purpose of causing such employee or group or committee directly or indirectly to influence any other employees in the exer-

73 Stat. 538.

cise of the right to organize and bargain collectively through representatives of their own choosing; or

"(4) to any officer or employee of a labor organization engaged in an industry affecting commerce with intent to influence him in respect to any of his actions, decisions, or duties as a representative of employees or as such officer or employee of such labor organization.

"(b)(1) It shall be unlawful for any person to request, demand, receive, or accept, or agree to receive or accept, any payment, loan, or delivery of any money or other thing of value prohibited by subsection (a).

"(2) It shall be unlawful for any labor organization, or for any person acting as an officer, agent, representative, or employee of such labor organization, to demand or accept from the operator of any motor vehicle (as defined in part II of the Interstate Commerce Act) employed in the transportation of property in commerce, or the employer of any such operator, any money or other thing of value payable to such organization or to an officer, agent, representative or employee thereof as a fee or charge for the unloading, or in connection with the unloading, of the cargo of such vehicle: Provided, That nothing in this paragraph shall be construed to make unlawful any payment by an employer to any of his employees as compensation for their services as employees.

"(c) The provisions of this section shall not be applicable (1) in respect to any money or other thing of value payable by an employer to any of his employees whose established duties include acting openly for such employer in matters of labor relations or personnel administration or to any representative of his employees, or to any officer or employee of a labor organization, who is also an employee or former employee of such employer, as compensation for, or by reason of, his service as an employee of such employer; (2) with respect to the payment or delivery of any money or other thing of value in satisfaction of a judgment of any court or a decision or award of an arbitrator or impartial chairman or in compromise, adjustment, settlement, or release of any claim, complaint, grievance, or dispute in the absence of fraud or duress; (3) with respect to the sale or purchase of an article or commodity at the prevailing market price in the regular course of business; (4) with respect to money deducted from the wages of employees in payment of membership dues in a labor organization: *Provided*, That the employer has received from each employee, on whose account such deductions are made, a written assignment which shall not be irrevocable for a period of more than one year, or beyond the termination date of the applicable collective agreement, whichever occurs sooner; (5) with respect to money or other thing of value paid to a trust fund established by such representative, for the sole and exclusive benefit of the employees of such employer, and their families and dependents (or of such employees, families, and dependents jointly with the employees of other employers making similar payments, and their families and dependents): *Provided*, That (A) such payments are held in trust for the purpose of paying, either from principal or income or both, for the benefit of employees, their families and dependents, for medical or hospital care, pensions on retirement or death of employees, compensation for injuries or illness resulting from occupational activity or insurance to provide any of the foregoing, or unemployment benefits or life insurance, disability and sickness insurance, or accident insurance; (B) the detailed basis on which such payments are to be made is specified in a written agreement with the employer, and employees and employers are equally represented in the administration of such fund, together with such neutral persons as the representatives of the employers and the representatives of employees may agree upon and in the event of the employer and employee groups deadlock on the administration of such fund and there are no neutral persons empowered to break such deadlock, such agreement provides that the two groups shall agree on an impartial umpire to decide such dispute, or in event of their failure to agree within a reasonable length of time, an impartial umpire to decide such dispute shall, on petition of either group, be appointed by the district court of the United States for the district where the trust fund has its principal office, and shall also contain provisions for an annual audit of the trust fund, a statement of the results of which shall be available for inspection by interested persons at the principal office of the trust fund and at such other places as may be designated in such written agreement; and (C) such payments as are intended to be used for the purpose of providing pensions or annuities for employees are made to a separate trust which provides that the funds held therein cannot be used for any purpose other than paying such pensions or annuities; or (6) with respect to money or other thing of value paid by any employer to a trust fund established by such representative for the purpose of pooled vacation, holiday, severance or similar benefits, or defraying costs of apprenticeship or other training programs: *Provided*, That the requirements of clause (B) of the proviso to clause (5) of this subsection shall apply to such trust funds."

73 Stat. 539.

TITLE VI—MISCELLANEOUS PROVISIONS
Investigations
(29 U.S.C. 521)

SEC. 601. (a) The Secretary shall have power when he believes it necessary in order to determine whether any person has violated or is about to violate any provision of this Act (except title I or amendments made by this Act to other statutes) to make an investigation and in connection therewith he may enter such places and inspect such records and accounts and question such persons as he may deem necessary to enable him to determine the facts relative thereto. The Secretary may report to interested persons or officials concerning the facts required to be shown in any report required by this Act and concerning the reasons for failure or refusal to file such a report or any other matter which he deems to be appropriate as a result of such an investigation.

(b) For the purpose of any investigation provided for in this Act, the provisions of sections 9 and 10 (relating to the attendance of witnesses and the production of books, papers, and documents) of the Federal Trade Commission Act of September 16, 1914, as amended (15 U.S.C. 49, 50), are hereby made applicable to the jurisdiction, powers, and duties of the Secretary or any officers designated by him.

Extortionate Picketing
(29 U.S.C. 522)

SEC. 602. (a) It shall be unlawful to carry on picketing on or about the premises of any employer for the purpose of, or as part of any conspiracy or in furtherance of any plan or purpose for, the personal profit or enrichment of any individual (except a bona fide increase in wages or other employee benefits) by taking or obtaining any money or other thing of value from such employer against his will or with his consent.

(b) Any person who willfully violates this section shall be fined not more than $10,000 or imprisoned not more than twenty years, or both.

Retention of Rights Under Other Federal and State Laws
(29 U.S.C. 523)

SEC. 603. (a) Except as explicitly provided to the contrary, nothing in this Act shall reduce or limit the responsibilities of any labor organization or any officer, agent, shop steward, or other representative of a labor organization, or of any trust in which a labor organization is interested, under any other Federal law or under the laws of any State, and, except as explicitly provided to the contrary, nothing in this Act shall take away any right or bar any remedy to which members of a labor organization are entitled under such other Federal law or law of any State.

(b) Nothing contained in titles I, II, III, IV, V, or VI of this Act shall be construed to supersede or impair or otherwise affect the provisions of the Railway Labor Act, as amended, or any of the obligations, rights, benefits, privileges, or immunities of any carrier, employee, organization, representative, or person subject thereto; nor shall anything contained in said titles (except section 505) of this Act be construed to confer any rights, privileges, immunities, or defenses upon employers, or to impair or otherwise affect the rights of any person under the National Labor Relations Act, as amended.

Effect on State Laws
(29 U.S.C. 524)

SEC. 604. Nothing in this Act shall be construed to impair or diminish the authority of any State to enact and enforce general criminal laws with respect to robbery, bribery, extortion, embezzlement, grand larceny, burglary, arson, violation of narcotics laws, murder, rape, assault with intent to kill, or assault which inflicts grievous bodily injury, or conspiracy to commit any of such crimes.

Service of Process
(29 U.S.C. 525)

SEC. 605. For the purposes of this Act, service of summons, subpena, or other legal process of a court of the United States upon an officer or agent of a labor organization in his capacity as such shall constitute service upon the labor organization.

Administrative Procedure Act
(29 U.S.C. 526)

SEC. 606. The provisions of the Administrative Procedure Act shall be applicable to the issuance, amendment, or rescission of any rules or regulations, or any adjudication, authorized or required pursuant to the provisions of this Act. 60 Stat. 237; 5 U.S.C. 1001 note.

Other Agencies and Departments
(29 U.S.C. 527)

SEC. 607. In order to avoid unnecessary expense and duplication of functions among Government agencies, the Secretary may make such arrangements or agreements for cooperation or mutual assistance in the performance of his functions under this Act and the functions of any such agency as he may find to be practicable and consistent with law. The Secretary may utilize the facilities or services of any department, agency, or establishment of the United States or of any State or political subdivision of a State, including the services of any of its employees, with the lawful consent of such department, agency, or establishment; and each department, agency, or establishment of the United States is authorized and directed to cooperate with the Secretary and, to the extent permitted by law, to provide such information and facilities as he may request for his assistance in the performance of his functions under this Act. The Attorney General or his representative shall receive from the Secretary for appropriate action such evidence developed in the performance of his functions under this Act as may be found to warrant consideration for criminal prosecution under the provisions of this Act or other Federal law. 73 Stat. 541.

Criminal Contempt
(29 U.S.C. 528)

SEC. 608. No person shall be punished for any criminal contempt allegedly committed outside the immediate presence of the court in connection with any civil action prosecuted by the Secretary or any other person in any court of the United States under the provisions of this Act unless the facts constituting such criminal contempt are established by the verdict of the jury in a proceeding in the district court of the United States, which jury shall be chosen and empaneled in the manner prescribed by the law governing trial juries in criminal prosecutions in the district courts of the United States.

Prohibition on Certain Discipline by Labor Organization
(29 U.S.C. 529)

SEC. 609. It shall be unlawful for any labor organization, or any officer, agent, shop steward, or other representative of a labor organization, or any employee thereof to fine, suspend, expel, or otherwise discipline any of its members for exercising any right to which he is entitled under the provisions of this Act. The provisions of section 102 shall be applicable in the enforcement of this section.

Deprivation of Rights Under Act by Violence
(29 U.S.C. 530)

SEC. 610. It shall be unlawful for any person through the use of force or violence, or threat of the use of force or violence, to restrain, coerce, or intimidate, or attempt to restrain, coerce, or intimidate any member of a labor organization for the purpose of interfering with or preventing the exercise of any right to which he is entitled under the provisions of this Act. Any person who willfully violates this section shall be fined not more than $1,000 or imprisoned for not more than one year, or both.

Separability Provisions
(29 U.S.C. 531)

Sec. 611. If any provision of this Act, or the application of such provision to any person or circumstances, shall be held invalid, the remainder of this Act or the application of such provision to persons or circumstances other than those as to which it is held invalid, shall not be affected thereby.

TITLE VII—AMENDMENTS TO THE LABOR MANAGEMENT RELATIONS ACT, 1947, AS AMENDED

Federal-State Jurisdiction

29 U.S.C. 164.

Sec. 701. (a) Section 14 of the National Labor Relations Act, as amended, is amended by adding at the end thereof the following new subsection:

"(c)(1) The Board, in its discretion, may, by rule of decision or by published rules adopted pursuant to the Administrative Procedure Act, decline to assert jurisdiction over any labor dispute involving any class or category of employers, where, in the opinion of the Board, the effect of such labor dispute on commerce is not sufficiently substantial to warrant the exercise of its jurisdiction: *Provided,* That the Board shall not decline to assert jurisdiction over any labor dispute over which it would assert jurisdiction under the standards prevailing upon August 1, 1959.

73 Stat. 542.

"(2) Nothing in this Act shall be deemed to prevent or bar any agency or the courts of any State or Territory (including the Commonwealth of Puerto Rico, Guam, and the Virgin Islands), from assuming and asserting jurisdiction over labor disputes over which the Board declines, pursuant to paragraph (1) of this subsection, to assert jurisdiction."

29 U.S.C. 153.

(b) Section 3(b) of such Act is amended to read as follows:

"(b) The Board is authorized to delegate to any group of three or more members any or all of the powers which it may itself exercise. The Board is also authorized to delegate to its regional directors its powers under section 9 to determine the unit appropriate for the purpose of collective bargaining, to investigate and provide for hearings, and determine whether a question of representation exists, and to direct an election or take a secret ballot under subsection (c) or (e) of section 9 and certify the results thereof, except that upon the filing of a request therefor with the Board by any interested person, the Board may review any action of a regional director delegated to him under this paragraph, but such a review shall not, unless specifically ordered by the Board, operate as a stay of any action taken by the regional director. A vacancy in the Board shall not impair the right of the remaining members to exercise all of the powers of the Board, and three members of the Board shall, at all times, constitute a quorum of the Board, except that two members shall constitute a quorum of any group designed pursuant to the first sentence thereof. The Board shall have an official seal which shall be judicially noticed."

29 U.S.C. 159

Economic Strikers

29 U.S.C. 159.

Sec. 702. Section 9(c)(3) of the National Labor Relations Act, as amended, is amended by amending the second sentence thereof to read as follows: "Employees engaged in an economic strike who are not entitled to reinstatement shall be eligible to vote under such regulations as the Board shall find are consistent with the purposes and provisions of this Act in any election conducted within twelve months after the commencement of the strike."

Vacancy in Office of General Counsel

SEC. 703. Section 3(d) of the National Labor Relations Act, as amended, is amended by adding after the period at the end thereof the following: "In case of a vacancy in the office of the General Counsel the President is authorized to designate the officer or employee who shall act as General Counsel during such vacancy, but no person or persons so designated shall so act (1) for more than forty days when the Congress is in session unless a nomination to fill such vacancy shall have been submitted to the Senate, or (2) after the adjournment sine die of the session of the Senate in which such nomination was submitted." 29 U.S.C. 153.

Boycotts and Recognition Picketing

SEC. 704. (a) Section 8(b)(4) of the National Labor Relations Act, as amended, is amended to read as follows: 29 U.S.C. 158.

"(4)(i) to engage in, or to induce or encourage any individual employed by any person engaged in commerce or in an industry affecting commerce to engage in, a strike or a refusal in the course of his employment to use, manufacture, process, transport, or otherwise handle or work on any goods, articles, materials, or commodities or to perform any services; or (ii) to threaten, coerce, or restrain any person engaged in commerce or in an industry affecting commerce, where in either case an object thereof is— 73 Stat. 543.

"(A) forcing or requiring any employer or self-employed person to join any labor or employer organization or to enter into any agreement which is prohibited by section 8(e);

"(B) forcing or requiring any person to cease using, selling, handling, transporting, or otherwise dealing in the products of any other producer, processor, or manufacturer, or to cease doing business with any other person, or forcing or requiring any other employer to recognize or bargain with a labor organization as the representative of his employees unless such labor organization has been certified as the representative of such employees under the provisions of section 9: *Provided,* That nothing contained in this clause (B) shall be construed to make unlawful, where not otherwise unlawful, any primary strike or primary picketing;

"(C) forcing or requiring any employer to recognize or bargain with a particular labor organization as the representative of his employees if another labor organization has been certified as the representative of such employees under the provisions of section 9;

"(D) forcing or requiring any employer to assign particular work to employees in a particular labor organization or in a particular trade, craft, or class rather than to employees in another labor organization or in another trade, craft, or class, unless such employer is failing to conform to an order or certification of the Board determining the bargaining representative for employees performing such work: *Provided,* That nothing contained in this subsection (b) shall be construed to make unlawful a refusal by any person to enter upon the premises of any employer (other than his own employer), if the employees of such employer are engaged in a strike ratified or approved by a representative of such employees whom such employer is required to recognize under this Act: *Provided further,* That for the purposes of this paragraph (4) only, nothing contained in such paragraph shall be construed to prohibit publicity, other than picketing, for the purpose of truthfully advising the public, including consumers and members of a labor organization, that a product or products are produced by an employer with whom the labor organization has a primary dispute and are distributed by another employer, as long as such publicity does not have an effect of inducing any individual employed by any person other than the primary employer in the course of his employment to refuse to pick up, deliver, or transport any goods, or not to perform any services, at the establishment of the employer engaged in such distribution;".

29 U.S.C. 158.

(b) Section 8 of the National Labor Relations Act, as amended, is amended by adding at the end thereof the following new subsection:

"(e) It shall be an unfair labor practice for any labor organization and any employer to enter into any contract or agreement, express or implied, whereby such employer ceases or refrains or agrees to cease or refrain from handling, using, selling, transporting or otherwise dealing in any of the products of any other employer, or to cease doing business with any other person, and any contract or agreement entered into heretofore or hereafter containing such an agreement shall be to such extent unenforcible and void: *Provided*, That nothing in this subsection (e) shall apply to an agreement between a labor organization and an employer in the construction industry relating to the contracting or subcontracting of work to be done at the site of the construction, alteration, painting, or repair of a building, structure, or other work: *Provided further*, That for the purposes of this subsection (e) and section 8(b)(4)(B) the terms 'any employer', 'any person engaged in commerce or any industry affecting commerce', and 'any person' when used in relation to the terms 'any other producer, processor, or manufacturer', 'any other employer', or 'any other person' shall not include persons in the relation of a jobber, manufacturer, contractor, or subcontractor working on the goods or premises of the jobber or manufacturer or performing parts of an integrated process of production in the apparel and clothing industry: *Provided further*, That nothing in this Act shall prohibit the enforcement of any agreement which is within the foregoing exception."

73 Stat. 544.

(c) Section 8(b) of the National Labor Relations Act, as amended, is amended by striking out the word "and" at the end of paragraph (5), striking out the period at the end of paragraph (6), and inserting in lieu thereof a semicolon and the word "and", and adding a new paragraph as follows:

"(7) to picket or cause to be picketed, or threaten to picket or cause to be picketed, any employer where an object thereof is forcing or requiring an employer to recognize or bargain with a labor organization as the representative of his employees, or forcing or requiring the employees of an employer to accept or select such labor organization as their collective bargaining representative, unless such labor organization is currently certified as the representative of such employees:

"(A) where the employer has lawfully recognized in accordance with this Act any other labor organization and a question concerning representation may not appropriately be raised under section 9(c) of this Act,

"(B) where within the preceding twelve months a valid election under section 9(c) of this Act has been conducted, or

"(C) where such picketing has been conducted without a petition under section 9(c) being filed within a reasonable period of time not to exceed thirty days from the commencement of such picketing: *Provided*, That when such a petition has been filed the Board shall forthwith, without regard to the provisions of section 9(c)(1) or the absence of a showing of a substantial interest on the part of the labor organization, direct an election in such unit as the Board finds to be appropriate and shall certify the results thereof: *Provided further,* That nothing in this subparagraph (C) shall be construed to prohibit any picketing or other publicity for the purpose of truthfully advising the public (including consumers) that an employer does not employ members of, or have a contract with, a labor organization, unless an effect of such picketing is to induce any individual employed by any other person in the course of his employment, not to pick up, deliver or transport any goods or not to perform any services.

"Nothing in this paragraph (7) shall be construed to permit any act which would otherwise be an unfair labor practice under this section 8(b)."

(d) Section 10(1) of the National Labor Relations Act, as amended, is amended by adding after the words "section 8(b)," the words "or section 8(e) or section 8(b)(7)," and by striking out the period at the end of the third sentence and inserting in lieu thereof a colon and the following: *"Provided further,* That such officer or regional attorney shall not apply for any restraining order under section 8(b)(7) if a charge against the employer under section 8(a)(2) has been filed and after the preliminary investigation, he has reasonable cause to believe that such charge is true and that a complaint should issue." 29 U.S.C. 160. 73 Stat. 545.

(e) Section 303(a) of the Labor Management Relations Act, 1947, is amended to read as follows: 29 U.S.C. 187.

"(a) It shall be unlawful, for the purpose of this section only, in an industry or activity affecting commerce, for any labor organization to engage in any activity or conduct defined as an unfair labor practice in section 8(b)(4) of the National Labor Relations Act, as amended."

Building and Construction Industry

SEC. 705. (a) Section 8 of the National Labor Relations Act, as amended by section 704(b) of this Act, is amended by adding at the end thereof the following new subsection: 29 U.S.C. 158.

"(f) It shall not be an unfair labor practice under subsections (a) and (b) of this section for an employer engaged primarily in the building and construction industry to make an agreement covering employees engaged (or who, upon their employment, will be engaged) in the building and construction industry with a labor organization of which building and construction employees are members (not established, maintained, or assisted by any action defined in section 8(a) of this Act as an unfair labor practice) because (1) the majority status of such labor organization has not been established under the provisions of section 9 of this Act prior to the making of such agreement, or (2) such agreement requires as a condition of employment, membership in such labor organization after the seventh day following the beginning of such employment or the effective date of the agreement, whichever is later, or (3) such agreement requires the employer to notify such labor organization of opportunities for employment with such employer, or gives such labor organization an opportunity to refer qualified applicants for such employment, or (4) such agreement specifies minimum training or experience qualifications for employment or provides for priority in opportunities for employment based upon length of service with such employer, in the industry or in the particular geographical area: *Provided,* That nothing in this subsection shall set aside the final proviso to section 8(a)(3) of this Act: *Provided further,* That any agreement which would be invalid, but for clause (1) of this subsection, shall not be a bar to a petition filed pursuant to section 9(c) or 9(e)."

(b) Nothing contained in the amendment made by subsection (a) shall be construed as authorizing the execution or application of agreements requiring membership in a labor organization as a condition of employment in any State or Territory in which such execution or application is prohibited by State or Territorial law.

Priority in Case Handling

29 U.S.C. 160.

SEC. 706. Section 10 of the National Labor Relations Act, as amended, is amended by adding at the end thereof a new subsection as follows:

"(m) Whenever it is charged that any person has engaged in an unfair labor practice within the meaning of subsection (a)(3) or (b)(2) of section 8, such charge shall be given priority over all other cases except cases of like character in the office where it is filed or to which it is referred and cases given priority under subsection (1)."

73 Stat. 546.

Effective Date of Amendments

SEC. 707. The amendments made by this title shall take effect sixty days after the date of the enactment of this Act and no provision of this title shall be deemed to make an unfair labor practice, any act which is performed prior to such effective date which did not constitute an unfair labor practice prior thereto.

Approved September 14, 1959.

Method Used for Main Body of
Department of Labor Study[1]

Our first task was to select the unions that would comprise our sample. We made our selection after extended discussions with our two senior legal consultants and a half dozen or so knowledgeable lawyers and past and present DOL officials recommended to us by our consultants.

We included twelve unions in our study, selected because they reflected a mix of industry groups: five manufacturing, four building and construction trades, one government, and two service unions. Most were affiliated with the AFL-CIO, but unaffiliated unions were also represented. Some have been involved in extensive litigation or Department of Labor (DOL) investigations related to the LMRDA; others have not. In all, the unions we chose represented 36.2 percent of all union members covered under the Act.[2] They range in size from four unions with under 250,000 members, to four with a membership range between 250,000 and 750,000 and four with over 750,000 members. All of them have subordinate units nationwide.

The cases cited in the DOL's annual publications detailing the activity under the LMRDA—the so-called Compliance Reports—indicate that the twelve unions in our sample accounted for approximately one third of all Title I litigation, as well as one third of Section 201(c), Title III, and Title IV suits brought. They also were involved in just over one third of the Title V civil suits cited, and exactly one third of all criminal actions, primarily allegations of embezzlement of union funds. This suggests that the impact of the LMRDA reported by our sample neither over- nor underrepresents actual over-all union experience under the Act and is, in fact, quite representative.

After close consultation with our advisors, we determined that the most logical and fruitful approach to our study would be by means of personal interviews. Gross statistics are insensitive to the particular characteristics and situations of individual unions, ignoring their structure, the composition and political consciousness of their membership, and the

---

1. Because the nature of the method used to analyze the data compiled from the three surveys of the Survey Research Center (University of Michigan) was so different from that employed in the rest of the study, it is described separately in appendix G.
2. U.S. Department of Labor, Bureau of Labor Statistics, *Directory of National Unions and Employee Associations, 1973* (Washington, D.C.: U.S. Department of Labor, 1976) Supplement 3. The members are distributed among 20,853 locals.

economic environment in which they function. The impossibility of controlling all relevant variables and the fact that even the most basic statistical data were largely unavailable, led to the conclusion that the personal interview method would provide the most meaningful data base.

Before beginning our interviews, and during the course of them, we gathered over 750 pieces of background material concerning the unions being studied, as well as analyses of the history and enforcement of the Act made by academicians, practitioners, and those charged with administering the Act. Relevant court decisions were also included. In addition, the material included books, pamphlets, articles from law reviews and other periodicals; internal DOL memoranda and printed material that either focus upon the impact of the Act or are intended to aid those affected by it; and individual unions' constitutions, bylaws, convention reports and proceedings, and the pamphlets and memoranda issued by those organizations to inform and guide their officers and members concerning the Act. The reading and analysis of that material not only served to give us historical background concerning the unions studied, and with regard to the Act itself, but also helped to pinpoint criticism leveled at the statutue or the interpretation of it. It also helped to educate us as to the problems that have been encountered by unions in attempting to comply with the Act, and the steps taken to cope with those problems.

After determining how we would approach the topic, we sent an outline describing our proposed study design to the appropriate DOL officials, and received their formal approval of it.

Interviews

In each union we interviewed members of the legal staff of the parent organization and in some cases (where a local union's counsel had been directly involved in LMRDA cases on behalf of the local) we interviewed the counsel for the local as well. The union officers and staff contacted at the top level were those in key policy-making positions, who have had extensive experience with both relevant court decisions and DOL enforcement policies. The intermediate and local level union officers contacted were again those who had had extensive experience with DOL enforcement of the Act.

In addition, we spoke to dissident members[3] in those same unions, as well as to their key advocates—those retained as counsel by the dissidents, and prominent spokesmen on their behalf. To determine the Act's effect from the vantage point of its enforcers, we also interviewed a number of past and present DOL officials.

The interviews often lasted for six hours or more; the number of representatives interviewed is set out below, according to category.

---

3. We defined "dissident members" as those who have been involved in litigation against their unions.

Union lawyers	32
Parent body officers and staff	18
Intermediate and local union officers	32[4]
Dissident members	13
Advocates for dissidents	7
DOL spokesmen	32

All eighty-two nondissident union spokesmen were drawn from the twelve unions in our sample. The average number per union was approximately seven, rather evenly divided between lawyers, parent union officials, and intermediate or local union officers. The thirteen dissidents were also all members of the unions in our sample. In that case, however, the distribution among the twelve unions was less even. In four unions, we interviewed no dissidents because, based on our interviews and the court cases, we could not identify any. The highest number of dissidents we interviewed from any one organization was three. All of the advocates for dissidents have acted as counsel for or spoken out on behalf of at least one of the dissidents in our sample.

We interviewed seventeen past and present DOL national office staff who have been, or are now, among the key administrators of the Act. We also considered it to be very important to become acquainted with the work of the agency personnel charged with the initial responsibility for investigating allegations that the Act has been violated, to learn what problems they have and what changes they would suggest. Therefore, we also interviewed DOL staff in the field.

Given the time limits under which we worked, it was clear that we could not visit all twenty-four area offices. Nor could we hope to speak to all of the some 600 DOL field staff members. Thus we had to be extremely selective. We first narrowed our choice to the area offices with the broadest experience in the conduct of investigations involving our twelve sample unions. Within that group, we singled out those offices in which both the union and dissident spokesmen we interviewed told us that they had received the fairest, most evenhanded treatment. In every case, personnel in those offices had also been cited to us as among the most competent by knowledgeable national office personnel. What we were interested in, then, was to interview field personnel whose enforcement of the Act came as close to adhering to the intent of the statute as possible, in the eyes of all who had come in contact with them—union officers, lawyers, dissidents, and their national office supervisors. Thus, the fifteen field office staff members that we interviewed, drawn from six area offices, are clearly not a random sample of DOL field personnel, nor were they intended to be. We therefore caution that the statements made by them may not be representative.

Once we began the field interviews, it became clear that the work of

---

4. Intermediate and local union officers were not separated in these figures because in many instances those interviewed served in both capacities.

the regional solicitors' offices and that of the area offices are often interrelated. We therefore added representatives of the two regional solicitors' offices most often cited to us by the area office personnel we had spoken to. For the most part, however, we did not include Labor-Management Services Administration (LMSA) regional office personnel in our survey, since they are not immediately involved in the receipt of complaints regarding alleged LMRDA violations and the investigation of such allegations. While they are responsible for making recommendations to the regional solicitor and the national office of the LMSA, they do not have final responsibility for the action taken on such complaints.

While our primary interest was in those who have been directly affected by, or who are charged with enforcement of, the Act, we also interviewed some dozen carefully selected employer spokesmen to obtain their views on the impact of the statute, particularly with reference to its effect on the collective bargaining process. Given the more limited nature of the topic covered, those interviews were somewhat shorter in length, though comparable in depth, to those with labor spokesmen or DOL representatives.

In addition, we considered it important to follow up the extensive reading we had done in legal periodicals with personal interviews with some of the leading scholars who have written the most concerning the Act, and who have displayed a continuing interest in it. The discussions with those academicians were quite lengthy, averaging four hours and, in one case, consuming closer to eight.

Measurement of Impact

The bulk of the statistical data we have used came from the DOL Compliance Reports or other DOL publications and records and from our comparison of the language of the constitutions and bylaws of the unions in our sample. In no case could we rely on that data alone to measure the impact of the Act on any aspect of the internal operation of labor unions. In each case, we had to supplement the statistical data with the impressions, memories, estimates, and beliefs of those we interviewed. Thus, while the statistics were extremely valuable to us, much of what we "measured" in the course of this study was subjective, rather than objective. In a study of this kind that is inevitable.

Moreover, insofar as those interviewed reached consensus on the effect of the Act on some aspect of current union practices—as they did on matters such as the improved financial record keeping, the greater care taken in handling union funds, the increased awareness of correct election procedures, and the more conscientious review of internal election appeals—our findings can be said to approach an objective measurement.

Where there was disagreement among those we contacted, we had to reckon with the differences in point of view, occupation, position, and outlook of those we interviewed, and weigh their statements accordingly.

This we did. We believe that by using the personal interview method, rather than relying wholly on the answers to written questionnaires, we were able to make such judgments more effectively than would otherwise have been the case.

Wherever possible, we have indicated alternate or additional methods of breaking down data that the DOL might wish to consider implementing to make the task of statistical measurement an easier one. However, even if such data were to become available, those statistics would still not be adequate to serve as the sole basis for measuring the impact of a piece of legislation, its interpretation and administration, upon the internal functioning of an organization. Much still depends upon what the administrators and interpreters of a statute believe the effect of it ought to be, and whether or not their perception of the law's intent differs from that held by the members of the organization the legislation is intended to regulate. In short, if the regulators often differ among themselves and, as a group, differ with those being regulated as to the function and purpose of a law—as is true in the case of the legislation we have been studying— purely objective measurement of the impact of that law is impossible.

With the help of our senior legal consultants, we designed separate questionnaires for lawyers, union officers, and DOL field personnel; these are reproduced in appendices C, D, and E. The questions were designed to elicit from those interviewed their assessment of the actual effect of the Act on the internal operations of labor unions, as well as the impact on those organizations of subsequent court interpretations and of DOL enforcement and administration of the Act.

What we attempted to learn was (1) whether or not these respondents have experienced or observed an actual impact and, if so, in what way; (2) whether they consider the impact, if any, beneficial or harmful; and (3) what changes, if any, should be made in either the language of the Act or in its enforcement, interpretation, or administration, and why.

We should emphasize that those sets of questions served only as a starting point for our interviews. Very few of our contacts stayed solely within the confines of the original set of questions posed. As time went on and new ideas and suggestions were given to us, we incorporated them into the questions we asked during the course of the interviews. (This also entailed recontacting those already interviewed, to ascertain their views concerning the additional ideas given us since the initial interview.)

Rather than preparing two additional sets of questions for the dissidents and for their advocates, we used the union officer or the lawyer questionnaire as a starting point in each interview, but concentrated primarily on what each could tell us from his own experience as a dissident or dissident advocate. In interviewing academicians and management spokesmen, we asked them what, from their experience, they thought the impact of the Act had been, what had led them to their conclusions, and what suggestions, if any, they had for change.

Confidentiality of Sources

We promised confidentiality to all the persons we interviewed, as well as to the organizations they represent, and have honored that promise. Therefore, at no time have we given the sources we used when discussing what we were told, except in the most general terms.

Survey Questionnaires

In order to test rank and file union member assessment of the impact of the Act, we formulated questions to be included in three University of Michigan Survey Research Center studies:

1. The Quality of Life survey, with 1,300 participants, 266 of them union members
2. The Summer 1975 Interim Telephone Survey, with 1,365 participants, 207 of them union members
3. The Omnibus Study, with 1,500 participants, 204 of them union members

The Quality of Life survey was made in the greater Detroit metropolitan area, encompassing three counties in and around Detroit. The other two surveys were conducted on a nationwide basis. Over-all, the union members in our selected unions comprised approximately one third of the total number of union member respondents reached by the surveys. By inserting questions in those three surveys, we were able to obtain information from 677 union members who would have been difficult to reach in any other way. We have included the questions we used in those surveys as appendix F; the methods used to analyze the survey data are discussed separately in appendix G.

We quoted quite liberally from the persons we interviewed. Each quotation was carefully chosen on the basis that it capsulized a viewpoint expressed by a particular segment of our interviewees, in each case identified as such. Our decision to quote rather than paraphrase those views grew out of our desire—nurtured by an eighteen-month investigation of our interviewees' experiences under the Act—to report the flavor as well as the facts of those experiences and observations.

Questionnaire for Union Lawyers

I. Nature of the union: composition of membership; how centralized or decentralized is it with regard to decision-making power; what was, historically, the interrelationship between the international, intermediate and local bodies; and has there been any change in that interrelationship since the enactment of LMRDA?

II. What changes did you advise your clients to make in order to comply with the original Act OR with later interpretations (made either by the courts or the DOL)? e.g., changes in:

(a) accounting procedures and records-keeping procedures;

(b) language of constitution and by-laws; (As to these, were such changes made on an *ad hoc* basis in response to specific problems or as an overall revision of the international's constitution and by-laws? Were model by-laws and constitutional changes suggested to the intermediate and local bodies?)

(c) qualifications for voting and office-holding;

(d) election procedures;

(e) how convention delegates' votes were to be counted;

(f) campaign rights of candidates (e.g., distribution of campaign literature; examination of membership lists, use of union journals prior to elections);

(g) purposes for which the union could spend money, in light of Section 501 (e.g., the payment of legal fees of union officers in criminal and civil cases, expense accounts, political expenditures);

(h) the grounds and procedures for the imposition of trusteeships;

(i) internal appellate procedures (and were such changes suggested because of increased use of those procedures);

(j) conduct of disciplinary proceedings.

To what extent do you consider that the changes made liberalized union rules, such as those covering eligibility to run for office, as against a tightening up, such as the imposition of additional eligibility requirements?

III. Did you find any resistance to making such changes and, if so, why and at what levels? What measures did you take to counter such resistance?

IV. What problems—internal and/or external—have your clients encountered in attempting to comply with the Act?

V. What aids have been available—internal and external (e.g., technical assistance, either within the union or from the DOL)? How effective have these been? [Note: If the internal aids were in writing, in the form of memoranda, booklets, model bylaws, etc., we asked for copies.]

VI. What are your views as to:
(a) the role of the courts in shaping the Act?
(b) the role of the DOL in interpreting and enforcing the Act?

VII. If you could rewrite the Act or make changes in emphasis with regard to its interpretation and/or enforcement, what would you suggest be done (e.g., changes in the issuance of "last clear chance" letters, and the way records are kept at the Silver Spring LMWP [now Office of Labor-Mangement Standards Enforcement] offices with respect to reports filed)?

VIII. What do you think the REAL impact of the Act has been, as against a "window-dressing" impact? Can you give concrete examples of REAL impact, whether for good or ill (e.g., has Title I in fact been an impediment to responsible collective bargaining as is sometimes contended? Has *Cole* v. *Hall* increased Title I court cases due to the ruling that the court "may" award attorney's fees, or have those fears faded away? Has Title II imposed an undue burden on smaller locals, as originally feared—have there been, for example, a number of mergers because of it)?

IX. Have opposition tickets been more frequent and more persistent since 1959 and, if so, what level has been most affected? Do you think that the "outs" have found it easier to become the "ins" within unions since 1959? In other words, how have opposition slates fared?

X. Has there been an increase in the number of complaints that have gone through the *internal* appellate procedure (and been settled internally, so that no court or DOL records would reflect them) since 1959? If so, has the greatest increase been in disciplinary appeals? Election appeals? Financial mishandling appeals? What is your opinion on the state of the law with respect to the exhaustion of internal union remedies?

XI. What historians (either official, such as a research director, or unofficial, such as a union member with an unusually good memory) could you suggest who might be able to pinpoint pre- and post-1959 differences?

XII. What international officers would be good to talk to (e.g., those directly involved in internal appellate procedures, overseeing election procedures, record-keeping and filing of reports) to find out what they think [expletives deleted, please] about the Act, its interpretation and enforcement?

XIII. What intermediate level union officers would be good to interview?

XIV. What local union officers would be good to contact with regard to the above because they have been directly involved in LMRDA related matters?

XV. How do you evaluate the caliber of Labor Department personnel, specifically the Compliance Officers (e.g., as to knowledge of the law, knowledge of the internal workings of unions, their investigatory skills)?

Questionnaire for Union Officials

I. (a) What changes can you think of that were made by your union to comply with the original Act? e.g.,
   (1) in the language of the constitution and by-laws;
   (2) in financial record-keeping procedures;
   (3) in election procedures;
   (4) in the imposition and duration of trusteeships;
   (5) in the internal appeals machinery;
   (6) in the disciplinary trial procedures;
   (7) in the procedures for levying initiation fees, dues and assessments.
   (b) What changes were made subsequently to comply with later court decisions or DOL interpretations affecting the Act?
II. What was the attitude of your members toward making any of the above changes? Did it differ among levels? If so, why?
III. What problems, if any, has your union encountered in attempting to comply with the Act? (e.g., is it common for local union officers to require help, either from a CPA or from the International Secretary-Treasurer's Office, in filling out their LM-3 forms? If so, can you suggest ways in which the form could be simplified so that such aid would not be necessary?)
IV. What aids have been made available to you (either from your own legal counsel or accountants or from the DOL) to help your union comply with the Act? How have you used them most effectively?
V. What effect, for good or ill, do you think those changes have had on your union? e.g.,
   (a) are trusteeships imposed more or less frequently?
   (b) do you get more or fewer internal complaints now? If more, has the greatest increase been in disciplinary appeals? In election appeals? In financial mishandling appeals?
   (c) have or have not the appeals procedures, both disciplinary and election, been speeded up?
   (d) have there been more or fewer court cases brought by members dissatisfied with the internal "verdict"?
   (e) have opposition tickets been more or less frequent in union elections? At what level?
   (f) have opposition tickets fared better or worse since 1959?
   (g) are members more or less anxious to run for union office at the local level? (The latter has been contended, particularly with

regard to small locals where the perquisites of office-holding are minimal.)

(h) are union meetings better or more poorly attended? Why?

(i) has the nature of those meetings changed? (e.g., more unruly, less so?)

(j) are those who attend meetings more or less openly critical of the leadership?

(k) has insistence on ratification of negotiated contract terms increased or decreased? If members do have the right to ratify contracts, has there been an increase or decrease in turn-downs?

(l) has there been an increase or decrease in mergers of small locals? If so, why?

(m) do members ask to see the union's financial reports more or less frequently? If more, do you ever get complaints from incumbent officers that dissidents use that tactic as an election device?

(n) has the Act imposed restraints on what union officers can spend union money for? If so, what has been the impact of them, for good or ill? Why?

(o) has it changed the procedures by which such expenditures can be made?

VI. If you have indicated, as to Question V, that the Act itself, and subsequent interpretations of it, have had an impact on the internal operations of your union, would you think that other factors may also have played a part in effectuating those changes? (e.g., "turbulent times," younger members are more willing to "buck the establishment," changes in the over-all economic picture.)

VII. If you do think other factors have been operative, do you think they have played a greater, equal, or lesser role than has the Act?

VIII. What are your views as to:

(a) the role of the courts in shaping the Act?

(b) the role of the DOL in interpreting and enforcing the Act?

IX. Overall, what do you think the ACTUAL impact of the Act has been, if any, on labor unions generally, as against "window dressing" impact? e.g.,

(a) what specifically has its impact been, if any, in protecting individual rank-and-file rights more effectively?

(b) what specifically has its impact been, if any, on collective bargaining?

X. What would you estimate to be the effect on your union of complying with the Act, in terms of financial cost or benefit? Can you point to specific additional expenditures or savings? e.g., for

(a) legal advice?

(b) bookkeeping charges and/or accountant's fees?

(c) changes, if any, in election procedures?

XI. Overall, if you could rewrite the Act or make changes in emphasis with regard to its interpretation and/or enforcement, what would you suggest be done?

XII. What historians (either official, such as research director; or unofficial, such as union member with an unusually good memory) could you suggest who might be able to pinpoint other pre- and post-1959 changes?

XIII. What other union officers, including intermediate and local level officers, would be good to talk to, (e.g., those directly involved in internal appeals procedures, overseeing elections, filing of reports) to get their views on the Act and its interpretation and enforcement?

Questionnaire for Department of Labor Field Office Personnel

I. Describe what you do—what do you concentrate on most and why? How much time is devoted to LMRDA problems? Which loom largest, next largest, etc.?

II. How do you fulfill the objective of expanding the rank-and-file union member's knowledge of his rights under the Act and Executive Order? What do you do in the way of "technical assistance" effort?

III. Title I: Describe what you do—what, related to this Title, requires the most time? Has FLMR [Federal Labor-Management Relations] increased your workload? (Have you always given advice on Title I problems?) What types of Title I complaints do you get most? Any numbers? (e.g., how many of each type per year—or does it vary between years? If the latter, have you any idea why?) What do you think of the suggestion that has been made that DOL should administer Title I, or part of it? (Exclusively?) What problems would you have if it did?

IV. Title II: Describe what you do—what, relative to Title II, requires the most time? Could more be done with this (e.g., more spot audits; do more with Section 203)?

V. Title III: Describe what you do—what, relative to this Title, requires the most time? Do you think enough is done with this? (Have you any files we could look at?)

VI. Title IV: Describe what you do—what, relative to this Title, requires the most time? What problems have you encountered and what are possible solutions? Have you an estimate of the number of reruns that have overturned previous results?

VII. Title V: Describe what you do—what, relative to the Title, requires the most time? Would you like direct, rather than Section 601, access to it—to administer it directly? (If so, should it be an exclusive right?) What problems would you foresee if you did so?

VIII. Title VI: Describe what you do—what, relative to this Title, requires the most time? Should Section 601 be used more to investigate pre-election? What do you do with Sections 609 and 610?

IX. How do you conceive of your role in administering the Act?

X. If you had more people and more money, what would you do with them and it?

XI. If you could restructure DOL enforcement and administration from top to bottom, what would you do to do your job more effectively (e.g., any bottlenecks you now encounter that you would eliminate; any paperwork that you would eliminate; would you eliminate time limits in election investigations; are you troubled if your recommendations are not taken; would you change the Solicitor's role; do you feel a need for better communication between levels of operation)?

XII. Should some other agency administer the Act? (e.g., aren't there inherent problems in having the same agency try to protect individual members' rights and at the same time consider the union's need to function effectively as a collective bargaining instrument?) Do you find different emphasis as to enforcement and administration depending on who is in office—or does it stay pretty much the same year in and year out?)

XIII. Are there any changes in policy, language, or court interpretations that you would make if you could?

XIV. What do you think the actual impact has been of the Act, and how could it become more effective? (Has it had an adverse effect on collective bargaining? Has it protected individual members' rights?)

XV. Even given your theoretical preferences and given political realities, should the Act and its current administration be left alone? (Can you live with it as it is?) Are you able to "bend" the current language? If so, what language, and how do you do it? Is there something to be *lost* by changing the language? If so, what language?

Questionnaire for Union Rank and File Members

There follows the portion of the 1975 Omnibus Study questionnaire that applied to this study. The questions for the Quality of Life survey and the Summer 1975 Interim Telephone Survey were identical to those reproduced below. In the Summer 1975 Interim Telephone Survey, the respondents were telephoned and the answers were open-ended. However, the responses were coded to correspond to the categories used in the other two surveys.

The Questionnaire

D1. INTERVIEWER CHECKPOINT

☐ 1. R IS CURRENTLY DOING SOME WORK FOR PAY; ON STRIKE; SICK LEAVE

☐ 2. R IS TEMPORARILY LAID OFF; UNEMPLOYED

☐ 3. ALL OTHERS ──────➤ TURN TO P. 46, SECTION E

D2. Are you a member of a labor union or organization? (INCLUDE TEACHERS AND NURSES ASSOCIATIONS.)

| 1. YES | | 5. NO | ──➤ TURN TO P. 46, SECTION E

D3. What union do you belong to? (WRITE OUT NAME.)

_____

D4. And what local or lodge do you belong to? (PROBE FOR NUMBER, OR NAME IF NUMBER IS NOT KNOWN.)

_____

D5. In general, how active are you in union activities, such as attending meetings, and participating in elections regularly—would you say you are very active, fairly active, somewhat active, fairly inactive, or not at all active?

1. VERY   2. FAIRLY   3. SOMEWHAT   4. FAIRLY   5. NOT AT ALL
   ACTIVE   ACTIVE   ACTIVE   INACTIVE   ACTIVE

D6. Could you go to your union's office and look at the union's financial reports if you wanted to?

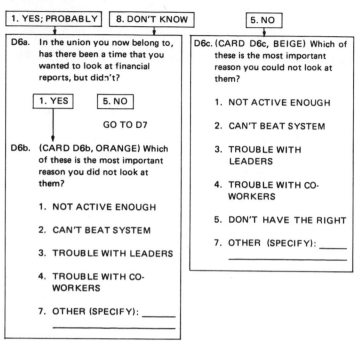

| 1. YES; PROBABLY | 8. DON'T KNOW | 5. NO |

D6a. In the union you now belong to, has there been a time that you wanted to look at financial reports, but didn't?

| 1. YES | 5. NO |

GO TO D7

D6b. (CARD D6b, ORANGE) Which of these is the most important reason you did not look at them?

1. NOT ACTIVE ENOUGH

2. CAN'T BEAT SYSTEM

3. TROUBLE WITH LEADERS

4. TROUBLE WITH CO-WORKERS

7. OTHER (SPECIFY): _____

D6c. (CARD D6c, BEIGE) Which of these is the most important reason you could not look at them?

1. NOT ACTIVE ENOUGH

2. CAN'T BEAT SYSTEM

3. TROUBLE WITH LEADERS

4. TROUBLE WITH CO-WORKERS

5. DON'T HAVE THE RIGHT

7. OTHER (SPECIFY): _____

D7. Could you speak up at union meetings if you thought the officers were not representing the members' interests well enough?

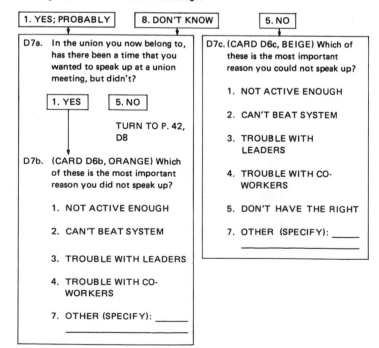

| 1. YES; PROBABLY | 8. DON'T KNOW | 5. NO |

D7a. In the union you now belong to, has there been a time that you wanted to speak up at a union meeting, but didn't?

| 1. YES | 5. NO |

TURN TO P. 42, D8

D7b. (CARD D6b, ORANGE) Which of these is the most important reason you did not speak up?

1. NOT ACTIVE ENOUGH

2. CAN'T BEAT SYSTEM

3. TROUBLE WITH LEADERS

4. TROUBLE WITH CO-WORKERS

7. OTHER (SPECIFY): _____

D7c. (CARD D6c, BEIGE) Which of these is the most important reason you could not speak up?

1. NOT ACTIVE ENOUGH

2. CAN'T BEAT SYSTEM

3. TROUBLE WITH LEADERS

4. TROUBLE WITH CO-WORKERS

5. DON'T HAVE THE RIGHT

7. OTHER (SPECIFY): _____

D8. Could you nominate, campaign and vote for someone other than the people in office at the next union election if you were unhappy with those now in office?

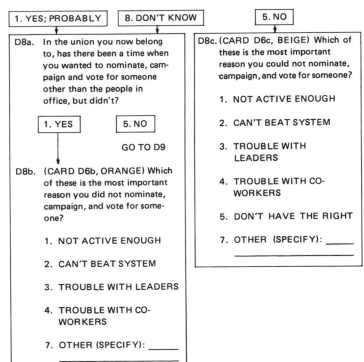

| 1. YES; PROBABLY | 8. DON'T KNOW | 5. NO |

D8a. In the union you now belong to, has there been a time when you wanted to nominate, campaign and vote for someone other than the people in office, but didn't?

| 1. YES | 5. NO |

GO TO D9

D8b. (CARD D6b, ORANGE) Which of these is the most important reason you did not nominate, campaign, and vote for someone?

1. NOT ACTIVE ENOUGH

2. CAN'T BEAT SYSTEM

3. TROUBLE WITH LEADERS

4. TROUBLE WITH CO-WORKERS

7. OTHER (SPECIFY): _____

D8c. (CARD D6c, BEIGE) Which of these is the most important reason you could not nominate, campaign, and vote for someone?

1. NOT ACTIVE ENOUGH

2. CAN'T BEAT SYSTEM

3. TROUBLE WITH LEADERS

4. TROUBLE WITH CO-WORKERS

5. DON'T HAVE THE RIGHT

7. OTHER (SPECIFY): _____

D9. Could you run for union office if you wanted to?

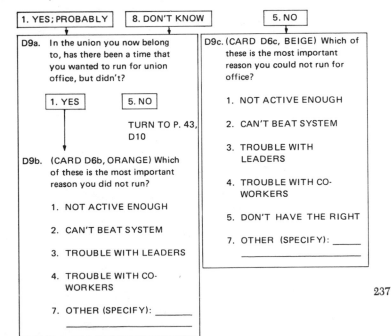

| 1. YES; PROBABLY | 8. DON'T KNOW | 5. NO |

D9a. In the union you now belong to, has there been a time that you wanted to run for union office, but didn't?

| 1. YES | 5. NO |

TURN TO P. 43, D10

D9b. (CARD D6b, ORANGE) Which of these is the most important reason you did not run?

1. NOT ACTIVE ENOUGH

2. CAN'T BEAT SYSTEM

3. TROUBLE WITH LEADERS

4. TROUBLE WITH CO-WORKERS

7. OTHER (SPECIFY): _____

D9c. (CARD D6c, BEIGE) Which of these is the most important reason you could not run for office?

1. NOT ACTIVE ENOUGH

2. CAN'T BEAT SYSTEM

3. TROUBLE WITH LEADERS

4. TROUBLE WITH CO-WORKERS

5. DON'T HAVE THE RIGHT

7. OTHER (SPECIFY): _____

237

D10. Could you do something about it if you thought there was something wrong with the way your union's elections were run?

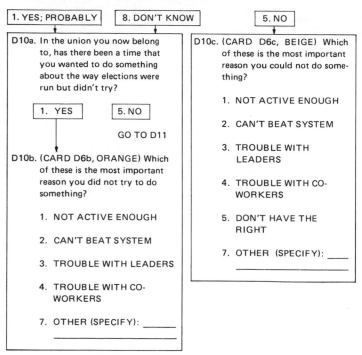

| 1. YES; PROBABLY | 8. DON'T KNOW | 5. NO |

D10a. In the union you now belong to, has there been a time that you wanted to do something about the way elections were run but didn't try?

1. YES   5. NO

GO TO D11

D10b. (CARD D6b, ORANGE) Which of these is the most important reason you did not try to do something?

1. NOT ACTIVE ENOUGH

2. CAN'T BEAT SYSTEM

3. TROUBLE WITH LEADERS

4. TROUBLE WITH CO-WORKERS

7. OTHER (SPECIFY): _____

D10c. (CARD D6c, BEIGE) Which of these is the most important reason you could not do something?

1. NOT ACTIVE ENOUGH

2. CAN'T BEAT SYSTEM

3. TROUBLE WITH LEADERS

4. TROUBLE WITH CO-WORKERS

5. DON'T HAVE THE RIGHT

7. OTHER (SPECIFY): ____

D11. Could you protest at a union meeting if you thought your union was using your dues money to support political candidates or parties you didn't agree with?

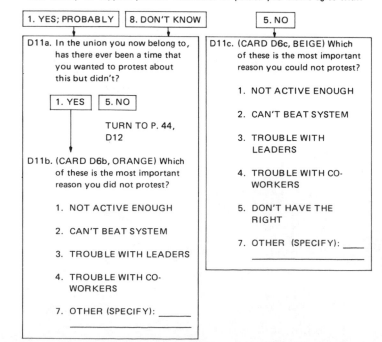

| 1. YES; PROBABLY | 8. DON'T KNOW | 5. NO |

D11a. In the union you now belong to, has there ever been a time that you wanted to protest about this but didn't?

1. YES   5. NO

TURN TO P. 44, D12

D11b. (CARD D6b, ORANGE) Which of these is the most important reason you did not protest?

1. NOT ACTIVE ENOUGH

2. CAN'T BEAT SYSTEM

3. TROUBLE WITH LEADERS

4. TROUBLE WITH CO-WORKERS

7. OTHER (SPECIFY): _____

D11c. (CARD D6c, BEIGE) Which of these is the most important reason you could not protest?

1. NOT ACTIVE ENOUGH

2. CAN'T BEAT SYSTEM

3. TROUBLE WITH LEADERS

4. TROUBLE WITH CO-WORKERS

5. DON'T HAVE THE RIGHT

7. OTHER (SPECIFY): ____

D12. Do you know much about the Landrum-Griffin Act—officially called the Labor-Management Reporting and Disclosure Act of 1959?

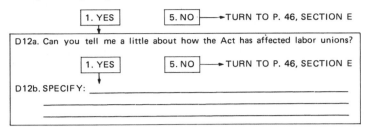

D13. Do you think the Landrum-Griffin Act has made your union officers <u>more</u> honest, <u>less</u> honest, or <u>hasn't it made any difference?</u>

| 1. MORE HONEST | 5. LESS HONEST | 3. NO DIFFERENCE | 8. DON'T KNOW |

D14. Has it made your union leaders <u>more</u> likely to listen to union members' wishes, <u>less</u> likely, or <u>hasn't it made any difference?</u>

| 1. MORE LIKELY | 5. LESS LIKELY | 3. NO DIFFERENCE | 8. DON'T KNOW |

D15. Has it given members of your union <u>more</u> control over how their dues money is spent, <u>less</u> control, or <u>hasn't it made any difference?</u>

| 1. MORE CONTROL | 5. LESS CONTROL | 3. NO DIFFERENCE | 8. DON'T KNOW |

D16. Has it given members of your union <u>more</u> freedom to speak out, <u>less</u> freedom, or <u>hasn't it made any difference?</u>

| 1. MORE FREEDOM | 5. LESS FREEDOM | 3. NO DIFFERENCE | 8. DON'T KNOW |

D17. If you wanted to become a union officer, has the Landrum-Griffin Act made it <u>easier</u>, made it <u>harder</u>, or <u>hasn't it made any difference?</u>

| 1. EASIER | 5. HARDER | 3. NO DIFFERENCE | 8. DON'T KNOW |

D18. Has it made it <u>easier</u> for you to go to the union offices and look at union financial reports if you want to, made it <u>more difficult,</u> or <u>hasn't it made any difference?</u>

| 1. EASIER | 5. MORE DIFFICULT | 3. NO DIFFERENCE | 8. DON'T KNOW |

Data Compiled from the Three Surveys

As reported at the beginning of this volume, to supplement the information obtained from personal interviews, we prepared questions on internal union activities, to be asked of rank and file union members, for incorporation in three surveys which were undertaken by the University of Michigan's Survey Research Center. The same set of questions was included in all three surveys. The three were:

The Detroit metropolitan area Quality of Life survey, completed in March, 1975, with 1,300 participants, 266 (20.49%) of them union members.

The nationwide Summer of 1975 Interim Telephone Survey, from which we received data in the late fall of 1975, with 1,365 respondents, 207 (15.16%) of them union members.

The nationwide Omnibus Study, from which we received final results in early 1976, with 1,500 participants, 204 (13.60%) of them union members.

Approximately one third of the rank and file members contacted by the three surveys were members of the twelve unions earlier selected for intensive study.

A Word of Caution

That only 677 (16.25 percent) of the total of 4,165 respondents in the three surveys were union members highlights a fact we would like to stress. The two national surveys were stratified to assure proportionate representation of U.S. households by geographic location, degree of urbanization, and social and economic levels. In the southern region, they were further stratified by race. Similarly, the Detroit survey sample was stratified to allow adequate representation both of residents of the city of Detroit and of those of the surrounding area, as well as of various social and economic subgroups. None of the surveys was designed to reach a representative cross section of this country's union members. This fact is reflected in the proportion of union members reached by each survey. In Detroit, where the population is heavily unionized, 20.46 percent of the respondents were union members, in contrast to the 14.34 percent found in the combined national surveys. Thus, the reader should be cautious in using the data compiled and the conclusions reached based on the survey responses. The respondents are not necessarily representative of all union members in this country, nor of those covered under the LMRDA. They are representative of union members in a cross section of U.S. households (tables 7 and 8).

Table 9 lists the names of the unions to which at least one survey respondent belonged, the number of members interviewed from each, and characteristics of each organization relevant to this study. Because of the disproportionate number of respondents reached from certain unions—either underrepresenting or overrepresenting the total membership—and the fact that some unions were not represented at all, table 9 gives additional evidence that the respondents reached are not representative of all American labor union members, nor of those covered under the LMRDA. Moreover, the number listed as being members of local unions directly affiliated with the AFL-CIO seems inordinately high. While it is, of course, possible that that figure is accurate, it seems more likely that either the respondents were too vague in answering the question posed or that the interviewers were too willing to accept "AFL-CIO" as a complete response.

In addition, we were unable to identify the unions named by seventy-one of the respondents, since none of those organizations are listed in the latest supplement to the *Directory of National Unions and Employee Associations* then available.[1] From the names of the organizations given to the interviewers by the respondents, those unidentifiable unions appear to be either small independents or newly organized white collar and/or public sector unions. However, since we could not identify them precisely, we preferred to exclude their seventy-one members from our union-related analysis. Those respondents do remain in the survey analysis, however.

Detroit Survey Respondents Compared with Those of National Surveys

Because of Detroit's distinguishing characteristics—lengthy and extensive unionization and the predominant presence of the United Automobile Workers—tests of distribution (Chi-square tests) were performed comparing the Detroit union members' responses with those of the national surveys. The tests compared the responses on three demographic characteristics (race, education, and age) and three nondemographic characteristics (union activity, freedom to participate in union affairs, and knowledge of LMRDA).[2]

The null hypothesis stated that there was no significant difference between the two groups, with "significant" defined as attaining a significance level of .05 or less.

---

1. U.S. Department of Labor, Bureau of Labor Statistics, *Directory of National Unions and Employee Associations, 1973* (Washington, D.C.: U.S. Department of Labor, 1976) Supplement 3.
2. See discussion at *The Questions Used* below for elaboration of these variables.

TABLE 7. Profile of Respondents

	All Respondents	LMRDA-covered Respondents
A. *Gender*	N=676*	N=491*
Male	471 (69.67%)	379 (77.19%)
Female	205 (30.33%)	112 (22.81%)
B. *Race*	N=676*	N=491*
White	526 (77.81%)	388 (79.02%)
Black	139 (20.56%)	93 (18.94%)
Other	11 (1.63%)	10 (2.04%)
C. *Average age*	N=677	N=492
Years	39.65	39.73
D. *Region (Interim and Omnibus Studies only)*	N=411	N=300
West	71 (17.27%)	56 (18.67%)
North central	156 (38.44%)	125 (41.66%)
Northeast	103 (25.06%)	63 (21.00%)
South	79 (19.22%)	56 (18.67%)
E. *Statutory coverage where union identifiable*	N=606	N=492
LMRDA covered	492 (81.19%)	492 (100.00%)
E.O. 11491 covered	8 (1.32%)	—
Quasi-covered†	61 (10.06%)	—
Not covered	45 (7.43%)	—
F. *Affiliation with AFL-CIO where union identifiable*	N=606	N=492
Yes	361 (59.57%)	294 (59.75%)
No	245 (40.43%)	198 (40.24%)
G. *Sector where union identifiable*	N=606	N=492
Public	114 (18.81%)	—
Private or quasi-public‡	492 (81.19%)	492 (100.00%)
H. *Activity level*	N=676*	N=492
Very	89 (13.17%)	58 (11.78%)
Fairly	131 (19.38%)	90 (18.29%)
Somewhat	126 (18.64%)	92 (18.69%)
Fairly inactive	115 (17.01%)	90 (18.29%)
Not	215 (31.80%)	162 (32.92%)
I. *Freedom score*	N=677	N=492
Six	310 (45.79%)	213 (43.29%)
Five	172 (25.41%)	134 (27.23%)
Four	93 (13.74%)	72 (14.63%)
Three	50 (7.38%)	40 (8.13%)
Two	22 (3.25%)	14 (2.84%)

TABLE 7—Continued

	All Respondents	LMRDA-covered Respondents
One	12 (1.77%)	9 (1.82%)
Zero	18 (2.65%)	10 (2.03%)
J. Familiarity with		
LMRDA	N=671**	N=492
Yes	59 (8.79%)	45 (9.15%)
No	612 (91.21%)	447 (90.85%)
K. Respondents 44 years		
of age or less	N=419††	N=304‡‡
Yes	27 (6.44%)	17 (5.59%)
No	392 (93.56%)	287 (94.41%)
L. Respondents over 44		
years of age	N=252	N=184
Yes	32 (12.70%)	28 (15.22%)
No	220 (87.30%)	156 (84.78%)

* In each case, characteristic not ascertained for one respondent.

† Unions, such as AFSCME, where some locals have private sector members.

‡ Government corporations, such as railroads and the U.S. Post Office.

** Five respondents not ascertained; one coded DK.

†† Knowledge of Act not ascertained for six respondents.

‡‡ Knowledge of Act not ascertained for four respondents.

The tests revealed that on only one variable—race—did the Detroit respondents' characteristics vary significantly from those of the respondents on the national survey. Not surprisingly, the Detroit survey returns included a higher proportion of black union members (37% black compared to 8% black in the national surveys) (table 10).

Further investigation of the disparity between the two groups' racial distributions—a comparison of the responses of Detroit's white union members with those of the national surveys' white union members, and likewise for the blacks—revealed a significant difference only in education levels between the Detroit black respondents and the blacks in the national surveys (table 11).

Of the black respondents in the national surveys, 62 percent have thirteen years or more of education compared to 29 percent in that classification among the Detroit survey blacks. This is probably a sampling problem, given that only twenty-nine blacks were reached in the national survey (or 8 percent of all union member respondents reached). Because blacks make up so much larger a proportion of the Detroit survey respondents (90 respondents or 37 percent), and because their education levels are virtually the same as those of white Detroit respondents (Chi-square = 1.0968, significance level = .7779, d.f. = 3, N=242), the over-all difference between the Detroit and national surveys in terms of education is not significant (table 10).

TABLE 8. Activity Level of Respondents

	Very Active	Fairly Active	Somewhat Active	Fairly Inactive	Not Active	Total Percentage
A. All respondents, all surveys (N=676)*	89 (13.17%)	131 (19.38%)	126 (18.64%)	115 (17.01%)	215 (31.80%)	100.00
B. Statutory coverage (N=606)†						
LMRDA (N=492)	58 (11.79%)	90 (18.29%)	92 (18.70%)	90 (18.29%)	162 (32.93%)	100.00
E.O. 11491 (N=8)	0	1 (12.50%)	3 (37.50%)	1 (12.50%)	3 (37.50%)	100.00
Quasi-covered (N=61)	9 (14.75%)	11 (15.25%)	10 (16.39%)	14 (22.95%)	17 (27.87%)	99.99
Not covered (N=45)	11 (24.44%)	11 (27.66%)	13 (28.88%)	1 (2.21%)	9 (20.00%)	99.98
C. AFL-CIO affiliation (N=606)†						
Yes (N=361)	43 (11.91%)	68 (18.84%)	56 (15.51%)	75 (20.78%)	119 (32.96%)	100.00
No (N=245)	35 (14.28%)	45 (18.37%)	62 (25.31%)	31 (12.65%)	72 (29.39%)	100.00
D. Sector (N=606)†						
Public (N=114)	29 (25.44%)	16 (14.03%)	26 (22.81%)	23 (20.18%)	20 (17.54%)	100.00
Private or quasi-public (N=492)	58 (11.79%)	90 (18.29%)	92 (18.70%)	90 (18.29%)	162 (32.93%)	100.00
E. Gender (N=675)‡						
Male (N=470)	67 (14.26%)	92 (19.57%)	88 (18.72%)	83 (17.66%)	140 (29.79%)	100.00
Female (N=205)	21 (10.24%)	39 (19.02%)	38 (18.54%)	32 (15.61%)	75 (36.59%)	100.00
F. Race (N=675)‡						
White (N=526)	59 (11.22%)	109 (20.72%)	102 (19.39%)	89 (16.92%)	167 (31.75%)	100.00
Black (N=138)	30 (21.74%)	21 (15.22%)	21 (15.22%)	22 (15.94%)	44 (31.88%)	100.00
Other (N=11)	0	1 (9.09%)	3 (27.27%)	3 (27.27%)	4 (36.36%)	99.99

G. Age (N=676)*						
18–25 (N=98)	8 (8.16%)	14 (14.28%)	21 (21.42%)	18 (18.36%)	37 (37.75%)	99.97
26–39 (N=255)	44 (17.25%)	54 (21.18%)	41 (16.08%)	46 (18.04%)	70 (27.45%)	100.00
40–55 (N=236)	26 (11.01%)	52 (22.03%)	55 (23.30%)	36 (15.25%)	67 (28.38%)	99.97
56–65 (N=76)	9 (11.84%)	10 (13.15%)	9 (11.84%)	14 (18.42%)	34 (44.73%)	99.98
66+ (N=10)	2 (20.00%)	1 (10.00%)	0	1 (10.00%)	6 (60.00%)	100.00
H. Education (N=673)**						
0–8 (N=70)	9 (12.85%)	14 (20.00%)	12 (17.14%)	10 (14.28%)	25 (35.71%)	99.98
9–12 (N=395)	44 (11.14%)	80 (20.25%)	78 (19.75%)	64 (16.20%)	129 (32.66%)	100.00
13–16 (N=147)	24 (16.32%)	24 (16.32%)	21 (14.28%)	32 (21.76%)	46 (31.29%)	99.97
17+ (N=61)	12 (19.67%)	13 (21.31%)	15 (24.59%)	8 (13.11%)	13 (21.31%)	99.99
I. Income						
Quality of Life (1973) (N=266)						
Less than $6,000 (N=34)	5 (14.70%)	2 (5.88%)	7 (20.58%)	2 (5.88%)	18 (52.94%)	99.98
$6,000–$9,999 (N=38)	6 (15.78%)	4 (10.52%)	7 (18.42%)	10 (26.31%)	11 (28.94%)	99.97
$10,000–14,999 (N=89)	14 (15.73%)	16 (17.97%)	20 (22.47%)	14 (15.73%)	25 (28.08%)	99.98
$15,000+ (N=105)	18 (17.14%)	18 (17.14%)	24 (22.85%)	17 (16.19%)	28 (26.66%)	99.98
Omnibus (1974) (N=203)*						
Less than $6,000 (N=45)	3 (6.67%)	2 (4.44%)	7 (15.56%)	5 (11.11%)	28 (62.22%)	100.00
$6,000–$9,999 (N=47)	4 (8.51%)	12 (25.53%)	11 (23.40%)	10 (21.27%)	10 (21.27%)	99.98
$10,000–14,999 (N=62)	9 (14.51%)	13 (20.96%)	12 (19.35%)	11 (17.74%)	17 (27.41%)	99.97
$15,000+ (N=49)	10 (20.40%)	7 (14.28%)	11 (22.44%)	8 (16.32%)	13 (26.53%)	99.97
J. Region						
Omnibus and Interim only (All regions)						
(N=410)*	46 (11.22%)	91 (22.20%)	68 (16.58%)	72 (17.56%)	133 (32.44%)	100.00
West (N=71)	7 (9.86%)	10 (14.08%)	11 (15.49%)	17 (23.94%)	26 (36.62%)	99.99

TABLE 8—Continued

	Very Active	Fairly Active	Somewhat Active	Fairly Inactive	Not Active	Total Percentage
North central (N=158)	16 (10.13%)	28 (17.72%)	29 (18.35%)	35 (22.15%)	50 (31.65%)	100.00
Northeast (N=102)*	13 (12.75%)	32 (31.37%)	15 (14.71%)	11 (10.78%)	31 (30.39%)	100.00
South (N=79)	10 (12.66%)	21 (26.58%)	13 (16.46%)	9 (11.39%)	26 (32.91%)	100.00
Quality of Life (All north central) (N=266)	43 (16.16%)	40 (15.04%)	58 (21.80%)	43 (16.16%)	82 (30.82%)	99.98
K. Knew about LMRDA (N=670)††						
Yes (N=59)	17 (28.81%)	16 (27.11%)	9 (15.26%)	8 (13.55%)	9 (15.26%)	99.99
No (N=611)	72 (11.78%)	115 (18.82%)	117 (19.15%)	107 (17.51%)	200 (32.73%)	99.99
L. Union size (N=600)‡‡						
1–49,999 (N=31)	2 (6.45%)	4 (12.90%)	5 (16.13%)	2 (6.45%)	18 (58.06%)	99.99
50,000–499,999 (N=220)	26 (11.81%)	47 (21.36%)	36 (16.36%)	46 (20.90%)	65 (29.54%)	99.97
500,000–999,999 (N=115)	13 (11.30%)	19 (16.52%)	15 (13.04%)	24 (20.86%)	44 (38.26%)	99.98
1,000,000+ (N=234)	35 (14.95%)	43 (18.37%)	60 (25.64%)	34 (14.52%)	62 (26.49%)	99.97
M. Freedom score (N=676)*						
Six (N=310)	64 (20.64%)	73 (23.54%)	55 (17.74%)	50 (16.12%)	68 (21.93%)	99.97
Five (N=172)	17 (9.88%)	33 (19.18%)	35 (20.34%)	39 (22.67%)	48 (27.90%)	99.97
Four (N=93)	3 (3.22%)	9 (9.67%)	25 (26.88%)	18 (19.35%)	38 (40.86%)	99.98
Three (N=50)	3 (6.00%)	11 (22.00%)	8 (16.00%)	5 (10.00%)	23 (46.00%)	100.00
Two (N=22)	2 (9.09%)	3 (13.63%)	2 (9.09%)	2 (9.09%)	13 (59.09%)	99.99
One (N=12)	0	2 (16.66%)	0	1 (8.33%)	9 (75.00%)	99.99
Zero (N=17)	0	0	1 (6.00%)	0	16 (94.00%)	100.00
Total (N=676)	89 (13.16%)	131 (19.38%)	126 (18.64%)	115 (17.01%)	215 (31.80%)	99.99

* Activity level not ascertained for one respondent.
† Respondents whose unions were identifiable.
‡Characteristic not ascertained for one respondent, and activity level not ascertained for one black male.
** Activity level not ascertained for one respondent, and education level not ascertained for three others.
†† Activity level not ascertained for one respondent, and knowledge of the Act not ascertained for six others.
‡‡ Respondents whose unions were identifiable, and size of union b...

TABLE 9. Characteristics of Unions Covered in the Three Surveys

Union Name	Number of Respondents in all Surveys	Economic Sector*	Union Size†	Affiliation with AFL-CIO	Statutory Coverage‡	Amount of LMRDA Litigation (Number of Cases Decided)
Amalgamated Clothing Workers of America	7	Private	365,000	Yes	LMRDA	8
Amalgamated Meat Cutters and Butcher Workmen of North America	17	Private	528,631	Yes	LMRDA	3
Amalgamated Transit Union	1	Private	130,000	Yes	LMRDA	3
American Federation of Government Employees	6	Gov't	292,809	Yes	E.O.	IA
American Federation of Grain Millers	1	Private	36,000	Yes	LMRDA	0
American Federation of Musicians	4	Private	315,000	Yes	LMRDA	19
American Federation of State, County and Municipal Employees	25	Gov't	529,035	Yes	Quasi	7
American Federation of Teachers	34	Gov't	248,521	Yes	Quasi	1
American Flint Glass Workers' Union of North America	2	Private	N.A.	Yes	LMRDA	0
American Postal Workers Union	5	Private	238,763	Yes	LMRDA	1
Associated Actors and Artistes of America	2	Private	63,000	Yes	LMRDA	0
Bakery and Confectionary Workers' International Union of America	4	Private	145,836	Yes	LMRDA	4
Bricklayers, Masons and Plasterers' International Union of America	7	Private	149,000	Yes	LMRDA	4
Brotherhood; Railway Carmen of the United States and Canada	1	Private	103,992	Yes	LMRDA	4
Brotherhood of Railway, Airline and Steamship Clerks, Freight Handlers, Express and Station Employees	4	Private	238,355	Yes	LMRDA	2

TABLE 9—Continued

Union Name	Number of Respondents in all Surveys	Economic Sector*	Union Size†	Affiliation with AFL-CIO	Statutory Coverage‡	Amount of LMRDA Litigation (Number of Cases Decided)
Civil Service Employees Ass'n. (NYS)	2	Gov't	202,000	No	Non	IA
Communications Workers of America	15	Private	443,278	Yes	LMRDA	3
Connecticut State Employees Association	1	Gov't	25,500	No	Non	IA
Directors Guild of America, Inc.	2	Private	3,842	No	LMRDA	0
Glass Bottle Blowers Association of the United States and Canada	2	Private	78,883	Yes	LMRDA	11
Hotel and Restaurant Employees and Bartenders International Union	8	Private	458,029	Yes	LMRDA	13
Insurance Workers International Union	1	Private	23,556	Yes	LMRDA	2
International Air Line Pilots Association	2	Private	27,639	Yes	LMRDA	2
International Alliance of Theatrical Stage Employees and Moving Picture Machine Operators of the United States and Canada	1	Private	62,000	Yes	LMRDA	9
International Association of Bridge, Structural and Ornamental Iron Workers	5	Private	175,611	Yes	LMRDA	8
International Association of Fire Fighters	2	Gov't	160,258	Yes	Quasi	IA
International Association of Machinists and Aerospace Workers	9	Private	757,564	Yes	LMRDA	25
International Brotherhood of Boilermakers, Iron Shipbuilders, Blacksmiths, Forgers and Helpers	2	Private	132,000	Yes	LMRDA	15
International Brotherhood of Electrical Workers	30	Private	956,579	Yes	LMRDA	24

Union						
International Brotherhood of Painters and Allied Trades	4	Private	207,844	Yes	LMRDA	21
International Brotherhood of Teamsters, Chauffeurs, Warehousemen and Helpers of America	46	Private	1,854,659	No	LMRDA	57
International Chemical Workers Union	2	Private	84,949	Yes	LMRDA	1
International Ladies' Garment Workers Union	1	Private	427,568	Yes	LMRDA	0
International Leather Goods, Plastic and Novelty Workers' Union	2	Private	39,200	Yes	LMRDA	0
International Longshoremen's and Warehousemen's Union	3	Private	58,000	No	LMRDA	0
International Printing Pressmen and Assistants' Union of North America	1	Private	100,000	Yes	LMRDA	5
International Typographical Union	5	Private	115,273	Yes	LMRDA	2
International Union of Electrical, Radio and Machine Workers	5	Private	290,000	Yes	LMRDA	8
International Union of Elevator Constructors	1	Private	17,683	Yes	LMRDA	0
International Union of Operating Engineers	9	Private	401,537	Yes	LMRDA	34
International Union, United Automobile, Aerospace and Agricultural Implement Workers of America	139	Private	1,393,501	No	LMRDA	15
International Union, United Plant Guard Workers of America	1	Private	20,000	No	LMRDA	0
Laborers' International Union of North America	1	Private	600,000	Yes	LMRDA	25
Massachusetts State Employees Association	1	Gov't	10,000	No	Non	IA
Michigan State Employees Association	3	Gov't	18,000	No	Non	IA
National Association of Government Employees	2	Gov't	100,000	No	E.O.	IA
National Association of Letter Carriers of the United States of America	13	Private	220,000	Yes	LMRDA	0

TABLE 9—Continued

Union Name	Number of Respondents in all Surveys	Economic Sector*	Union Size†	Affiliation with AFL-CIO	Statutory Coverage‡	Amount of LMRDA Litigation (Number of Cases Decided)
National Education Association	33	Gov't	1,165,615	No	Non	IA
Ohio Civil Service Employees Association	1	Gov't	33,500	No	Non	IA
Pattern Makers' League of North America	3	Private	11,311	Yes	LMRDA	0
Retail Clerks International Association	17	Private	633,221	Yes	LMRDA	9
Retail, Wholesale and Department Store Union	2	Private	197,840	Yes	LMRDA	0
Service Employees' International Union	2	Private	484,000	Yes	LMRDA	2
Sheet Metal Workers International Association	4	Private	153,000	Yes	LMRDA	4
The Wood, Wire and Metal Lathers International Union	1	Private	13,767	Yes	LMRDA	4
Tobacco Workers International Union	1	Private	33,565	Yes	LMRDA	2
Transport Workers' Union of America	1	Private	150,000	Yes	LMRDA	4
United Association of Journeymen and Apprentices of the Plumbing and Pipe Fitting Industry of the United States and Canada	11	Private	228,000	Yes	LMRDA	8
United Brotherhood of Carpenters and Joiners of America	16	Private	820,000	Yes	LMRDA	42
United Cement, Lime and Gypsum Workers International Union	2	Private	36,644	Yes	LMRDA	0
United Electrical, Radio and Machine Workers of America	2	Private	165,000	No	LMRDA	0
United Furniture Workers of America	1	Private	30,503	Yes	LMRDA	0

United Glass and Ceramic Workers of North America	1	Private	42,943	Yes	LMRDA	0
United Mine Workers of America	4	Private	213,113	No	LMRDA	33
United Papermakers and Paperworkers	4	Private	389,427	Yes	LMRDA	1
United Rubber, Cork, Linoleum and Plastic Workers of America	3	Private	182,949	Yes	LMRDA	1
United Shoe Workers of America	3	Private	35,000	Yes	LMRDA	0
United Steelworkers of America	16	Private	1,400,000	Yes	LMRDA	37
United Telegraph Workers	1	Private	18,000	Yes	LMRDA	0
United Transportation Union	4	Private	248,088	Yes	LMRDA	10
Utah State Employees Association	1	Gov't	8,598	No	Non	IA
Utility Workers Union of America	5	Private	60,000	Yes	LMRDA	1
American Federation of Labor and Congress of Industrial Organizations (directly affiliated)§	21	Private	55,000	Yes	LMRDA	0
United Farmworkers of America§	1	Private	20,000	Yes	LMRDA	0
Police Officers Association§	3	Gov't	N.A.	No	Non	IA

Note: E.O. means Executive Order No. 11491; Quasi means quasi-covered; IA means inappropriate; N.A. means not ascertained; Non means noncovered.

* "Private" includes government corporations.

† Figures taken from U.S. Department of Labor, Bureau of Labor Statistics, *Directory of National Unions and Employee Associations, 1973* (Washington, D.C.: U.S. Department of Labor, 1975), Part 2.

‡ Those unions listed as "noncovered" were not covered under either LMRDA or Executive Order No. 11491 at the time their member respondents were interviewed.

§Not listed in *Directory of National Unions and Employee Associations* at time of surveys.

TABLE 10. Detroit Survey Respondents Compared with National Survey Respondents

Variable	Chi-square	Significance Level	d.f.	Number
Education*	1.6803	.6413	3	605
Age†	6.8490	.1441	4	606
Freedom	6.5474	.3647	6	606
Knowledge of LMRDA	0.73671×10^{-1}	.7861	1	601
Race	75.516	< .0001	1	595
Activity‡	2.4875	.2883	2	606

*To ensure minimum expected frequencies in each cell, education was categorized as follows: 1–8 years, 9–12 years, 13–16 years, 17 years and over.
†To ensure minimum expected frequencies in each cell, age was divided as follows: 18–25 years, 26–39 years, 40–55 years, 56–65 years, 66 years and over.
‡When activity is treated as a five-category variable ("very active," "fairly active," "somewhat active," "fairly inactive," and "inactive"), the Detroit survey respondents are somewhat more "very active" (16% compared to 11% in the national surveys), significant at the .05 level. (Chi-square = 10.116; significance level = .0385; d.f. = 4; N=606.) However, in the national surveys, there are considerably more "fairly active" respondents (22% compared to 14% in the Detroit survey), suggesting that, given the similarity of the two categories, the two groups' activity behavior is much the same. When activity is treated as a three-category variable ("high," "medium," and "low"), the groups are not statistically different. (Chi-square = 2.4875; significance level = .2883; d.f. = 2; N=606.)

TABLE 11. Detroit and National Respondents Compared Within Racial Groups

Variable	Chi-square	Significance Level	d.f.	Number
		White Respondents		
Activity	9.1248	.0581	4	476
Knowledge of LMRDA	0.90929	.3403	1	472
Education	1.7792	.6195	3	475
Age	6.6875	.1534	4	476
Freedom	4.4491	.6161	6	476
		Black Respondents		
Activity	2.5552	.6348	4	119
Knowledge of LMRDA	1.4022	.2364	1	118
Education	9.0990	.0280	3	119
Age*	5.7050	.1269	3	119
Freedom†	1.4679	.4800	2	119

*To ensure the minimum expected frequency in each cell, age was divided into the following categories: 18–25 years, 26–39 years, 40–55 years, 56 years and over.
†To ensure the minimum expected frequency in each cell, freedom was divided into the following categories: 0–2, 3–4, 5–6.

Thus the Detroit survey respondents do not differ significantly from the national survey respondents in any relevant or significant way, based on our criteria. Throughout the analysis the three surveys are treated as one.

Respondents of Selected Unions Compared to Those of Nonselected Unions

To test the representativeness of the twelve selected unions, tests of distribution were performed on four demographic and three nondemographic variables. These tests revealed that the two groups differed significantly on only one variable—race (table 12).

TABLE 12. Respondents of Selected and Nonselected Unions Compared (LMRDA-covered Unions Only)*

Variables	Chi-square	Significance Level	d.f.	Number
Freedom	12.359	.0544	6	290
Activity	4.0937	.3935	4	290
Knowledge of LMRDA	0.51934	.4711	1	290
Education†	1.8297	.6085	3	290
Sex	0.15040×10^{-2}	.9691	1	289
Age‡	0.63026	.9596	4	290
Race	8.9793	.0027	1	290

*Data are from national surveys.
†To ensure minimum expected frequencies in each cell of the contingency table, education was separated into groups which were considered reasonable categories for contrast: 1–8 years of education, 9–12 years, 13–16 years, and 17 years and over.
‡To ensure minimum expected frequencies in each cell, age was divided into the following categories: 18–25 years, 26–39 years, 40–55 years, 56–65 years, and 66 years and over.

A greater proportion of the respondents from the selected unions were black than of respondents from the nonselected unions (14.5 percent compared to 4.4 percent). This is explained by the fact that there are several large industrial unions among the selected unions in which blacks are heavily represented. Moreover, because of the size of those unions, there was a greater probability that members of those unions would be reached by the surveys. Those two factors account for the higher proportion of blacks among the respondents of the selected unions. The racial difference is examined more closely below (table 13).

The blacks from the selected unions do not differ significantly from those from the nonselected unions on any of the variables examined. The white respondents of the two groups differ significantly on one variable. The whites from the nonselected unions have freedom values somewhat higher than those from the selected unions (77.6 percent of the nonselected unionists having scores of five or six compared to 65.2 percent of

TABLE 13. Respondents of Selected and Nonselected Unions Compared According to Racial Group (LMRDA-covered Unions Only)*

Variables	Chi-square	Significance Level	d.f.
	Black Respondents (N = 26)		
Freedom	0.29323	.9622	3
Activity†	2.0508	.7264	2
Knowledge of LMRDA	0.88859×10^{-2}	.9249	1
Education‡	1.0793	.7821	3
Sex	0.2172×10^{-1}	.8828	1
Age**	0.13229×10^{-1}	.9084	2
	White Respondents (N = 264)		
Freedom	15.489	.0168	6
Activity†	2.5631	.6334	4
Knowledge of LMRDA	1.1053	.2964	1
Education‡	3.7478	.2900	3
Sex	0.07245	.7874	1
Age**	0.85524	.9309	4

*Data are from national survey.
†To ensure minimum expected frequency in each cell, activity was categorized as follows: "very and fairly active," "somewhat active," "fairly inactive and inactive."
‡To ensure minimum expected frequency in each cell, education was separated into the following categories: 1–8 years, 9–12 years, 13–16 years and 17 years and over.
**To ensure minimum expected frequency in each cell, age was separated as follows: for blacks, 18–39 years, 40 years and over; for whites, 18–25 years, 26–39 years, 40–55 years, 56–65 years, 66 years and over.

those from selected unions.) This accounts for the nearly significant difference on the freedom score Chi-square test between the respondents of the selected compared to nonselected over-all. The direction of the freedom distributions is very similar, however (89.9 percent of all respondents of nonselected unions, compared to 84 percent of all respondents of selected unions, have freedom scores of five or six). Thus, the selected unions proved not to differ in any significant way from the nonselected unions, as far as could be determined by the survey results.

The Questions Used

With the help of the staff of the Survey Research Center, long experienced in designing questionnaires, we determined what questions to use and how to pose them. Before each survey went into the field, the questions were pretested at least once. The questions as finally developed, together with the instructions to the interviewers, appear in appendix F.

The interviewer first established that the participant was a union member, and then determined the organization to which he belonged at the time of the interview (appendix F, questions D2–D4). Retired members were not included, while members on layoff at the time of the interview were.

Next, the interviewer sought the respondent's own view of his level of union activism, ranging from "very active" through "fairly active," "somewhat active," "fairly inactive," to "not active" (appendix F, question D5). We included that question in order to see if there was a correlation between a member's level of activism and his knowledge of the Act.

Whether or not union members know they have rights derived specifically from the LMRDA is less important than that they know that they have those rights at all (tables 14, 15, and 16). Thus, questions D6 through D11 focused upon the basic rights the statute was designed to guarantee to the individual union member: his right to look at his union's financial reports; his free speech rights; his ability to participate fully in union elections either in terms of nominating, campaigning, and voting for others or in terms of running for office himself; his right to protest following a union election if he believes there were irregularities in the conduct of that election; and his ability to protest the use of his union dues for contributions to political causes he personally does not favor.

If the respondent answered that he could not exercise one of those rights, he was asked to tell the interviewer why not. He was given six options from which to select the most important reason for his inhibition: not active enough, can't beat the system, trouble with leaders, trouble with co-workers, don't have a right, or "other." (If he chose "other," he was asked to be specific.)

TABLE 14. Union Members' Rights as Perceived by All Respondents in All Surveys (N = 677)

| | Basis for Freedom Score* | | | |
Question	Yes	No	Don't Know	Total Percentage
(D6) Look at financial reports (N=672)†	446(66.37%)	76(11.31%)	150(22.32%)	100.00
(D7) Speak up at meetings (N=672)†	623(92.71%)	26 (3.87%)	23 (3.42%)	100.00
(D8) Nominate, campaign, and vote (N=672)†	594(88.39%)	38 (5.65%)	40 (5.95%)	99.99
(D9) Run for office (N=670)†	539(80.45%)	89(13.28%)	42 (6.27%)	100.00
(D10) Change elections (N=670)†	499(74.48%)	107(15.97%)	64 (9.55%)	100.00
(D11) Protest dues (N=666)†	597(89.64%)	45 (6.76%)	24 (3.60%)	100.00
Total (N=4,022)	3,298(82.00%)	381 (9.47%)	343 (8.53%)	100.00

*Each Yes answer scored one point; thus, the highest possible score was six.
†In each case, the difference between 677 and the figure shown represents the number of participants whose responses were not ascertained.

TABLE 15. Union Members' Rights Perceived by Respondents, According to Whether Respondent Did or Did Not Profess Knowledge of LMRDA

Question	Knowledgeable (N=59)	Not Knowledgeable (N=612)*
(D6) Look at financial reports	(N=59)	(N=609)
Yes	45 (76.27%)	401 (65.84%)
No	6 (10.16%)	70 (11.49%)
DK	8 (13.55%)	138 (22.66%)
Total	99.99%	99.99%
(D7) Speak up	(N=59)	(N=610)
Yes	57 (96.61%)	565 (92.62%)
No	2 (3.38%)	24 (3.93%)
DK	0	21 (3.44%)
Total	99.99%	99.99%
(D8) Nominate, campaign, and vote	(N=59)	(N=610)
Yes	56 (94.91%)	537 (88.03%)
No	2 (3.38%)	36 (5.90%)
DK	1 (1.69%)	37 (6.06%)
Total	99.98%	99.99%
(D9) Run for office	(N=59)	(N=608)
Yes	53 (89.83%)	485 (79.77%)
No	6 (10.16%)	83 (13.65%)
DK	0	40 (6.58%)
Total	99.99%	100.00%
(D10) Change elections	(N=59)	(N=608)
Yes	48 (81.35%)	450 (74.01%)
No	9 (15.25%)	98 (16.12%)
DK	2 (3.38%)	60 (9.87%)
Total	99.98%	100.00%
(D11) Protest dues	(N=59)	(N=606)
Yes	53 (89.83%)	543 (89.60%)
No	6 (10.16%)	39 (6.44%)
DK	0	24 (3.96%)
Total	99.99%	100.00%

*Not ascertained = 6. Where N is less than 612, the difference is accounted for by not ascertained responses throughout column.

TABLE 16.   Union Members' Perceptions of Inability to Act*

Question	"No, I Could Not...."	"Yes, I Have Wanted to but Did Not...."	Total
(D6) Look at financial reports (N=672)	76 (11%)	30 (4%)	106 (15%)
(D7) Speak up (N=672)	26 (4%)	85 (13%)	111 (17%)
(D8) Nominate, campaign, and vote (N=672)	38 (6%)	50 (7%)	88 (13%)
(D9) Run for office (N=670)	89 (13%)	23 (3%)	112 (16%)
(D10) Change elections (N=670)	107 (16%)	26 (4%)	133 (20%)
(D11) Protest dues (N=666)	45 (7%)	29 (4%)	74 (11%)

*"Not ascertained" deleted.

The answers to those six questions formed the basis for each respondent's so-called freedom score. Each "yes" answer to one of the six questions earned the respondent one point. Thus, if his answer to each of the six questions was affirmative, he received the highest possible score—six. (We were interested in sorting out only those respondents who had a clear awareness of their rights. Thus, only those who said "yes" received a positive score.) On the other hand, if he said "no" or "don't know" to all six questions, he was given the lowest freedom score—zero. (The composite freedom score is shown in table 17.)

We were also concerned to learn not only whether the respondent felt free to exercise these rights per se, but whether or not he had ever felt inhibited from exercising them in the union he belonged to at the time of the interview. For example, if he answered "yes" when asked whether or not he could look at his union's financial reports if he wanted to, he was then queried as to whether or not, as a practical matter, he had ever wanted to do so in his present union, but had decided against it. (We did not ask if there had ever been a time when he wanted to do something and actually did it, because we were interested in what factor inhibited members.) If he responded that there had been a time that he wanted to but did not, he was then again asked to select the most important reason he had not done so, this time from among five choices: not active enough, can't beat the system, trouble with leaders, trouble with co-workers, or "other." (As before, if he gave "other" as the reason, he was asked to elaborate.) Tables 18, 19, 20, and 21 show the breakdown both separately (the "no" as distinct from the "yes, there was a time") and as a composite of the two responses, by reason. Tables 18 and 19 give that information for all respondents, table 20 for those who indicated some knowledge of the Act, and table 21 for those who did not.

TABLE 17. Freedom Scores

	Six	Five	Four	Three	Two	One	Zero	Total Percentage
A. All respondents, all surveys (N=677)	310 (45.86%)	172 (25.44%)	93 (13.76%)	50 (7.40%)	22 (3.25%)	12 (1.78%)	18 (2.51%)	100.00
B. Statutory coverage (N=606)*								
LMRDA (N=492)	213 (43.29%)	134 (27.24%)	72 (14.63%)	40 (8.13%)	14 (2.85%)	9 (1.83%)	10 (2.03%)	100.00
E.O. 11491 (N=8)	4 (50.00%)	2 (25.00%)	1 (12.50%)	0	0	0	1 (12.50%)	100.00
Quasi-covered (N=61)	33 (54.09%)	12 (19.67%)	11 (18.03%)	2 (3.28%)	3 (4.92%)	0	0	99.99
Not covered (N=45)	29 (64.44%)	9 (20.00%)	2 (4.44%)	2 (4.44%)	1 (2.22%)	0	2 (4.44%)	99.98
C. AFL-CIO affiliation (N=606)*								
Yes (N=361)	177 (49.03%)	85 (23.55%)	56 (15.51%)	23 (6.37%)	10 (2.77%)	6 (1.66%)	4 (1.11%)	100.00
No (N=245)	102 (41.63%)	72 (29.39%)	30 (12.24%)	21 (8.57%)	8 (3.27%)	3 (1.22%)	9 (3.67%)	99.99
D. Sector (N=606)*								
Public (N=114)	66 (57.89%)	23 (20.18%)	14 (12.28%)	4 (3.51%)	4 (3.51%)	0	3 (2.63%)	100.00
Private or quasi-public (N=492)	213 (43.29%)	134 (27.24%)	72 (14.63%)	40 (8.13%)	14 (2.85%)	9 (1.83%)	10 (2.03%)	100.00
E. Gender (N=676)†								
Male (N=471)	228 (48.41%)	116 (24.63%)	62 (13.16%)	34 (7.22%)	15 (3.18%)	6 (1.27%)	10 (2.12%)	99.99
Female (N=205)	81 (39.51%)	56 (27.32%)	31 (15.12%)	16 (7.80%)	7 (3.41%)	6 (2.93%)	8 (3.90%)	99.99

F. Race (N=676)†								
White (N=526)	244 (46.39%)	129 (24.52%)	75 (14.26%)	36 (6.84%)	19 (3.61%)	10 (1.90%)	13 (2.47%)	99.99
Black (N=139)	64 (46.04%)	39 (28.06%)	15 (10.79%)	14 (10.07%)	2 (1.44%)	0	5 (3.60%)	100.00
Other (N=11)	2 (18.18%)	4 (36.36%)	2 (18.18%)	0	1 (9.09%)	2 (18.18%)	0	99.99
G. Age (N=676)†								
18–25 (N=98)	32 (32.65%)	22 (22.44%)	18 (18.36%)	14 (14.28%)	6 (6.12%)	2 (2.04%)	4 (4.08%)	99.97
26–39 (N=256)	117 (45.70%)	62 (24.21%)	37 (14.45%)	17 (6.64%)	11 (4.29%)	5 (1.95%)	7 (2.73%)	99.97
40–55 (N=236)	126 (53.38%)	62 (26.27%)	28 (11.86%)	14 (5.93%)	1 (0.42%)	3 (1.27%)	2 (0.84%)	99.97
56–65 (N=76)	31 (40.79%)	24 (31.58%)	10 (13.15%)	4 (5.26%)	3 (3.95%)	1 (1.32%)	3 (3.95%)	100.00
66+ (N=10)	4 (40.00%)	2 (20.00%)	0	1 (10.00%)	1 (10.00%)	1 (10.00%)	1 (10.00%)	100.00
H. Education (N=674)‡								
0–8 (N=70)	28 (40.00%)	20 (28.57%)	8 (11.42%)	8 (11.42%)	1 (1.42%)	3 (4.28%)	2 (2.85%)	99.96
9–12 (N=396)	170 (42.92%)	110 (27.77%)	57 (14.39%)	28 (7.07%)	13 (3.28%)	7 (1.76%)	11 (2.77%)	99.96
13–16 (N=147)	69 (46.93%)	31 (21.08%)	23 (15.64%)	13 (8.84%)	7 (4.76%)	2 (1.36%)	2 (1.36%)	99.97
17+ (N=61)	43 (70.49%)	9 (14.75%)	4 (6.55%)	1 (1.63%)	1 (1.63%)	0	3 (4.91%)	99.96
I. Income								
Quality of Life (N=266)								
Less than $6,000 (N=34)	11 (32.35%)	8 (23.52%)	7 (20.58%)	2 (5.88%)	2 (5.88%)	1 (2.94%)	3 (8.82%)	99.97
$6,000–$9,999 (N=38)	20 (52.63%)	9 (23.68%)	4 (10.52%)	5 (13.15%)	0	0	0	99.98
$10,000–$14,999 (N=89)	42 (47.19%)	23 (25.84%)	11 (12.35%)	9 (10.11%)	2 (2.24%)	0	2 (2.24%)	99.97
$15,000+ (N=105)	54 (51.42%)	24 (22.85%)	12 (11.42%)	6 (5.71%)	5 (4.76%)	0	4 (3.80%)	99.96

TABLE 17—Continued

	Six	Five	Four	Three	Two	One	Zero	Total Percentage
Omnibus (1974) (N=204)								
Less than $6,000 (N=46)	6 (13.04%)	11 (23.91%)	10 (21.73%)	6 (13.04%)	4 (8.69%)	3 (6.52%)	6 (13.04%)	99.97
$6,000-$9,999 (N=47)	15 (31.91%)	21 (44.68%)	5 (10.63%)	4 (8.51%)	1 (2.12%)	0	1 (2.12%)	99.97
$10,000-$14,999 (N=62)	35 (56.45%)	16 (25.80%)	5 '(8.06%)	2 (3.22%)	2 (3.22%)	2 (3.22%)	0	99.97
$15,000+ (N=49)	28 (57.14%)	9 (18.36%)	8 (16.32%)	3 (6.12%)	1 (2.04%)	0	0	99.98
J. Region								
(Interim and Omnibus only) (All regions)								
(N=411)	183 (44.53%)	108 (26.28%)	59 (14.36%)	28 (6.81%)	13 (3.16%)	11 (2.68%)	9 (2.19%)	100.01
West (N=71)	30 (42.25%)	17 (23.94%)	10 (14.08%)	6 (8.45%)	4 (5.64%)	4 (5.64%)	0	100.00
North central (N=158)	66 (41.77%)	46 (29.11%)	24 (15.17%)	11 (6.96%)	3 (1.90%)	4 (2.53%)	4 (2.53%)	99.97
Northeast (N=103)	48 (46.60%)	31 (30.10%)	15 (14.56%)	2 (1.94%)	3 (2.91%)	2 (1.94%)	2 (1.94%)	99.99
South (N=79)	39 (49.38%)	14 (17.72%)	10 (12.66%)	9 (11.39%)	3 (3.79%)	1 (1.26%)	3 (3.79%)	99.99
Quality of Life (All north central) (N=266)	127 (47.74%)	64 (24.06%)	34 (12.78%)	22 (8.27%)	9 (3.38%)	1 (0.37%)	9 (3.38%)	99.98

K. Knew about LMRDA (N=671)**

Yes (N=59)	34 (57.63%)	13 (22.03%)	8 (13.56%)	3 (5.08%)	1 (1.69%)	0	0	99.99
No (N=612)	276 (45.09%)	158 (25.81%)	85 (13.88%)	47 (7.67%)	21 (3.43%)	12 (1.96%)	13 (2.12%)	99.96

L. Union size (N=600)††

1–49,999 (N=31)	14 (45.16%)	12 (38.71%)	1 (3.22%)	1 (3.22%)	1 (3.22%)	1 (3.22%)	1 (3.22%)	99.97
50,000–499,999 (N=220)	119 (54.09%)	48 (21.82%)	32 (14.55%)	13 (5.91%)	2 (0.91%)	3 (1.36%)	3 (1.36%)	100.00
500,000–999,999 (N=115)	50 (43.48%)	26 (22.61%)	20 (17.39%)	9 (7.82%)	8 (6.96%)	1 (0.87%)	1 (0.87%)	100.00
1,000,000+ (N=234)	93 (39.74%)	70 (29.91%)	32 (13.68%)	21 (8.97%)	7 (2.99%)	4 (1.71%)	7 (2.99%)	99.99

M. Activity level, all surveys (N=676)‡

Very active (N=89)	64 (71.91%)	17 (19.10%)	3 (3.37%)	3 (3.37%)	2 (2.25%)	0	0	100.00
Fairly active (N=131)	73 (55.72%)	33 (25.19%)	9 (6.87%)	11 (8.40%)	3 (2.29%)	2 (1.53%)	0	100.00
Somewhat active (N=126)	55 (43.65%)	35 (27.78%)	25 (19.84%)	8 (6.35%)	2 (1.59%)	0	1 (0.79%)	100.00
Fairly inactive (N=115)	50 (43.48%)	39 (33.91%)	18 (15.65%)	5 (4.35%)	2 (1.74%)	1 (0.87%)	0	100.00
Not active (N=215)	68 (31.63%)	48 (22.32%)	38 (17.67%)	23 (10.70%)	13 (6.05%)	9 (4.19%)	16 (7.44%)	100.00

*Respondents whose unions were identifiable.

†Characteristic not ascertained for one respondent.

‡Characteristic not ascertained for three respondents.

**Characteristic not ascertained for six respondents.

††Respondents whose unions were identifiable and size of organization known.

TABLE 18. Respondents' Reasons for "No" or "Yes, but" Responses (DK's Deleted)

Question	Not Active Enough	Can't Beat System	Trouble with Leaders	Trouble with Co-workers	No Right	Other*	Total Percentage
(D6) Look at financial reports							
No (N=65) (+11 NA)	13 (20.00%)	22 (33.85%)	11 (16.92%)	4 (6.15%)	7 (10.77%)	8 (12.31%)	100.00
Yes, but (N=30) (+2 NA; +1 DK)	14 (46.67%)	5 (16.67%)	2 (6.66%)	1 (3.33%)		8 (26.66%)	99.99
(D7) Speak up							
No (N=22) (+4 NA)	3 (13.64%)	9 (40.91%)	7 (31.82%)	0	2 (9.09%)	1 (4.54%)	100.00
Yes, but (N=85) (+3 NA; 3 DK)	28 (32.94%)	26 (30.59%)	10 (11.76%)	7 (8.24%)		14 (16.47%)	100.00
(D8) Nominate, campaign, and vote							
No (N=32) (+6 NA)	17 (53.12%)	5 (15.63%)	5 (15.63%)	2 (6.25%)	1 (3.12%)	2 (6.25%)	100.00
Yes, but (N=50) (+2 NA; 2 DK)	15 (30.00%)	18 (36.00%)	4 (8.00%)	3 (6.00%)		10 (20.00%)	100.00
(D9) Run for office							
No (N=73) (+16 NA)	53 (72.60%)	6 (8.22%)	3 (4.11%)	1 (1.37%)	3 (4.11%)	7 (9.59%)	100.00
Yes, but (N=23) (+1 NA)	8 (34.78%)	4 (17.39%)	2 (8.70%)	2 (8.70%)		7 (30.43%)	100.00
(D10) Change elections							
No (N=92) (+15 NA)	30 (32.61%)	40 (43.48%)	11 (11.95%)	4 (4.35%)	3 (3.26%)	4 (4.35%)	100.00
Yes, but (N=26) (+1 NA)	9 (34.61%)	9 (34.61%)	2 (7.69%)	1 (3.85%)		5 (19.23%)	99.99
(D11) Protest dues							
No (N=35) (+10 NA)	8 (22.86%)	14 (40.00%)	6 (17.14%)	0	2 (5.71%)	5 (14.29%)	100.00
Yes, but (N=29) (+1 NA)	6 (20.69%)	17 (58.62%)	3 (10.34%)	1 (3.45%)		2 (6.90%)	100.00
Total (N=562)	204 (36.30%)	175 (31.14%)	66 (11.74%)	26 (4.63%)	18 (3.20%)	73 (12.99%)	100.00

Note: NA means not ascertained; DK means don't know.
*See text for discussion of "other" reasons.

TABLE 19. Combined Tabulation of "No" and "Yes, but" Responses, by Reason (DK, NA Deleted)

Question	Not Active Enough	Can't Beat System	Trouble with Leaders	Trouble with Co-workers	No Right	Other*	Total Percentage
(D6) Look at financial reports (N=95)	27 (28.42%)	27 (28.42%)	13 (13.68%)	5 (5.26%)	7 (7.37%)	16 (16.84%)	99.99
(D7) Speak up (N=107)	31 (28.97%)	35 (32.71%)	17 (15.89%)	7 (6.54%)	2 (1.87%)	15 (14.02%)	100.00
(D8) Nominate, campaign, and vote (N=82)	32 (39.02%)	23 (28.05%)	9 (10.98%)	5 (6.10%)	1 (1.22%)	12 (14.63%)	100.00
(D9) Run for office (N=96)	61 (63.54%)	10 (10.42%)	5 (5.21%)	3 (3.12%)	3 (3.12%)	14 (14.58%)	99.99
(D10) Change elections (N=118)	39 (33.05%)	49 (41.52%)	13 (11.02%)	5 (4.24%)	3 (2.54%)	9 (7.63%)	100.00
(D11) Protest dues (N=64)	14 (21.88%)	31 (48.44%)	9 (14.06%)	1 (1.56%)	2 (3.12%)	7 (10.94%)	100.00
Total (N=562)	204 (36.30%)	175 (31.14%)	66 (11.74%)	26 (4.63%)	18 (3.20%)	73 (12.99%)	100.00

*See text for discussion of "other" reasons.

TABLE 20. LMRDA-Knowledgeable Respondents' Reasons for "No" or "Yes, but" Responses (DK, NA Deleted)

Question	Not Active Enough	Can't Beat System	Trouble with Leaders	Trouble with Co-workers	No right	Other*	Total Percentage
(D6) Look at financial reports							
No (N=6)	1 (16.67%)	1 (16.67%)	1 (16.67%)	1 (16.67%)	2 (33.33%)	0	100.01
Yes, but (N=1)	0	1 (100.00%)	0	0	0	0	100.00
(D7) Speak up							
No (N=2)	1 (50.00%)	0	1 (50.00%)	0	0	0	100.00
Yes, but (N=12) (+1 DK)	4 (33.33%)	4 (33.33%)	0	1 (8.33%)	0	3 (25.00%)	99.99
(D8) Nominate, campaign, and vote							
No (N=2)	1 (50.00%)	0	1 (50.00%)	0	0	0	100.00
Yes, but (N=8)	2 (25.00%)	5 (62.50%)	0 ·	1 (12.50%)	0	0	100.00
(D9) Run for office							
No (N=4) (+2 NA)	3 (75.00%)	0	0	0	0	1 (25.00%)	100.00
Yes, but (N=3) (+1 NA)	0	0	1 (33.33%)	0	0	2 (66.67%)	100.00
(D10) Change elections							
No (N=8) (+1 NA)	1 (12.50%)	2 (25.00%)	2 (25.00%)	1 (12.50%)	1 (12.50%)	1 (12.50%)	100.00
Yes, but (N=4)	1 (25.00%)	2 (50.00%)	0	0	0	1 (25.00%)	100.00
(D11) Protest dues							
No (N=2) (+3 NA)	0	2 (100.00%)	0	0	0	0	100.00
Yes, but (N=2)	1 (50.00%)	1 (50.00%)	0	0	0	0	100.00
Total							
No (N=25)	7 (28.00%)	5 (20.00%)	5 (20.00%)	3 (8.00%)	3 (12.00%)	3 (12.00%)	100.00
Yes, but (N=30)	8 (26.67%)	13 (43.33%)	1 (3.33%)	2 (6.67%)	0	6 (20.00%)	100.00

265

"No" and "Yes, but" Responses Combined Tabulation

(D6) Look at financial reports (N=7)	1 (14.29%)	2 (28.57%)	1 (14.29%)	1 (14.29%)	2 (28.57%)	0	100.01
(D7) Speak up (N=14)	5 (35.71%)	4 (28.57%)	1 (7.14%)	1 (7.14%)	0	3 (21.43%)	99.99
(D8) Nominate, campaign, and vote (N=11)	3 (27.27%)	5 (45.45%)	1 (9.09%)	1 (9.09%)	0	1 (9.09%)	99.99
(D9) Run for office (N=7)	3 (42.86%)	0	1 (14.28%)	0	0	3 (42.86%)	100.00
(D10) Change elections (N=12)	2 (16.67%)	4 (33.33%)	2 (16.67%)	1 (8.33%)	1 (8.33%)	2 (16.67%)	100.00
(D11) Protest dues (N=4)	1 (25.00%)	3 (75.00%)	0	0	0	0	100.00
Total (N=55)	15 (27.27%)	18 (32.73%)	6 (10.91%)	4 (7.27%)	3 (5.45%)	9 (16.36%)	99.99

Note: NA means not ascertained; DK means don't know.
*See text for discussion of "other" reasons.

TABLE 21. Respondents' Reasons for "No" or "Yes, but" Responses by Those Who Were Not Familiar with LMRDA (DK, NA Deleted)

Question	Not Active Enough	Can't Beat System	Trouble with Leaders	Trouble with Co-workers	No Right	Other*	Total Percentage
(D6) Look at financial reports							
No (N=59)	12 (20.34%)	21 (35.59%)	10 (16.95%)	3 (5.08%)	5 (8.47%)	8 (13.56%)	99.99
Yes, but (N=29)	14 (48.27%)	4 (13.79%)	2 (6.90%)	1 (3.45%)		8 (27.59%)	100.00
(D7) Speak up							
No (N=20)	2 (10.00%)	9 (45.00%)	6 (30.00%)	0	2 (10.00%)	1 (5.00%)	100.00
Yes, but (N=73)	24 (32.88%)	22 (30.14%)	10 (13.70%)	6 (8.22%)		11 (15.07%)	100.01
(D8) Nominate, campaign, and vote							
No (N=30)	16 (53.33%)	5 (16.67%)	5 (16.67%)	2 (6.67%)	1 (3.33%)	1 (3.33%)	100.00
Yes, but (N=42)	13 (30.95%)	13 (30.95%)	4 (9.52%)	2 (4.76%)		10 (23.81%)	99.99
(D9) Run for office							
No (N=69)	50 (72.46%)	6 (8.69%)	3 (4.35%)	1 (1.45%)	3 (4.35%)	6 (8.69%)	99.99
Yes, but (N=20)	8 (40.00%)	4 (20.00%)	1 (5.00%)	2 (10.00%)		5 (25.00%)	100.00
(D10) Change elections							
No (N=84)	29 (34.52%)	38 (45.24%)	9 (10.71%)	3 (3.57%)	2 (2.38%)	3 (3.57%)	99.99
Yes, but (N=22)	8 (36.36%)	7 (31.82%)	2 (9.09%)	1 (4.54%)		4 (18.18%)	99.99
(D11) Protest dues							
No (N=32)	8 (25.00%)	12 (37.50%)	5 (15.62%)	0	2 (6.25%)	5 (15.62%)	99.99
Yes, but (N=27)	5 (18.52%)	16 (59.26%)	3 (11.11%)	1 (2.70%)		2 (7.41%)	100.00
Total							
No (N=294)	117 (39.80%)	91 (30.95%)	38 (12.93%)	9 (3.06%)	15 (5.10%)	24 (8.16%)	100.00
Yes, but (N=213)	72 (33.80%)	66 (30.98%)	22 (10.33%)	13 (6.10%)		40 (18.78%)	99.00

267

"No" and "Yes, but" Responses Combined Tabulation

(D6) Look at financial reports (N=88)	26 (29.54%)	25 (28.41%)	12 (13.64%)	4 (4.54%)	5 (5.68%)	16 (18.18%)	99.99
(D7) Speak up (N=93)	26 (27.96%)	31 (33.33%)	16 (17.20%)	6 (6.45%)	2 (2.15%)	12 (12.90%)	99.99
(D8) Nominate, campaign, and vote (N=72)	29 (40.28%)	18 (25.00%)	9 (12.50%)	4 (5.55%)	1 (1.39%)	11 (15.28%)	100.00
(D9) Run for office (N=89)	58 (65.17%)	10 (11.23%)	4 (4.49%)	3 (3.37%)	3 (3.37%)	11 (12.36%)	99.99
(D10) Change elections (N=106)	37 (34.90%)	45 (42.45%)	11 (10.38%)	4 (3.77%)	2 (1.89%)	7 (6.60%)	99.99
(D11) Protest dues (N=59)	13 (22.03%)	28 (47.46%)	8 (13.56%)	1 (1.69%)	2 (3.39%)	7 (11.86%)	99.99
Total (N=507)	189 (37.28%)	157 (30.97%)	60 (11.83%)	22 (4.34%)	15 (2.96%)	64 (12.62%)	100.00

*See text for discussion of "other" reasons.

After having determined whether or not the survey respondent knew that he had certain basic rights as a union member, and whether or not he believed that he could exercise them, we then sought to find out whether or not he knew the statutory source of those rights. Question D12 ("Do you know much about the Landrum-Griffin Act . . . ?") was designed to elicit whether or not the respondent *thought* he knew something about the Act. Questions D12a and D12b (asking for greater specificity) were intended to obtain, in the respondent's own words, his actual understanding of the statute. The remaining questions, D13 through D18, all concerned with aspects of the Act's possible impact on the internal operation of labor unions, were asked only of those survey respondents who professed some knowledge of the Act, based on an affirmative answer to question D12. Subsequent to the completion of the surveys, we checked the answers to question D12b, and recoded the responses to eliminate the question D13 through D18 answers of those respondents who in fact were not familiar with the LMRDA. (Some confused it with the Taft-Hartley Act, others with right-to-work legislation, and still others with statutes prohibiting public employee strikes.)

Thus, table 22 gives the breakdown of answers to questions D13 through D18 for only those respondents who actually had some knowledge of the scope of the LMRDA. The responses are further subdivided to show the Act's impact on labor unions as perceived by all respondents who correctly identified the statute and those who are covered under the Act. Tables 23 and 24 break down the answers still further between those respondents who were over forty-four years of age at the time they were questioned and those who were forty-four years of age or younger; in addition, they give the respondents' activity level by freedom score.

As can be seen from Table 22, only fifty-nine (9 percent of the 677 union members who were interviewed in the course of the three surveys) were familiar with the LMRDA. Among those fifty-nine, a higher proportion were over forty-four years of age than were forty-four or younger (54 percent as against 46 percent). This was to be expected because the older group would be more likely to have been aware of the Act's passage and to have experienced whatever changes resulted from its enactment than would those who entered the work force after 1959.

Since a union member's knowledge of the LMRDA is less important than his feeling free to exercise the rights accorded under it, the freedom score assumes some importance. As table 17 (category A) indicates, 46 percent of the union member respondents interviewed believed that they have a right to do all six things: look at their union's financial records; speak up at meetings; nominate, campaign, and vote for the union officer candidates of their choice; run for union office themselves; protest election irregularities; and protest dues expenditures for political purposes they do not favor. The fact that many of the respondents had a sense of

TABLE 22. Impact of Act as Perceived by Respondents Who Knew of LMRDA (N=59)

Question	More/Easier	Same	Less/Harder	Don't Know	Total Percentage
A. All Respondents					
(D13) Officers honest (N=55) (+4 NA)	13 (23.64%)	34 (61.81%)	2 (3.64%)	6 (10.91%)	100.00
(D14) Listen (N=56) (+3 NA)	19 (33.93%)	30 (53.57%)	1 (1.79%)	6 (10.71%)	99.99
(D15) Control dues (N=55) (+4 NA)	18 (32.73%)	29 (52.73%)	1 (1.81%)	7 (12.73%)	100.00
(D16) Speak (N=55) (+4 NA)	15 (27.27%)	35 (63.64%)	2 (3.64%)	3 (5.45%)	100.00
(D17) Become officer (N=55) (+4 NA)	9 (16.36%)	35 (63.64%)	2 (3.64%)	9 (16.36%)	100.00
(D18) Look at reports (N=55) (+4 NA)	18 (32.73%)	29 (52.73%)	1 (1.81%)	7 (12.73%)	100.00
B. LMRDA-Covered Respondents Only (N=45)					
(D13) Officers honest (N=43) (+2 NA)	11 (25.58%)	26 (60.46%)	1 (2.32%)	5 (11.63%)	99.99
(D14) Listen (N=44) (+1 NA)	14 (31.82%)	23 (52.27%)	1 (2.27%)	6 (13.64%)	100.00
(D15) Control dues (N=43) (+2 NA)	15 (34.88%)	22 (51.16%)	0	6 (13.95%)	99.99
(D16) Speak (N=43) (+2 NA)	11 (25.58%)	27 (62.79%)	2 (4.65%)	3 (6.98%)	100.00
(D17) Become officer (N=43) (+2 NA)	7 (16.28%)	27 (62.79%)	1 (2.32%)	8 (18.60%)	99.99
(D18) Look at reports (N=43) (+2 NA)	14 (32.56%)	23 (53.49%)	1 (2.32%)	5 (11.63%)	100.00

Note: NA means not ascertained.

TABLE 23. Impact of Act as Perceived by, and Activity/Freedom Levels of, Respondents over Age Forty-four Who Knew of LMRDA

Question	More/Easier	Same	Less/Harder	Don't Know	Total Percentage
	A. Impact on Respondent's Own Union (N=32)				
(D13) Officers honest (N=31) (+1 NA)	7 (22.58%)	21 (67.74%)	2 (6.45%)	1 (3.22%)	99.99
(D14) Listen (N=32)	12 (37.50%)	16 (50.00%)	1 (3.12%)	3 (9.38%)	100.00
(D15) Control dues (N=32)	12 (37.50%)	16 (50.00%)	0	4 (12.50%)	100.00
(D16) Speak (N=32)	9 (28.12%)	22 (68.75%)	0	1 (3.12%)	99.99
(D17) Become officer (N=32)	5 (15.62%)	23 (71.88%)	1 (3.12%)	3 (9.38%)	100.00
(D18) Look at reports (N=32)	10 (31.25%)	19 (59.38%)	1 (3.12%)	2 (6.25%)	100.00
Total (N=191)*	55 (28.79%)	117 (61.26%)	5 (2.62%)	14 (7.33%)	100.00
	B. Impact of LMRDA-covered Respondent's Own Union (N=28)				
(D13) Officers honest (N=27) (+1 NA)	7 (25.92%)	18 (66.67%)	1 (3.70%)	1 (3.70%)	99.99
(D14) Listen (N=28)	11 (39.28%)	13 (46.43%)	1 (3.57%)	3 (10.71%)	99.99
(D15) Control dues (N=28)	11 (39.28%)	13 (46.43%)	0	4 (14.28%)	99.99
(D16) Speak (N=28)	8 (28.57%)	19 (67.86%)	0	1 (3.57%)	100.00
(D17) Become officer (N=28)	4 (14.28%)	20 (71.43%)	1 (3.57%)	3 (10.71%)	99.99
(D18) Look at report (N=28)	9 (32.14%)	16 (57.14%)	1 (3.57%)	2 (7.14%)	99.99
Total (N=167)*	50 (29.94%)	99 (59.28%)	4 (2.39%)	14 (8.38%)	99.99

Activity Level	Score							Total Percentage
	Six	Five	Four	Three	Two	One	Zero	
C. Activity × Freedom Score, All Respondents Above (N=32)								
Very active (N=9)	7 (77.78%)	2 (22.22%)	0	0	0	0	0	100.00
Fairly active (N=8)	5 (62.50%)	2 (25.00%)	0	1 (12.50%)	0	0	0	100.00
Somewhat active (N=5)	3 (60.00%)	2 (40.00%)	0	0	0	0	0	100.00
Fairly inactive (N=5)	2 (40.00%)	2 (40.00%)	1 (20.00%)	0	0	0	0	100.00
Not active (N=5)	2 (40.00%)	0	2 (40.00%)	1 (20.00%)	0	0	0	100.00
D. Activity × Freedom Score, LMRDA-covered Respondents (N=28)								
Very active (N=7)	5 (71.43%)	2 (28.57%)	0	0	0	0	0	100.00
Fairly active (N=8)	5 (62.50%)	2 (25.00%)	0	1 (12.50%)	0	0	0	100.00
Somewhat active (N=4)	2 (50.00%)	2 (50.00%)	0	0	0	0	0	100.00
Fairly inactive (N=4)	1 (25.00%)	2 (50.00%)	1 (25.00%)	0	0	0	0	100.00
Not active (N=5)	2 (40.00%)	0	2 (40.00%)	1 (10.00%)	0	0	0	100.00

Note: NA means not ascertained.

*N = Number of responses to questions regarding impact.

TABLE 24. Impact of Act as Perceived by, and Activity/Freedom Levels of, Respondents Age Forty-four or Less Who Knew of LMRDA

Question	More/Easier	Same	Less/Harder	Don't Know	Total Percentage
		A. Impact on Respondent's Own Union (N=27)			
(D13) Officers honest (N=24) (+3 NA)	6 (25.00%)	13 (54.17%)	0	5 (20.83%)	100.00
(D14) Listen (N=24) (+3 NA)	7 (29.17%)	14 (58.33%)	0	3 (12.50%)	100.00
(D15) Dues (N=23) (+4 NA)	7 (30.43%)	13 (56.52%)	0	3 (13.04%)	99.99
(D16) Speak (N=23) (+4 NA)	6 (26.09%)	13 (56.52%)	2 (8.69%)	2 (8.69%)	99.99
(D17) Become officer (N=23) (+4 NA)	4 (17.39%)	12 (52.17%)	1 (4.35%)	6 (26.09%)	100.00
(D18) Look at reports (N=23) (+4 NA)	8 (34.78%)	10 (43.48%)	0	5 (21.74%)	100.00
Total (N=140)	38 (27.14%)	75 (53.57%)	3 (2.14%)	24 (17.14%)	99.99
		B. Impact on LMRDA-covered Respondent's Own Union (N=17)			
(D13) Officers honest (N=16) (+4 NA)	4 (25.00%)	8 (50.00%)	0	4 (25.00%)	100.00
(D14) Listen (N=16) (+1 NA)	3 (18.75%)	10 (62.50%)	0	3 (18.75%)	100.00
(D15) Dues (N=15) (+2 NA)	4 (26.67%)	9 (60.00%)	0	2 (13.33%)	100.00
(D16) Speak (N=15) (+2 NA)	3 (20.00%)	8 (53.33%)	2 (13.33%)	2 (13.33%)	99.99
(D17) Become officer (N=15) (+2 NA)	3 (20.00%)	7 (46.67%)	0	5 (33.33%)	100.00
(D18) Look at reports (N=15) (+2 NA)	5 (33.33%)	7 (46.67%)	0	3 (20.00%)	100.00
Total (N=92)	22 (23.91%)	49 (53.26%)	2 (2.17%)	19 (20.65%)	99.99

| | Score | | | | | | | Total |
Activity Level	Six	Five	Four	Three	Two	One	Zero	Percentage
	C. Activity × Freedom Score, All Respondents above (N=27)							
Very active (N=8)	5 (62.50%)	1 (12.50%)	2 (25.00%)	0	0	0	0	100.00
Fairly active (N=8)	6 (75.00%)	1 (12.50%)	0	1 (12.50%)	0	0	0	100.00
Somewhat active (N=4)	1 (25.00%)	2 (50.00%)	0	0	1 (25.00%)	0	0	100.00
Fairly inactive (N=3)	1 (33.33%)	0	2 (66.67%)	0	0	0	0	100.00
Not active (N=4)	2 (50.00%)	1 (25.00%)	1 (25.00%)	0	0	0	0	100.00
	D. Activity × Freedom Score, LMRDA-covered Respondents (N=17)							
Very active (N=5)	3 (60.00%)	1 (20.00%)	1 (20.00%)	0	0	0	0	100.00
Fairly active (N=2)	1 (50.00%)	0	0	1 (50.00%)	0	0	0	100.00
Somewhat active (N=3)	1 (33.33%)	2 (66.67%)	0	0	0	0	0	100.00
Fairly inactive (N=3)	1 (33.33%)	0	2 (66.67%)	0	0	0	0	100.00
Not active (N=4)	2 (50.00%)	1 (25.00%)	1 (25.00%)	0	0	0	0	100.00

Note: NA means not ascertained.

what rights they have within the union, while relatively few were aware of the Act, merely reflects the fact that people generally tend to be unfamiliar with the statutory basis for any number of rights that they nevertheless exercise and take for granted.

Summary of Survey Findings

Except for the emphasis on Title II and V rights and obligations on the part of those union members in the three surveys who answered question D12b correctly, the data we obtained held no real surprises.

We have discussed at various points in the text the survey findings which add to an understanding of the impact of specific sections of the Act. Since tables 25, 26, and 27 describe our findings fully, we will only highlight those items that seem to us to be the most significant in terms of the basic purpose of this portion of our study, i.e., the determination of what the rank and file union member respondents in the three surveys knew of their LMRDA rights, and what they believed the impact of the LMRDA had been on the internal operation of their own unions.

•A far greater number of union member respondents were aware of the rights they have under the Act than knew the statutory basis for them.

•Respondents who presumably were in the work force at the time the Act was passed (i.e., those over the age of forty-four) were much more knowledgeable concerning the Act itself than were the younger respondents.

•Those respondents who believed they could exercise the rights guaranteed under the Act (i.e., those with the highest freedom score) were also the most active within their unions. This was even more pronounced if, in addition, they knew something concerning the statute itself.

•About 30 percent of those who had specific knowledge about LMRDA felt it had not had any impact on their own unions in terms of the six main issues inquired of. Over-all, almost 60 percent of the answers regarding impact indicated "no change"; 37 percent indicated a favorable impact; and less than 3 percent indicated that the statute's effect on their unions had been adverse.

•Those respondents who knew something about the Act and believed its effect has been beneficial consider that the statute's greatest impact has been to make union officers more responsive, closely followed by the fact that union financial records are now more open to member scrutiny and the members are now more able to protest the expenditure of union dues for political purposes they do not favor. The statute has been least effective, according to this group of respondents, in making it possible for rank and file members to challenge the incumbent officers successfully.

•Consistent with the opinions expressed by those interviewed personally for the main report, union members in the surveys who said they "could not" or "did not" exercise their internal union rights overwhelmingly gave personal reasons—rather than intimidation by officers or co-workers—for not exercising them.

Comparison of Respondents Who Have Statutory Coverage of Rights with Those Who Do Not

Table 25 sets out a comparison of those union member respondents who did not belong to organizations covered by any type of federal legislation protecting union members' rights[3] (e.g., they were members of the National Education Association, state employee associations, certain public safety unions, etc. at the time they were interviewed) with both those whose unions were covered by some federal regulation, either the LMRDA or Executive Order No. 11491, and those belonging to unions whose parent bodies were then covered by the LMRDA (e.g., AFSCME, AFT) whether or not the individual respondent's local was covered.

TABLE 25. Results of the Chi-square Analysis of Respondents with Federally Legislated Rights Compared with Respondents without Such Rights

Variables	Chi-square Statistic	Significant Level	d.f.	Number
Activity	17.7150	.0014	4	606
Freedom*	9.4709	.0503	4	606
Age†	9.9722	.0188	3	606
Education‡	102.4700	<.0001	2	605
Race	7.9065	.0049	1	595
Union size	45.5080	<.0001	2	600

*To ensure minimum expected frequencies in each cell, freedom scores were categorized as follows: 0–2, 3, 4, 5, 6.
†To ensure minimum expected frequencies in each cell, age was categorized as follows: 18–25 years, 26–39 years, 40–55 years, 56 years and over.
‡To ensure minimum expected frequencies in each cell, education was categorized as follows: 1–12 years, 13–16 years, 17 years and over.

There was significant difference between the two groups on every variable except the freedom score, and even there the difference between the two was very nearly significant at the .05 level. The noncovered are more active (almost~79 percent considered themselves "very," "fairly," or

---

3. It may well be that state legislation protects some respondents that we have categorized as noncovered.

"somewhat" active, compared to less than 49 percent of those covered), and more free (85 percent have values of five or six, compared to just over 70 percent of the covered). However, those not covered either by the LMRDA or the Executive Order are also better educated (85 percent have values of thirteen years or more compared to 26 percent of the rest, and 47 percent have seventeen years or more compared to 7 percent of the covered). In addition, they are younger (72 percent are under forty years of age as compared to 50 percent of the others), and have proportionately more white respondents (96 percent as against 79 percent). The difference between the two groups, in terms of union size, is accounted for by the heavy representation of the National Education Association, which at the time of the interviews was clearly understood not to fall under either the Act or the Executive Order. That union, with over a million members, accounted for a total of 75 percent of the noncovered respondents. In contrast, only 36 percent of the respondents subject to some kind of federal regulation belonged to unions with over a million members.

Even when race, education, and age are controlled for, there is still a considerable difference in terms of freedom and activity between the noncovered public employees surveyed and those respondents who are clearly considered covered. For example, looking just at whites, aged twenty-six to thirty-nine, having thirteen to sixteen years of education (covered N=30, noncovered N=10), only 23.3 percent of the covered are "somewhat," "fairly," or "very" active, compared to 50 percent of the noncovered respondents in that category (Chi-square = 5.6508, significance level = .0593, d.f. = 2).[4]

Similarly, controlling for race, age, and education, the two groups differ significantly on freedom[5] (Chi-square = 4.8000, significance level = .0285, d.f. = 1): 60 percent of the covered had freedom scores of five or less as against 20 percent of the noncovered, and 40 percent of the covered had scores of six compared to 80 percent of the noncovered.

While the noncovered respondents possess more of the personal characteristics which correlated with greater freedom and activity, we do not conclude that federal regulation per se has had an adverse impact on covered members' freedom and activity. To draw that conclusion one would have to prove that the covered respondents have fared worse since the enactment of the LMRDA than before its passage, which is clearly not the case, based both on our main report findings and the data collected for this addendum.

Moreover, we cannot conclude that members who are not covered by

---

4. To ensure minimum expected frequencies, activity was separated into two categories: "active" (somewhat, fairly and very active) and "inactive" (fairly inactive and not active).

5. To ensure minimum expected frequencies, it was necessary to separate freedom into two categories: zero through five, and six.

federal regulation do not need to have their rights protected by law simply because their personal characteristics make it more likely that they will assert those rights themselves. While their greater sense of freedom may well result from their personal characteristics, their current level of activism may be attributable to the fact that the unions to which they belong are more recently established and, much like the unions in the southern region, are still embattled. Indeed, the noncovered, while often facing the same employer hostility as the southern trade unionists, are more likely to be confronted with greater hostility from the general public, nationwide.

Once public sector unionism at the state, county, and municipal levels becomes more acceptable to both employers and the public, one could expect that the noncovered members' level of activism would decrease. At that point, legislative protection of those union members' rights may well require congressional attention, just as did the rights of private sector trade unionists in the late 1950s.[6]

Correlation Summary

Chi-Square Tests

The Chi-square tests were performed to determine if a significant difference existed between the various groups of respondents within the variables shown in the first column of table 26 (e.g., white, black; male, female; public vs. private sector employee) on the two main variables of interest, freedom score and activity level.

The null hypothesis was that the groups within the first column variables were *not different* on the specified variable (i.e., freedom or activity). An attained significance level of .05 or less (underlined figures) was selected as the point at which the null hypothesis could be rejected and the conclusion could be made, with a 95 percent confidence level or better (or, stated another way, with a 5 percent or less error margin) that the two groups differed significantly, to a degree greater than would be achieved by chance alone.

---

6. While the respondents in the three surveys who are covered by Executive Order No. 11491 are too few to be considered representative, their low level of activism may reflect the fact that the transition from noncoverage to coverage was smoother than would normally be the case. Their supervisors had been well briefed beforehand as to what was expected of them in dealing with those they supervised. In addition, the federal government employees too had been informed of their rights and obligations under the executive order. That situation differs considerably from the barriers faced by teachers, police, firemen, and the like. The latter have usually had to contend with a much lower level of tolerance towards unionization and collective bargaining, both from their employers and the public at large.

TABLE 26. Chi-square Test Results

	Freedom*				Activity				Knowledge of LMRDA			
	χ^2	Sig. Lev.	d.f.	Number	χ^2	Sig. Lev.	d.f.	Number	χ^2	Sig. Lev.	d.f.	Number
Gender	1.8914	.3884	2	605	2.1081	.7159	4	605	6.67430	.0098	1	600
Race†												
Whites, blacks, other	11.1630	.0284	4	605	12.9160	.1148	8	605	.98640	.6107	2	600
Whites, blacks	2.1700	.3379	2	595	10.2410	.0366	8	595	$.21090 \times 10^{-1}$	.8845	1	590
Age‡	18.8010	.0045	6	606	27.4130	.0067	12	606	3.19990	.5250	4	601
Education	8.3955	.2105	6	605	10.1890	.5994	12	605	7.23950	.0648	3	600
Region**	3.0221	.8061	6	362	16.0660	.1882	12	362	.45996	.9246	3	362
Public v. private sector	2.8756	.2374	2	606	5.9650	.2017	4	606				
Affiliated v. unaffiliated	1.6480	.4387	2	606	13.9430	.0075	4	606	$.63609 \times 10^{-1}$	.8009	1	601
Knowledge of LMRDA	3.7447	.1583	2	601	16.8980	.0020	4	601				

*To ensure minimum expected frequencies in each cell of the contingency table, freedom was separated into "low" (values 0, 1, 2), "medium" (3, 4) and "high" (5, 6) categories.

†A significant difference is observed with regard to freedom when nonwhites other than blacks are included because the former, of whom there were only 10 respondents, had low freedom scores. The significant difference found between blacks and whites on activity is due to the inclusion here of the Detroit survey respondents. See discussion in text under "Detroit Survey Respondents Compared with Those of National Surveys."

‡To ensure minimum expected frequencies in each cell of the contingency table, age was divided into the following categories: 18–25 years, 26–39 years, 40–55 years, 56 years and over.

**The Detroit survey respondents were deleted for analysis of region.

Correlation Coefficient (r)

In order to determine the existence and intensity of linear relationships between pairs of variables, Pearson's product moment correlation coefficients were produced, pairing the freedom scores and activity levels of individuals with certain personal, demographic, and union characteristics (table 27). The correlation coefficient (r) measures the strength of the linear relationship, if any, between the two variables being correlated. A perfect relationship assumes one of two extreme values, −1 if the relationship is negative (the line slopes up to the left), and +1 if there is a positive relationship (the line slopes up to the right).

The square of the correlation coefficient (r^2), called the coefficient of determination, is the proportion of the variability in one variable which may be "explained" or "accounted for" by the linear relationship it has with the other variable (e.g., an $r^2 = .25$ would mean that 25 percent of the variability in the values of one variable is accounted for by its linear relationship with another).

The underlined correlation coefficients are those which are significant at at least the .05 level. The resulting coefficients of determination indicate that the proportions of variability accounted for within these pairs range from 1 percent (for age/freedom) to approximately 9 percent (for freedom/activity).

TABLE 27. Correlation Coefficients

	Freedom	*Activity**
Freedom	1	r=−.2911; p=0.01; r²=.0847
Activity*	r=−.2911; p=0.01; r²=.0847	1
Age	r=.1098; p=0.01; r²=.0120	r=.0344; p=NS
Education	r=.0267; p=NS	r=.0486; p=NS
Income† Detroit 1973	Rho=.1666; p=0.01	Rho=−.1330; p=0.05
National 1974	Rho=.3236; p=0.01	Rho=−.1825; p=0.05
Union size	r=−.1415; p=0.01; r²=.0200	r=−.0550; p=NS
Litigation‡	r=.0159; p=NS	r=.0781; p=NS

NS = Not significant at the 0.05 level.
*A negative correlation coefficient indicates a positive correlation because "high" activity was coded as a low number.
†Rank correlation (Spearman's Rho) was performed on income because the data was obtained in terms of ranges only. Activity was separated into high-medium-low categories.
‡LMRDA-covered respondents only.

Table of Cases

Principal cases are those with page references in italics.

Adamczewski v. International Association of Machinists (IAM), Local Lodge 1487, 103

Air Line Stewards and Stewardesses Association v. Transportation Workers Union, 137

Allen v. Iron Workers, Local 92, 81, 92

American Federation of Musicians v. Wittstein, 95

Arnold v. Meatcutters, 80

Axelrod v. Stultz, 81

Barbour v. Sheet Metal Workers, 92

Bausman v. National Cash Register Employees' Independent Union, 81

Blue v. Carpenters, 137

Boilermakers v. Braswell, *110, 113*

Boilermakers v. Hardeman, *110–18*

Boilermakers v. Rafferty, 84

Brennan v. Teamsters, Local 639, 66

Brennan v. United Steelworkers of America, *39*

Brennan v. United Steelworkers of America, AFL-CIO, Local 3911, 30

Brennan v. United Steelworkers of America, Local 5724, *30*

Brewery Bottlers and Drivers Union, Local 1345 v. International Brotherhood of Teamsters, 136

Broomer v. Schultz, 92, 126

Burch v. International Association of Machinists (IAM), 111

Burke v. Boilermakers, 111

Burton v. Independent Packinghouse Workers Union, 113

Calabrese v. United Association of Plumbers, 112

Calhoon v. Harvey, *42, 78–79*

Carpenters v. Brown, 138

Carrasquillo v. Sindicato, 111

Chicago Federation of Musicians, Local 10 vs. American Federation of Musicians, 138

Colorado Labor Council v. AFL-CIO, *4*

Conley v. Steelworkers, Local 1014, 162

Cornelio v. Carpenters, District Council of Philadelphia, 111

Cox v. Hutcheson, 136

Deacon v. Operating Engineers, Local 12, 92–93

DeCampli v. Greeley, 114

Degan v. Tugmen's and Pilots' Association, 93

Depew v. Edmiston, 78

Detroy v. American Guild of Variety Artists, 99, 112

Duncan v. Pennsylvania Shipbuilders, 112

Dunlop v. Bachowski, *31–32, 40, 47*

Dunlop v. United Steelworkers of America, Local 3489, *30*

Excelsior Underwear case. *See* NLRB v. Wyman Gordon Co.

Farnum v. Kurtz, 93
Farowitz v. Associated Musicians of New York, Local 802, 84, 92, 103
Federation of Teachers v. Miesen, 117
Ferger v. Iron Workers, Local 483, 81
Figueroa v. National Maritime Union, 112
Flaherty v. McDonald, 136
Ford v. Carpenters, Metropolitan District Council of Philadelphia, 96
Forline v. Helpers, Local 42, 137

Garret v. Dorosh, 78
Gartner v. Soloner, 91–92, 119
Gavin v. Iron Workers Union, 81
George v. Bricklayers' Union, 114
Giordani v. Upholsterers' Union, 93
Graham v. Soloner, 91

Hall v. Cole, *84, 119–20, 123*
Hayes v. International Brotherhood of Electrical Workers (IBEW), Local 481, 112
Hill v. Aro Corporation, 82
Hodgson v. Operating Engineers, Local 18, 79
Hodgson v. United Mine Workers of America, *66, 138, 140*
Hodgson v. United Steelworkers of America, 42
Hodgson v. United Steelworkers of America, Local Union 6799, *28–29, 33, 58, 60*
Holdeman v. O'Callaghan, 79
Hotel and Restaurant Employees' Union v. Del Valle, 137

Illario v. Frawley, 165
International Association of Machinists (IAM), Grand Lodge of the, v. King, *113–14*
International Association of Machinists, Lodge 702, v. Loudermilk, 93
International Brotherhood of Electrical Workers, Executive Board, Local 28 v. IBEW, *137*
International Brotherhood of Electrical Workers v. Illinois Bell Telephone, *103*

Jacques v. International Longshoremen's Association, Local 1418, 119
Jenette v. Ammons, 97

Kalish v. Hosier, 91
Kelsey v. International Alliance of Theatrical and Stage Employees, Philadelphia Local No. 8, 110
Kiepura v. United Steelworkers of America, Local 1091, 111
King decision. *See* IAM, Grand Lodge of the, v. King
King v. International Association of Machinists, 84
King v. Randazzo, 96–97

Lamb v. Carpenters, Local 1292, 117
Lassiter v. Walton, 134
Lenhart v. International Union of Operating Engineers, 77
Libutto v. Dibrizzi, 78
Lucy v. Richardson, 80
Lusk v. Plumbers, 81
Lux v. Blackman, 81

McDonald v. Oliver, 62, 143
McFarland v. Building Material Teamster Local 282, 92
McNail v. Meatcutters, 78

McNamara, Bernard W., v. Johnson, Robert, 160

Magelssen v. Plasterers, Local 518, 111

Mamula v. United Steelworkers of America, Local 1211, 113

Martire v. Laborers, 112, 114

Massey v. Curry, 136

Monborne v. United Mine Workers of America, District 2, *140, 144*

Morrissey v. National Maritime Union, 93, 112

Needham v. Isbister, 117

Nix v. Fulton Lodge, 93

NLRB v. International Union of Operating Engineers, Local 524, 134

NLRB v. Marine Shipbuilders, 99

NLRB v. Wyman Gordon Co., 35–36

Paige v. National Maritime Union, 112

Painters Union, Local No. 127 v. Painters, District Council of, No. 16, 94, 97

Parks v. International Brotherhood of Electrical Workers, 99–100, 112, 137

Peck v. Food Distributors, Local 138, 97

Purcell v. Keane, 138

Ranes v. Office Employees, Local 28, 96–97

Ransdell v. International Association of Machinists, Local Lodge 1904, 103

Retail Clerks, Local 648 v. RCIA, 114

Reyes v. Laborers, Local 16, 84

Rizzo v. Ammond, 136

Robins v. Schonfeld, 112

Ross v. International Brotherhood of Electrical Workers, *100*

Rota v. Railway Clerks, *96*

Ryan v. International Brotherhood of Electrical Workers, *100*

Sabolsky v. Budzanowski, 138

Salzhandler v. Caputo, *83, 114, 183*

Sawyers v. International Association of Machinists, Grand Lodge, 93

Schonfeld v. Penza, 117

Schuhardt v. Carpenters, Local 2834, 111

Schwartz v. Associated Musicians of Greater New York, Local 802, 96

Semancik v. United Mine Workers, District 5, *112*

Sertic v. Carpenters District Council, *96–97*

Sewell v. International Association of Machinists, Grand Lodge, *114–15*

Sheldon v. O'Callaghan, 80, 96

Sheridan v. United Brotherhood of Carpenters, Local 626, 114

Sordillo v. Sheet Metal Workers, Local Union No. 63, 92

Stachan v. Weber, 93

Steelworkers, Local 3489 v. Usery, *30, 33*

Steib v. International Longshoremen's Association, Local 1497, 96–97

Stettner v. Printing Pressmen, 80

Stout et al. v. Construction Laborers' Council, 82

Strauss v. International Brotherhood of Teamsters, 113

Tax Rank and File v. Van Ardsdale, 79

Telephone Workers, Local 2, v. International Brotherhood of Telephone Workers, 97, 119

Thomas v. Penn Supply and Metal Corporation, 82

Trbovich v. United Mine Workers of America, 30–33, 138

United Automobile Workers v. National Right to Work Legal Defense and Education Foundation, 103–4

United Mine Workers of America, Local Union 13410 v. UMWA, 137

United States v. Brown, 165

Usery v. Stove Workers, 29

Usery v. Teamsters, Local 639, 39

Usery v. Transit Union, Local 1205, 30, 42

Vaca v. Sipes, 82, 178

Valenta v. Dunlop and United Steelworkers of America, 32

Vars v. International Brotherhood of Boilermakers, 110, 113, 137

Verville v. International Association of Machinists, 103

Vestal v. International Brotherhood of Teamsters, 81

Wesling v. Waitresses Union, Local 305, 96

White v. King, 97

Wiglesworth v. Teamsters Local 592, 100

Williams v. International Typographical Union, 79, 96

Wirtz v. Glass Bottle Blowers Association, Local 153, 27–28, 32

Wirtz v. Hotel, Motel and Club Employees Union, Local 6, 29, 33, 62

Wirtz v. Independent Service Employees Union, 74

Wirtz v. International Longshoremen's Association, Local 1752, 62

Wirtz v. Ken-Lee, Inc., 154

Wirtz v. Laborers International Union of North America, Local Union No. 125, 28, 33

Wirtz v. National Welders Supply Company, 154

Wirtz v. Teamsters Industrial and Allied Employees Union Local 73, International Brotherhood of Teamsters, Chauffeurs, Warehousemen and Helpers of America, 62

Wood v. Dennis, 117

Yablonski v. United Mine Workers of America, 34, 38

Yanity v. Benware, 81

Index

Act of Vengeance, 162
American Arbitration Association, 53
American Civil Liberties Union, 74
American Federation of State, County and Municipal Employees, 4
Armbrister, Trevor, 162

Bartosic, Florian, 27
Bill of Rights. *See* Title I, Bill of Rights
Bureau of National Affairs, 51

Carey, James, 171
Civil rights legislation, 178
Commerce Clearing House, 51
Communist Party, 80, 165
Cornell University, 170

Dodd, Thomas, 145

Eisenhower, Dwight D., 2
Employee Retirement Income Security Act (1974) (ERISA), 2, 161, 178
Enforcement by the United States Department of Labor. *See* Title IV, Elections
Executive Order No. 11491 (1969), 2, 4, 41

Federal Bureau of Investigation, 156–57
Fiduciary responsibility. *See* Title V, Fiduciary Obligations
Financial reporting. *See* Title II, Financial Reporting
Fitzsimmons, Frank, 172

Free speech and assembly, 82–93. *See also* Title I, Bill of Rights

Goldwater, Barry, 62
Griffin, Robert, 76

Honest Ballot Association, 53
Humphrey, Hubert H., 2

International Brotherhood of Teamsters, 179–80; and Central States Pension Fund investigation, 168

Jennings, Paul, 171

Kuchel, Thomas, 76

Labor-Management Relations Act (1947) (Taft-Hartley Act), 74, 178; Section 301, 134; and union member discipline, 105
Labor-Management Reporting and Disclosure Act (1959) (LMRDA), 2–4; attorneys' fees awarded under, 119; impact of, on collective bargaining, 181–86; interviewees' assessment of impact of, 178–81; and limits on Department of Labor enforcement, 3–4; suggested amendments to, 4–5, 173–76, 186–87. *See also* Title I, Bill of Rights; Title II, Financial Reporting; Title III, Trusteeships; Title IV, Elections; Title V, Fiduciary Obligations; Title VI, Union Discipline
Labor's "Bill of Rights." *See* Title I, Bill of Rights

Landrum, Phillip, 76
Landrum-Griffin Act. *See* Labor-
    Management Reporting and Dis-
    closure Act

McBride, Lloyd, 125
McClellan, John L., 1, 75
McClellan Committee hearings, 1;
    trusteeship abuses found by,
    127–28
McDonald, David, and Abel, I. W.,
    election, 44
Member discipline. *See* Title V,
    Fiduciary Obligations

Nader, Ralph, 162
National Labor Relations Board, 3,
    154, 174–75
National Right to Work Legal De-
    fense Foundation, 103
Nixon, Richard, 172

Office of Labor-Management Stan-
    dards Enforcement, 2

Pension reform law (1974). *See*
    Employee Retirement Income
    Security Act
Perkins, Frances, 173
Postal Reorganization Act (1970), 4
President's Anti-Organized Crime
    Program, 2

Referendum ballot election versus
    convention election, 24–26
Reporting requirements. *See* Title
    II, Financial Reporting

Sadlowski, Edward, 125
Secretary of Labor, 45, 171, 187
Solicitor of Labor, 45, 171
Summers, Clyde, 109

Taft-Hartley Act. *See* Labor-Man-
    agement Relations Act

Time waivers, 48, 65–66. *See also*
    Title IV, Elections
Title I, Bill of Rights: enforcement
    of, 120–24; history of, 74–76;
    impact of, summarized, 126; sug-
    gested amendments, 120
——Section 101 (a) (1), Equal
    rights, 76–82; court interpreta-
    tions of, 77–82; and discrimina-
    tion in employment, 77, 81–82;
    and elections, 76–80, 82; impact
    of, 77, 82; restrictions on cover-
    age, 78–79, 80; and union meet-
    ings, participation in, 77, 81–82;
    and union membership, 77, 80–
    81; and voting, 79–80
——Section 101 (a) (2), Freedom
    of speech and assembly, 82–93,
    112–18; court interpretation of,
    83–84, 91–93, 114–15; impact
    of, 84–91; restrictions on cover-
    age, 83–85
——Section 101 (a) (3), Dues
    and initiation fees and assess-
    ments, 93–97; court interpreta-
    tion of, 95–97; impact of, 94, 97;
    and voting and dues, 93–96
——Section 101 (a) (4), Protec-
    tion of the right to sue, 98–104;
    court interpretation of, 98–100,
    102–4; and employer interfer-
    ence in unions, 98, 102–4; and
    exhaustion of union remedies,
    98–102; impact of, 100–102;
    and union member discipline,
    98–102
——Section 101 (a) (5), Internal
    union discipline, 104–18; court
    interpretation of, 110–13, 114–
    15; impact of, 105–6, 108–9,
    115–18; and union member dis-
    cipline, bases for, 104–13; and
    union staff discipline, 113–18
——Section 102, Civil enforce-
    ment, 118–19; court interpreta-

tion of, 119–20; impact of, 119–20; remedies under, 119

———Section 103, Retention of existing rights, 118

———Section 104, Enforcement by the Department of Labor, 74, 104, 120

———Section 105, Dissemination of information, 124–26

Title II, Financial Reporting, 119, 149–66; enforcement of, by the United States Department of Justice, 151; impact of, 160–63, 166; and reporting requirements for employers, 151, 153–55

———Enforcement of, by the United States Department of Labor, 149; and interpretation of Section 208 language, 153; and interviewees' assessment of reporting requirements, 149–56; and "spot audits," 155–56, 158; and use of Section 601 (general investigatory powers), 155–56

Title III, Trusteeships, 127–48; broadening the language of Section 302 of, 146–47; court interpretations of, 136–38; and Department of Labor report to Congress, 147–48, 187; enforcement of, by Department of Labor, 139–42; impact of, 129–36, 148; and lifting of the eighteen-month presumption of validity, 144–46; purposes for inclusion of, 128–29; reporting forms required under, 139, 141; Section 601 (general investigatory powers) cases, 129; suggested amendments to, 144–48

Title IV, Elections, 6–42; assessment of impact of, 32–33; and attorney's fees and other expenses, 38–39; and "bona fide candidate" and "adequate safe-guards," 34; court interpretations of, 26–27, 29–30, 32; and "determination" letters, 48; and elections, 8, 18, 21, 26–33, 43, 45, 48–55; and elimination of mailed notice requirement, 22–23; enforcement of, by the United States Department of Justice, 52, 55; and intermediate bodies included under Section 401 (c), 33–34; interviewees' assessment of, 18–26; language of, 22; and local union officers' terms, 23–24, 42; measuring impact of, 8–18, 21; and opposition candidates, 34–37; and post-election procedures, 45–48; and pre-election activity, 43–45, 53–54; restrictions on coverage of Title IV, 7–8, 78–79; Sections 401 (h) and 401 (i), 37–38; and standards set forth for elections, 6–7; suggested amendments to, 22–23, 33, 39–42; summarized, 21–26; and "summary of violations" letters, 46, 58, 60; and "voluntary compliance" agreements, 48

———enforcement by the United States Department of Labor, 2, 6, 7–8, 43, 45, 48, 53, 78; and authority to investigate pre-election complaints, 42, 53–54; impact of, summarized, 27, 71–73; and injunctive relief option, 42, 47; and internal assessment of agency conflict of interest, 176–77; interviewees' assessment of, 48, 52, 168–76; limits on, 149; non-Department of Labor interviewees' assessment of language, 68–71; and power to supervise any election upon request, 42, 52–53; recommended procedural changes, 187; and Titles I, II, III, V, 167–68; and use of Section 601

Title IV, Elections (*cont.*)
(general investigatory powers) in
election cases, 56–58, 167–68
Title V, Fiduciary Obligations,
119, 149–50, 156–58; and
"double dipping," 156–57; enforcement of, by the United
States Department of Justice,
150, 157; enforcement of, by the
United States Department of Labor, 157–58, 160; impact of, 160,
163–66; suggested amendments
to, 158–60, 164–66
Title VI, Union Discipline: Section 609, 104–9, 114–18; Section
610, 105. *See also* Title I, Bill of
Rights, Sections 101 (a) (2) and
(5)
Trusteeships. *See* Title III, Trusteeships

Union discipline. *See* Title I, Bill
of Rights; Title VI, Union
Discipline
Union elections. *See* Title IV,
Elections
Union meetings: attendance at,
88–89, 91; conduct of, 91–92;
nature of, 84–88. *See also* Title
I, Bill of Rights, Section 101 (1)
and (2)
Union pension fund reform law.
See Employee Retirement In-
come Security Act
United Mine Workers of America,

56, 162, 184; election case, 19,
168; election rerun, 27, 125;
trusteeship cases, 127, 140, 145–
46
United States Department of Jus-
tice, 3, 45, 174–75
United States Department of La-
bor, 2; Assistant Secretary for
Labor-Management Relations, 2,
171; Branch of Elections and
Trusteeships, 45–46; Bureau of
Labor-Management Reports, 2;
Labor-Management Services Ad-
ministration, 2, 187; Labor-
Management Standards Enforce-
ment, 45
United States Industrial Commis-
sion (1902) hearings, 1
United States Senate's Select
Committee on Improper Activi-
ties in the Labor or Management
Field. *See* McClellan Committee
hearings
United Steelworkers of America:
District 31 election rerun, 27,
125
University of Wisconsin, 170

Veterans' reemployment rights
program, 2, 51

Welfare and Pension Plan Disclosure Act (1958), 178

Yablonski murders, 56

DATE DUE